# The War List

*Battlefield Tactical Manual*

*Powerful Proclamations to Pray or Ponder*

**Susan B. Dobbs**

XULON PRESS

Xulon Press
2301 Lucien Way #415
Maitland, FL 32751
407.339.4217
www.xulonpress.com

Printed in the United States of America.

ISBN-13: 978-1-54566-362-2

# Dedication

*To the Most Magnificent Warrior of the Ages and the Great Ruling Monarch of the Universe, the King of Light and Glory, Jesus Christ.*

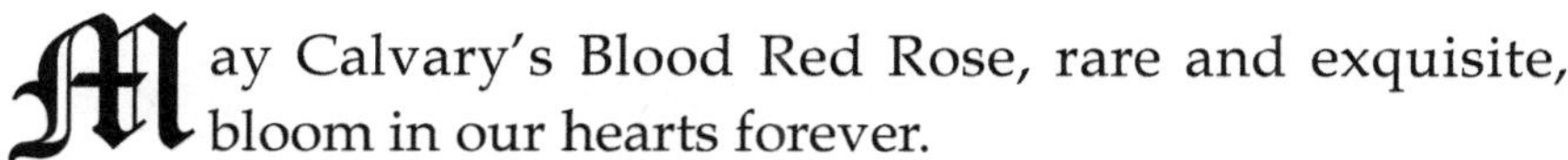

May Calvary's Blood Red Rose, rare and exquisite, bloom in our hearts forever.

~Charles Spurgeon

# Acknowledgments

To My Heaven-Sent Husband
Dr. Edwin Chappabitty Jr., MD
Honored Warrior and Esteemed Medicine Man
Who won the heart of your captive white princess.

Deepest gratitude to the Holy Spirit
for prompting me to write this book.

My son-in-law, Pastor Hadley, and daughter, Christie Baker,

Jennifer M. Lopez, and Caryl S. Smith,
for their tireless efforts regarding this project.

My two sons, J. Brandon Dobbs and R. Ashley Dobbs,
for their endless love and support.

May the legacy of this book be passed to my children
and grandchildren and all others its contents may touch.

# Arsenal/Armory of Choice Covenant Weapons

# Introduction

Many a battle has been fought to bring forth the manual you're holding in your hands. It was designed to be a great aid to you in your spiritual battles. The weapons presented in these pages were chosen to give you an optimal assortment to choose from so that you can most effectively fight your battles and conquer your enemies. Warriors, study and read with holy joy, for the battle belongs to the Lord.

Put your wholehearted trust and confidence in the Captain of your Salvation. He shall deliver your enemies into your hands. Enter each and every conflict with steadfast footing, a dauntless heart, and flaming zeal. You are waging Jehovah's war, and He has never lost a battle!

Although you will spend much time in battle mode, arming yourselves with effective spiritual weapons will allow you to avoid fatigue while crushing all clandestine assaults. May no cowardice be found among you.

Choose and use the necessary weapons, meditate out loud on the scriptures, ponder the corresponding quotes, relish the old hymns, and learn from the personalized weaponry and prayers.

Find your sacred space and your sacred stance, and launch into your territory of victory.

Sound the battle cry of alarm. Your Champion leads and goes before you!

Let us establish what we're fighting for: there is a heaven to gain and a hell to shun. Both are literal and eternal. There is a mighty kingdom of God to continue maintaining. The ground must be secured and expansion expedited on this earth.

No one earns Airborne Military Status overnight. Special Forces are not trained and equipped in a day. Navy SEALs aren't trained nor proven instantly. Air Force Thunderbirds don't reach a level of performance that's celebrated and admired in a quick fashion. There are no overnight successes on the battleground, either in the mortal world or the supernatural.

So when it comes to the spiritual battles of life, a solid foundation must be laid first and then built upon before the battle is entered. Consider Luke 14:31: "Which of you going to battle does not inspect or scrutinize a clear outcome to count the cost?"

Now we must be fitted. We need to be made capable, competent, and adept. We have to be molded to be powerful enough to fulfill the missions assigned to us. The ordnance depot of the Lord is fully stocked, and the weapons are ready for distribution.

Assess your position, warrior. You are more than likely emerging victorious from a tooth-and-nail, hard-fought battle or entering a heavy bombardment, preparing to engage the enemy of your soul. Perhaps you're resting in those times when your Leader deems it necessary you rest and recuperate. At ease, soldier!

Just in case you've been wrongly instructed that Satan and his minions don't exist, check your pulse and monitor your atmosphere. There is a very real, unending, long-standing hatred against all true committed Christians. This is a supernatural struggle of good against evil, of promises postponed, destinies blurred, relationships soured into ruination, wills pulverized, and sin looking ever so reasonable even delightful.

Realign yourself in your Holy Manual for further instructions. Your gallant Commander-in-Chief has equipped your DNA (both natural and supernatural) for this time in history. In His loving wisdom, He has carefully selected and determined each of your battles exactly to benefit you in the outcome. One size does not fit all. And why, you ask, are we presented with these battles? To conform you to the image of your Savior and to make you dependent on Him alone. This Mighty One is supremely Omnipotent, Omnipresence, and Omniscient.

# Weapon 1

# The Word

## *Scriptures*

For all have sinned and come short of the glory of God.

**Romans 3:23**

The Lord will command the blessing upon you in your storehouses and in all that you undertake, and He will bless you in the land which the Lord your God gives you.

**Deuteronomy 28:8 AMP**

The Sovereign Lord has given me a well-instructed tongue, to know the word that sustains the weary. He wakens me morning by morning, wakens my ear to listen like one being instructed.

**Isaiah 50:4 NIV**

Unto me, who am less than the least of all saints, is this grace given, that I should preach among the Gentiles the unsearchable riches of Christ.

**Ephesians 3:8**

And he sought God in the days of Zechariah, who had understanding in the visions of God: and as long as he sought the Lord, God made him to prosper.

**2 Chronicles 26:5**

Thy word is a lamp unto my feet, and a light unto my path.

**Psalm 119:105**

Ask and it will be given to you; seek and you will find; knock and the door will be opened to you.

**Matthew 7:7 NIV**

My Father, which gave them me, is greater than all; and no man is able to pluck them out of my Father's hand.

**John 10:29**

To appoint unto them that mourn in Zion, to give unto them beauty for ashes, the oil of joy for mourning, the garment of praise for the spirit of heaviness; that they might be called trees of righteousness, the planting of the Lord, that he might be glorified.

**Isaiah 61:3**

Look at the birds of the air, for they neither sow nor reap nor gather into barns; yet your heavenly Father feeds them. Are you not of more value than they?

**Matthew 6:26 NKJV**

For length of days, and long life, and peace, shall they add to thee.

**Proverbs 3:2**

The path of the righteous is like the morning sun, shining ever brighter till the full light of day.

**PROVERBS 4:18 NIV**

Wherefore lay apart all filthiness and superfluity of naughtiness, and receive with meekness the engrafted word, which is able to save your souls.

**JAMES 1:21**

The Lord is my light and my salvation; whom shall I fear? the Lord is my strength of my life; of whom shall I be afraid?

**PSALM 27:1**

My help comes from the Lord, who made heaven and earth!

**PSALM 121:2 NLT**

"For assuredly, I say to you, whoever says to this mountain, Be removed and be cast into the sea," and does not doubt in his heart, but believes that those things he says will be done, he will have whatever he says."

**MARK 11:23 NKJV**

From the dew of heaven and the richness of the earth, may God always give you abundant harvests of grain and bountiful new wine.

**GENESIS 27:28 NLT**

Death and Destruction lie open before the Lord—how much more do human hearts!

**PROVERBS 15:11 NIV**

Listening to gossip is like eating cheap candy; do you want junk like that in your belly?

**Proverbs 26:22 msg**

You must not turn away from any of the commands I am giving you today, nor follow after other gods and worship them.

**Deuteronomy 28:14 nlt**

Study this Book of Instruction continually. Meditate on it day and night so you will be sure to obey everything written in it. Only then will you prosper and succeed in all you do.

**Joshua 1:8 nlt**

And they that are Christ's have crucified the flesh with the affections and lusts.

**Galatians 5:24**

When my father and my mother forsake me, then the Lord will take me up.

**Psalm 27:10**

Ye are of God, little children, and have overcome them: because greater is he that is in you, than he that is in the world.

**1 John 4:4**

A calm and undisturbed mind and heart are the life and health of the body, but envy, jealousy, and wrath are like rottenness of the bones.

**Proverbs 14:30 amp**

My people have committed two sins: They have forsaken me, the spring of living water, and have dug their own cisterns, broken cisterns that cannot hold water.

**Jeremiah 2:13 NIV**

Pure religion and undefiled before God and the Father is this, To visit the fatherless and widows in their affliction, and to keep himself unspotted from the world.

**James 1:27**

This is the day which the Lord hath made; we will rejoice and be glad in it.

**Psalm 118:24**

I will instruct you and teach you in the way you should go; I will counsel you with My eye upon you.

**Psalm 32:8 AMP**

A father to the fatherless, a defender of widows, is God in his holy dwelling.

**Psalm 68:5 NIV**

Bless the Lord, O my soul; And all that is within me, bless His holy name! Bless the Lord, O my soul, and forget not all His benefits: Who forgives all your iniquities, Who heals all your diseases, Who redeems your life from destruction, Who crowns you with lovingkindness and tender mercies.

**Psalm 103:1–4 NKJV**

And it shall come to pass in that day, that his burden shall be taken away from off thy shoulder, and his yoke from off thy neck, and the yoke shall be destroyed because of the anointing.

**Isaiah 10:27**

Surely, he hath borne our griefs, and carried our sorrows: yet we did esteem him stricken, smitten of God, and afflicted.

**Isaiah 53:4**

## *Quotes: The Word*

A Bible that is falling apart usually belongs to someone who isn't. ~**Charles Spurgeon**

Half our fears arise from the neglect of the Bible. ~**Charles Spurgeon**

The Bible is the book of all others, to be read at all times and all conditions of human life. ~**John Quincy Adams**

Put your nose into the Bible every day. It is your spiritual food, then share it. Make a vow not to be a lukewarm Christian. ~**Kirk Cameron**

The smallest sin is an act of cosmic treason against a Holy God. ~**Jonathan Edwards**

I love to think of nature as an unlimited broadcasting system, from which God speaks to us every hour if we will only tune in. ~**George Washington Carver**

The secret of my success? It is simple. It is found in the Bible. ~**George Washington Carver**

My ground is the Bible. Yes, I am a Bible bigot. I follow it in all things both great and small. ~**John Wesley**

A child identifies his parents as God whether or not the adults want that role. Most children see God the way they perceive their earthly fathers. ~**James Dobson**

Every day that goes by without spiritual training for our children is a day never to be recaptured. ~**James Dobson**

Comfort is the god of our generation, so suffering is seen as a problem to be solved and not a providence from God. ~**Matt Chandler**

If you are not confident in the authority of scripture, you will be a slave to what sounds right. ~**Matt Chandler**

The Bible is the only book where the author is in love with the reader. ~**Unknown**

A man who is intimate with God is not intimidated by man. ~**Leonard Ravenhill**

God wants you to be a winner. He wants you to hook into those Beatitudes that will change your attitudes. ~**Marilyn Hickey**

Men do not reject the Bible because it contradicts itself, but because it contradicts them. ~**Paul Harvey**

Deeply consider that it is your duty and interest to read the Holy scriptures. ~**Adam Clarke**

Preach Christ, and if you must use words. Comforting others puts our pain in perspective. ~**Frank Peretti**

The Bible is no lazy man's book! Much of its treasures, like valuable minerals in the bowels of the earth, only yield themselves to the diligent seeker. ~**Arthur W. Pink**

It is a press from which will flow inexhaustible streams, through it God will spread His word. Rivers of truth will flow from it; a new star will scatter the darkness of ignorance, and cause a light not known before to shine among men. ~**Johannes Gutenberg**

There are more sure marks of authenticity in the Bible than any profane history. ~**Isaac Newton**

I have a fundamental belief in the Bible as the word of God written by those who were inspired, I study the Bible daily. ~**Isaac Newton**

Read your Bible; it is your roadmap through life. ~**George Foreman**

The Gospel is like water, no man invented it and no man can live without it. ~**Reinhard Bonnke**

In all my perplexities and distresses, the Bible has never failed to give me light and strength. ~**Robert E. Lee**

The Church is the one institution that exists for those outside it. ~**William Tyndale**

The highest service to which a man may obtain on earth is to preach the law of God. ~**John Wycliffe**

Anything you don't feed dies, we need to make time to feed ourselves spiritually. ~**Joyce Meyer**

Good things happen when you believe in God who always believes in you. ~**Unknown**

The Bible was not given to replace the miraculous; it was given to correct abuses. ~**Martyn Lloyd-Jones**

Good is not always God's will, but God's will is always good. ~**Watchman Nee**

The Bible is either absolute or obsolete. ~**Leonard Ravenhill**

All of us have mortal bodies, composed of perishable matter, but the soul lives forever; it is a portion of the Godhead housed in our bodies. ~**Josephus**

The tongue is a foolish creature that is more deadly than a rattlesnake and lurking behind the enameled fence of our teeth, it is always ready to strike. ~**John Hagee**

The Bible is the greatest of all books to study, it is the noblest of all pursuits to understand it, the highest of all goals. ~**Charles Ryrie**

Some read the Bible in Hebrew, some in Greek, I like to read mine in the Holy Spirit. ~**Smith Wigglesworth**

The living Word is able to destroy satanic forces. ~**Smith Wigglesworth**

God's Word is a treasure, a comfort for the soul, mind and spirit and heavenly medicine for the worried, stressed, over-burdened and troubled. Like a warm soothing breeze from the throne of God. ~**Dave Wilkerson**

The invisible realm is superior and far more real than the visible realm. ~**John Paul Jackson**

While love is one of God's attributes, it is not his only one. God is also Holy and just. ~**Robert Jeffress**

When God gives us a plan, he will only give us the best plans that lead to the greatest joy. ~**Michael Youssef**

If you're ever tempted to think you've blown it, reflect on the life of Simon Peter. ~**Michael Youssef**

The Bible begins with Paradise lost, it ends with Paradise regained when time, pain, suffering and debt will be a thing of the past. ~**Ron Rhoades**

Renewed Godlike thinking is a vital necessity to a successful Christian life. ~**Joyce Meyer**

To be a chaplain in your own home is a great honor! ~**Charles Spurgeon**

Nothing terrifies Satan more than a widespread hunger to know God and His word. ~**Mario Murillo**

The Gospel is good news of mercy to the undeserving. The symbol of the religion of Jesus is the cross, not the scales. ~**John Stott**

There are two things I do with the Gospel: I believe it and I behave like it. ~**Suzannah Wesley**

Scripture has power that is supernatural, soothing, convicting, transforming, life changing, timeless, timely and eternal. Nothing beats having the Word of God stored away in the chambers of your mind. It's like painting the inside of your mind with God's colors one brushstroke at a time. ~**Robert Morgan**

Men may not read the Gospel in sealskin or in cloth covers but they cannot get away from the Gospel in shoe leather. ~**Donald Barnhouse**

The great sin today in the Church is the man in the pew who is ignorant of the Bible. ~**J. Vernon McGee**

Grant that I may experience the power of your Word before I share it. ~**Christmas Evans**

It is destructive to add anything to Christ. ~**Richard Sibbes**

The Bible redirects my will, cleans my will, enlightens my mind and quickens my total being. ~**E. Stanley Jones**

Many good books you may visit but live in the Bible! ~**Charles Spurgeon**

The promises of God are our flotation devices that keep us from sinking when we face the waters of affliction. ~**Thomas Watson**

The best way to show the devil up is to speak God's word. ~**Joyce Meyer**

I will combine two ancient poems, the 23rd Psalm and the Lord's Prayer to follow a road map, a compass to the perfect prayer of restoration. This is the rabbi's prayer and the king's poem. May this recipe of the divine be medicine, life and health. A parallel splendor of the two is miraculous. ~**Mark Rutland**

Loneliness is not a lack of company, loneliness is a lack of purpose. ~**Guillermo Maldonado**

The God of the Bible is a God of covenant. No one reaches their destiny without walking with God in covenant. Every flower that blooms in the sacred scripture is planted in the soil of covenant. ~**John Hagee**

The Master architect of the ages created the universe and everything in it using his spoken word as his fingerprint. ~**John Hagee**

God never alters the role of righteousness to fit the man. Rather he alters the man to fit the role. ~**John Hagee**

Children represent God's most generous gift to us. ~**James Dobson**

The incredible, unforgettable Blood Red Rose of Calvary, our Everlasting Light, our Faithful Valley Walker, He who is our Holy and Hidden mystery, our Treasure, the Lofty Rock, the Fair Haven of rest, the Pure and Golden Joy of our lives, the Sweetest Consolation for our restless souls. May we ever speak and sing His eternal matchless, boundless love. He is our Majestic Sealed Perfection, the Blessed and only Supreme Potentate, the crowned Prince of Glory. ~**Anonymous**

Jehovah God has no equal, no rival, no match, no competitor, He is the all-sufficient one, the Supreme, Holy zenith of eternal glory! ~**Anonymous**

Bible prophecy should not be a playground for fanatics but a green pasture for disciples. ~**David Reagan**

The Word has the power to heal our souls: Dunamis (Greek) is dynamite power mode. Heaven's governmental powerhouse; anointing and soul healing mode, it is the resurrection power of God! Exocia (Greek) is the authority command mode, these power twins can soak our minds, wills and emotions and produce great victory! ~**Katie Souza**

Thoughts are the well my tongue draws from; therefore, the truest detergent is God's Word to wash our battle-weary minds. ~**Anonymous**

## Hymn: The Word

**O Word of God Incarnate**
O Word of God Incarnate
O Wisdom from above
O Truth unchanged, unchanging
O Light of our dark sky
We praise you for the radiance
from the hallowed page
A lantern for our footsteps
shines on from age to age
~**William Walsham How**, 1867 (public domain)

## Warrior's Prayer

We come to You, Mighty Champion God, seeking your face, watching and waiting for Your commands. Your Word is a fortifying sustenance as well as a sweet nectar. May it soothe the rough and jagged places in us as it toughens the soft and weak. The sprawling mysteries You have spoken are an ocean unexplored, uninhibited, where we are welcome, even urged, to immerse ourselves. Grant us deeper faith, clearer insight, and renewed fervent love for Your Word.

## Personalized Weaponry

As a "war baby" of WWII, I was ushered into a modest home of love and affection. At the time I was born, my dad was a young infantry/intelligence officer just returning from combat, distinguished and decorated. A few short years later, my younger brother was born, only to return to heaven at four months in May 1948, the exact time when Israel became a nation.

My grief-stricken parents moved to California, and we lived there for three years as they tried to ease the burden of their loss. On occasion, I was taken to Sunday school or church, and on one particularly timely visit, I emerged from Sunday school quoting Exodus 20:12—as a five-year-old! "Honor your father and your mother, so that you may live long in the land the Lord your God is giving you" (NIV). In one short hour, one patient Sunday school teacher had planted the *everlasting, ever-living Word* in my tender heart. Thus began the building, piece by piece, of my own personal arsenal of covenant Word weaponry.

Weave a beautiful blanket of Your Word, Lord, to wrap us warmly in Your love!

## WEAPON 2

# The Name

### *Scriptures*

The night is far spent, the day is at hand: let us therefore cast off the works of darkness and let us put on the armour of light.

**ROMANS 13:12**

Salvation is found in no one else, for there is no other name under heaven given to mankind by which we must be saved.

**ACTS 4:12 NIV**

Jesus answered, "I am the way and the truth and the life. No one comes to the Father except through me."

**JOHN 14:6 NIV**

For whosoever shall call upon the name of the Lord shall be saved.

**ROMANS 10:13**

No one is like you, Lord; you are great, and your name is mighty in power.

**JEREMIAH 10:6 NIV**

Trust ye in the Lord forever: for in the Lord Jehovah is everlasting strength.

**Isaiah 26:4**

Now we have received, not the spirit of the world, but the spirit which is of God; that we might know the things that are freely given to us of God.

**1 Corinthians 2:12**

"The Lord is my portion", says my soul, therefore, I hope in Him.

**Lamentations 3:24 NKJV**

Thanks be unto God for his unspeakable gift.

**2 Corinthians 9:15**

I have been crucified with Christ; it is no longer I who live, but Christ lives in me; and the life which I now live in the flesh I live by faith in the Son of God, who loved me and gave Himself for me.

**Galatians 2:20 NKJV**

In all these things we are more than conquerors through him who loved us.

**Romans 8:37 NIV**

From the end of the earth will I cry unto thee, when my heart is overwhelmed: lead me to the rock that is higher than I.

**Psalm 61:2**

Show me, Lord, my life's end and the number of my days; let me know how fleeting my life is.

**Psalm 39:4 NIV**

Because of the savour of thy good ointments thy name is as ointment poured forth, therefore do the virgins love thee.

**Song of Solomon 1:3**

You caused the springs and streams to gush forth, and you dried up rivers that never run dry.

**Psalm 74:15 NLT**

He is the Rock, his work is perfect: for all his ways are judgment: a God of truth and without iniquity, just and right is he.

**Deuteronomy 32:4**

Therefore, he is able to save completely those who come to God through him, because he always lives to intercede for them.

**Hebrews 7:25 NIV**

Therefore, if any man be in Christ, he is a new creature: old things are passed away; behold, all things are become new.

**2 Corinthians 5:17**

But as many as received Him, to them He gave the right to become children of God, to those who believe in His name.

**John 1:12 NKJV**

Give all your worries and cares to God, for he cares about you.

**1 Peter 5:7 NLT**

I am the Good Shepherd: the good shepherd giveth his life for the sheep.

**John 10:11**

Come unto me, all ye that labour and are heavy laden, and I will give you rest.

**Matthew 11:28**

For there is one God, and one mediator between God and men, the man Christ Jesus.

**1 Timothy 2:5**

Wherefore, holy brethren, partakers of the heavenly calling, consider the Apostle and High Priest of our profession, Christ Jesus.

**Hebrews 3:1**

But I have prayed for you, that your faith should not fail; and when you have returned to Me, strengthen your brethren.

**Luke 22:32 NKJV**

For in him dwelleth all the fulness of the Godhead bodily. And ye are complete in him, which is the head of all principality and power.

**Colossians 2:9–10**

His mouth is most sweet: yea, he is altogether lovely. This is my beloved, and this is my friend, O daughters of Jerusalem.

**Song of Solomon 5:16**

A man that hath friends must shew himself friendly: and there is a friend that sticketh closer than a brother.

**Proverbs 18:24**

The Lord will march forth like a mighty hero; he will come out like a warrior, full of fury. He will shout his battle cry and crush all his enemies.

**Isaiah 42:13**

Many of the scriptures above are reminders of the following attributes and names of God — The Lion of the Tribe of Judah, the Spotless Lamb of God that sits on the throne, the Eternal Conqueror, the Wonderful Counselor, the Prince of Peace, the Possessor of heaven and earth, the Mighty Man of War, the Friend who sticks closer than a brother, the King who reigns above and over all, the Altogether Lovely One is ever present through the power of the Spirit and he will never leave us or ever forsake us.

## *Quotes: The Name*

Jesus, the Wonderful one, He is greater than any ruler, Mightier than any warrior, Nobler than any king, Wiser than any sage, Bigger than any kingdom, Better than any crown, Lovelier than any name, worthy of worship and deserving of praise. ~**Roy Lessin**

Christ is the sharpest arrow in my quiver, the most powerful explosive in my arsenal, the one who can annihilate every avalanche of the enemy. ~**Steve Hill**

Christ, the grandest of the mighty. ~**Chadwick**

Every time you say the name of Jesus, you bring the fullness of Jehovah down to earth; every time you say Jesus, you move out of time into eternity. ~**Benny Hinn**

When we call upon his name **1**. We are admitting the bankruptcy of our name **2**. We identify with the person Jesus Christ **3**. We pray in his authority **4**. We submit to his will **5**. We are representing Him and His interests here on earth **6**. We pray expectantly. ~**Rick Ezell**

In Christ we become God's sons, man's servants and the devil's masters. ~**John G. Lake**

Take the words of Jesus and let them become the supreme court of the Gospel to you. ~**John G. Lake**

God has never, in the history of mankind, allowed his name to go long offended. ~**Dave Wilkerson**

To be a genuine Christian, you must believe the claims of Christ ~**Michael Youssef**

While many try to ignore Jesus, when he returns in power and might, this will be impossible. ~**Michael Youssef**

Smite all disease and sickness by the covenant healing name of God. ~**Anonymous**

The fullness and righteousness of Christ is our treasure in our trials. ~**Anonymous**

Jesus was and is the human embodiment of the eternal truth of God. ~**Unknown**

Christ is with us until the end of the age. Let his little flock; therefore, be bold. ~**William Tyndale**

Help me to be fully occupied with Christ, having great peace of heart and peace of mind. ~**Anonymous**

When we get connected to the one who created us, amazing things happen. ~**Joni Lamb**

Arise, believer, look at your Lord Jesus hitching his divine Godhead to the chariot of salvation. How vast his Grace. How firm his Faithfulness. Every drop of the Fathomless love of the Savior's heart is ours. Every sinew in the arm of his Might, every jewel in the Crown of his Majesty, as well as the immensity of divine knowledge and the sternness of divine justice is ours. ~**Charles Spurgeon**

Christ is the great steward of the infinite reaches of God's grace. ~**R. A. Torrey**

Jesus is not one of many ways to approach God, nor is he the best of several ways, he is the only way. ~**A. W. Tozer**

Freedom of fear takes spiritual strength, the kind of strength that can only be drawn from getting in touch with Christ within you. ~**Morris Cerullo**

Our Lord Jesus stoops down to where we are and offers his strong shoulders to us when we are weary and fearful. ~**Joseph Prince**

The Lord Jesus must have the crown of our hearts and life. He must be to us a precious fragrance, a rare ointment, a sturdy balm, an aromatic spice so very sweet. ~**Charles Spurgeon**

There is none like him, I would not exchange one smile of his lovely face for all the kingdoms of this world. ~**Samuel Rutherford**

The great tyrant has not forgotten your name and he desires your recapture, to re-enslave you, but the High Priest of your confession constantly prays for your faith not to fail you. ~**Charles Spurgeon**

Lord God Almighty, you are Supreme, Unquestionable, Unparalleled, Limitless, Infinite, Absolute, Magnificent, Dazzling, Ingenious, Timeless, Terrible, Unsearchable, Incomprehensible, Indescribable, Unfathomable, Matchless, Unswerving, Unending, Blazing and Flawless, Awesome, Pristine and Fascinating. ~**Joy Dawson**

The multifaceted wisdom of God, the incomprehensible riches of Christ, the God who sits high and looks low, is our ultimate Father, full of amazing endless love. Yet for those who hate him, and hate his word, and hate his people, there awaits a fiery and just judgment, by the Good and the Righteous Judge over all the earth. ~**Anonymous**

Lord, you are our exceeding great reward, the sunshine of our soul, the very light of life itself ~**Anonymous**

Knowing God and making Him know, receiving his blessing to be a blessing, fulfilling all the potential he has for my life; living a life of step-by-step obedient faith, a life of eternal significance. This is my Magnificent Obsession. ~**Anne Graham Lotz**

It makes no sense to name the name of Christian and not claim Christ. Jesus is not some magic charm to wear like jewelry. He is Lord! This name is to be written on our hearts in such a powerful way that it creates a profound experience of His peace. ~**William Wilberforce**

Victory begins with the name of Jesus on our lips and consummates by the nature of Christ in our hearts. ~**Francis Frangipane**

To holy people, the very name of Jesus is the name to feed upon, a man to transform us. His name can raise the dead and transfigure and beautify the living. ~**John Henry Newman**

Indeed, the mystery of Christ runs the risk of being disbelieved, precisely because it is so incredibly wonderful. ~**Cyril of Alexandria**

Hidden in the hollow of his Blessed Hand, no foe can follow, no traitor stand. Not a surge of worry, not a shade of care, not a blast of hurried can touch us there. ~**Frances Havergal**

He is the sun ever shining, the manna ever falling. The river of his bounty is always flowing, the rain of his grace is always dropping. ~**Charles Spurgeon**

Christ is the inviolable, the infallible truth, the never-ending life. ~**Thomas** à **Kempis**

I am an empty sinner. You are the full Christ.
~**Susannah Spurgeon**

If you are a church person and not a Jesus person, my heart hurts for you, it's like being engaged and never getting married, it's miserable! ~**Matt Chandler**

We need a holy addiction to his presence so that he becomes more important to us than oxygen. ~**Rick Joyner**

Don't hold on to religion and miss the joy of enjoying Jesus. ~**James Robison**

Every virtue has its origin in Christ. ~**Ambrose**

Are you Mrs. Dismal Forebodings, Sir Arrogant, Old Lord Fearing or Little Craven Fear? Would you rather be Mrs. Valiant or Grace and Glory or Joy, Peace and Love? The Good Shepherd is calling you to climb up from the Shadow Lands to His Mountain of Spices, come out of the Valley of Humiliation so that the fruit of the Spirit and the Spices of Solomon can reveal your human weaknesses and your great strengths! ~**Hannah Hurnard**

We who are saved are perpetually, endlessly and infinitely locked up in the person of Jesus Christ. He has become our realm of existence and habitation for all eternity. We are in him! ~**Rick Renner**

He who counts the stars and calls them all by name is in no danger of forgetting his cherished children. ~**Charles Spurgeon**

The great fights of afflictions have prepared you for the manifesting of His glory in His wonderful dealings with you! ~**Charles Spurgeon**

The Healer of the Nations shall lead his holy fighters to holy heights. ~**Anonymous**

Every day I need fresh, sustaining and undergirding strength from the Lord. ~**Anonymous**

## *Hymn: The Name*

**He Keeps Me Singing**
Jesus, Jesus, Jesus,
the sweetest name I know
Fills my every longing,
keeps me singing as I go
There's within my heart a melody,
Jesus whispers sweet and low,
"Fear not, I am with you,
peace be still in all of life's ebb and flow."
~**Luther Bridgers**, 1910 (public domain)

## *Personalized Weaponry*

Glorious Champion of right and unrelenting destroyer of wrong, You are our God! The lovely Lord Jesus, the Essence of Consolation and the all-prevailing Monarch, You are the right hand of Jehovah, the Master Connector, God of all creation, Lion of Judah and our soon-coming King.

Stolen years and shattered dreams are mended and restored by You, the Great Physician.

Our proud glistening adornment is Your majestic name, O Lord! Jesus, the Christ, the anointed One, is the name high above all and any names. There will come a day, very soon, when all three worlds—above, below, and earthly—will bow in either willing love or rank fear, but they will submit.

The beauty of His name enraptures us, and yet the sternness of His rod and staff comfort us in a most unusual way. He restores, rekindles, reinstates, remits, remakes, refreshes, and on it goes for the child of God.

Limitless is our Savior. He is our divine delight, and we are his. We are accepted in the Beloved. The Incarnate Deity is a multiplicity of safety and privilege that will never fail us.

Righteous Branch, the fourth Man in the fire, the Trusted Prophet, endlessly He rejoices over his people with gladness. He is the proven, qualified and authorized advocate who yearns to save; His name assures victory.

He has fashioned us of another Spirit; He will quieten us with His love; He has begotten us to a living hope.

His name has been joyfully proclaimed by new believers, militantly shouted by warriors, whispered by martyrs, murmured by dying saints, muffled by tribulations. It has been prayed, manifested, published, and revealed, never to be erased or faded from the landscape of humanity.

At the moment of conversion, we are marked in a supernatural and mysterious manner, sealed, imprinted, branded with our Savior's name. All realms recognize this "glory lightning" moment. Some rejoice; others shudder.

## WEAPON 3

# Love

### *Scriptures*

Greater love hath no man than this, that a man lay down his life for his friends.

**JOHN 15:13**

Every man according as he purposes in his heart, so let him give; not grudgingly, or of necessity: for God loveth a cheerful giver.

**2 CORINTHIANS 9:7**

For he that will love life, and see good days, let him refrain his tongue from evil, and his lips that they speak no guile.

**1 PETER 3:10**

Because of the Lord's great love, we are not consumed, for his compassions never fail.

**LAMENTATIONS 3:22 NIV**

In the same way, let your good deeds shine out for all to see, so that everyone will praise your heavenly Father.

**MATTHEW 5:16 NLT**

But I say unto you which hear, love your enemies, do good to them which hate you.

**LUKE 6:27**

Do not withhold good from those who deserve it when it's in your power to help them.

**PROVERBS 3:27 NLT**

And though I bestow all my goods to feed the poor, and though I give my body to be burned, but have not love, it profits me nothing.

**1 CORINTHIANS 13:3 NKJV**

Some of you will rebuild the deserted ruins of your cities. Then you will be known as a rebuilder of walls and a restorer of homes.

**ISAIAH 58:12 NLT**

The Lord on high is mightier than the noise of many waters, yea, than the mighty waves of the sea.

**PSALM 93:4**

And above all things have fervent love for one another, for love will cover a multitude of sins.

**1 PETER 4:8 NKJV**

If, however; you are fulfilling the royal law according to the Scripture, You shall love your neighbor as yourself you are doing well.

**JAMES 2:8 AMP**

For God hath not given us the spirit of fear; but of power, and of love, and of a sound mind.

**2 TIMOTHY 1:7**

There is no fear in love; but perfect love casteth out fear: because fear hath torment. He that feareth is not made perfect in love.

**1 John 4:18**

For God so loved the world, that he gave his only begotten Son, that whosoever believeth in him should not perish, but have everlasting life.

**John 3:16**

## *Quotes: Love*

Something in our nature cries out to be loved by another. Isolation is devastating to the human psyche. That is why solitary confinement is considered the cruelest of punishment. ~**Gary Chapman**

The love of God towards you is like the Amazon River flowing down to water a single daisy. ~**Anonymous**

God loves each of us as if there were only one of us. ~**Saint Augustine**

God loves us too much to indulge our every whim. ~**Max Lucado**

To proclaim a love so marvelous, that it can only be wondered at and rejoiced in with delight, is our great privilege. ~**Madeleine L'Engle**

Put together all the tenderest love you know of, multiply it by infinity, and you will just begin to see glimpses of the love and grace of God. ~**Hannah W. Smith**

We must develop a relationship with the Lord in which he is our first love. ~**T. L. Lowery**

Wise sayings often fall on barren ground, but a kind word is never thrown away. ~**Unknown**

Be patient and understanding, life is too short to be vengeful or malicious. ~**Phillips Brooks**

Spread love everywhere you go. Let no one ever come to you without leaving happier. ~**Mother Teresa**

Constant kindness can accomplish much. As the sun melts ice, kindness causes misunderstanding, mistrust and hostility to evaporate. ~**Phillips Brooks**

Love is the greatest force on earth to resist, limit and ultimately halt deadly progression. ~**James Robison**

Love is the grand motive of the plan of salvation. ~**Anonymous**

Today I will set my mind on how greatly loved and dearly prized I am! ~**Joseph Prince**

I have been seized by the power of a great affection. ~**Brennan Manning**

God loves you more in a moment than anybody else could in a lifetime. ~**Unknown**

God doesn't love some future version of you, He loves you now. ~**Matt Chandler**

God loves me, the beautiful Holy Creator and rescuer of everything loves me! ~**Unknown**

The colossal magnitude of the Son's love is manifested by his changelessness. ~**Jonathan Cahn**

The Maker of the Stars would rather die than live without you. That is a fact! ~**Max Lucado**

Love is not something you feel, it is something you do, expect a miracle. ~**Dave Wilkerson**

Every drop of the fathomless love of the Savior's heart is ours. His omnipotence, omniscience and omnipresence are all combined for our defense. ~**Charles Spurgeon**

Let us feel the fire of God's love, the sacred glow, the heat from his heavenly flame. ~**Anonymous**

God has unchanging, unconditional and irrevocable love for us. ~**Amy Carmichael**

Christ is the first and the last, and I am gathered up between as in great arms of eternal loving-kindness. ~**Amy Carmichael**

God's pleasure, delight, goodwill and acceptance is showered on us the moment we surrender to him. ~**David Jeremiah**

God's love is enormous, causing us to allow ourselves the luxury of his love! ~**David Jeremiah**

The most beautiful and exquisite love story of the ages, the magnificent story of the Gospel. We are the objects of the greatest and most stunning love ever known to man. ~**Anonymous**

God could not keep his love a secret, so he made creation. ~**Fulton Sheen**

God is especially fond of me and you, full of relentless affection. ~**Paul Young**

God is intrinsically involved in my life, climbing into the middle of my circumstances with impeccable timing. ~**Paul Young**

Just think, you're not here by chance, but by God's choosing. His hand formed you and made you the person that you are. He compares you to no one; you are one of a kind. You lack nothing that his grace cannot give you. He has allowed you to be here at this time in history, to fulfill his special purpose for this generation. ~**Unknown**

Every elegant detail of who you are was designed for the purposes of God. Thank you for being a light! May you experience his love and blessings today. Keep the faith. Do what you do, be who you are, walk in that sometimes blind, always beautiful obedience. Yes, you really are making a difference! ~**Holley Gerth**

God has given us two hands, one to receive and the other to give. ~**Billy Graham**

To prosper can mean getting pushed forward with love. ~**Anonymous**

Christ is the most wonderful example of ardor, vigor, strength of love, both to God and man that ever was. His holy love was stronger than death. ~**Jonathan Edwards**

The disappointments of life are simply the hidden appointments of love. ~**C. A. Fox**

God's outstanding love for you will break through all the walls you have built out of fear. It will soon penetrate and rule all your thoughts. ~**Morris Cerullo**

If there is anything that will make us blush in heaven, it will be the realization of how much we were loved on this earth but did not appreciate it. ~**R. T. Kendall**

Love is the oil of the spirit that gives all we do for Christ a fragrant aroma that draws people to him. ~**David Jeremiah**

A leisurely pace accomplishes more than hurried striving. ~**Sarah Young**

Give us dove's eyes that only see you, Lord! The dove mates for life and looks at no other! ~**Unknown**

Oh, love that will not let me go, I rest my weary soul in you! ~**George Matheson**

The more happiness you create for others, the more will be yours, a satisfaction no one can take from you. ~**Lloyd C. Douglas**

If you can't do great things, do little things with great love! ~**Mother Teresa**

We indwell a garden of grace. God's love sprouts around us like lilacs and towers over us like Georgia pines. ~**Max Lucado**

For all eternity God will lavish on us His honor and delight. ~**Bruce Wilkinson**

The amazing, endless, boundless love of God! The fortress of our salvation! ~**Unknown**

Let not the "fire of persecution" dry out your love for Christ. Nothing can separate our divinely welded hearts to His! ~**Charles Spurgeon**

May the fair star of Divine Love shine in your darkest night with serene splendor. May the haunting refrain of His love ravish our hearts with an acceleration previously unknown. ~**Anonymous**

Bright is the oasis that blooms in the desert but brighter and fairer is God's love in the midst of great sorrow. ~**Unknown**

Types of love from the Greek:
**Agape:** the God kind of unconditional love
**Phileo**: brotherly love
**Pragma**: everlasting commitment love
**Eros**: sensual love
**Storge**: love for a child
**Ludis**: childlike and fun loving
**Philautia**: love of self

## *Hymn: Love*

**Love Lifted Me**
I was sinking deep in sin,
Far from the peaceful shore.
Very deeply stained within,
Sinking to rise no more.
But the master of the sea
Heard my despairing cry.
From the waters lifted me
Now safe am I.
Love lifted me,
When nothing else could help,
love lifted me.
~**James Rowe**, 1912 (public domain)

## *Personalized Weaponry*

A parent's devotion can prove to be a pillar of strength for his or her child or children. In my case, my daddy was that strong, unchanging presence that I could always count on and look to for whatever challenge might present itself.

Major Robert A. Brigham (US Army Ret.) was a part of the "greatest generation." In the midst of the Great Depression years, he worked his way through college and came out with five degrees. But no sooner had he taken a position as a college professor than he was pulled by the call of duty into WWII. He experienced the horrors, which included his being wounded on a secret night mission that almost cost him his life.

I would come to learn that in spite of his heavy burdens, his loyalty to his family and his love for the Lord would rule his life. After having made peace with his Maker, he was instrumental in making sure I was in Sunday school and church regularly.

He was a student of the Word and would often preach at men's gatherings as well as church meetings. He used the slogan "Win with Brig" when he ran for public office in my hometown.

Brig was a man of varied interests. He loved to quote poetry and to recall Civil War battles and events. He settled the world's problems with the barber shop gang and followed that up with a cup of coffee and a piece of pie. A quiet, thought-focused game of solitaire seemed to calm his nerves. He loved to joke, and he often said, "Laugh a lot. It's good for what ails you." A rousing basketball game could get him cheering loudly at about the time everyone else got quiet, much to the embarrassment of a teenage daughter. He was a man who did love to eat and thoughtfully considered each meal. This came as a leftover from the Depression years, when food and money were scarce.

I remember well the years he spent driving me to school and to piano, dance, and voice lessons. He took me to dentists and doctors and hair appointments and on shopping excursions. He took me traveling and drove me to camp. He was there for my surgery, and afterward, he sat by my sickbed playing cards with me to help keep my spirits up.

He loved what he called, "the world of pink." I was his darling baby girl and, thankfully, he never let me forget it. In an age of one lone, permissive parenting school of thought, I look back on my dad as a man possessed of the innate ability to discipline with a firm yet gentle hand applied to the "seat of learning." He was never lacking in verbal affirmations and wise counsel as the years flew by. My dad loved his God, his family, and his country, and he served each extremely well.

He was the perfect example of the Heavenly Father's love, and that boosted my longing to know more about that love. Oh, that every child could have at least one parent readily prepared and willing to imprint a bestowed, spoken blessing on that child!

## WEAPON 4

# The Cross/Salvation

### *Scriptures*

For the preaching of the cross is to them that perish foolishness; but unto us which are saved it is the power of God.

**1 CORINTHIANS 1:18**

Blotting out the handwriting of ordinances that was against us, which was contrary to us, and took it out of the way, nailing it to his cross.

**COLOSSIANS 2:14**

And whosoever doth not bear his cross, and come after me, cannot be my disciple.

**LUKE 14:27**

Looking unto Jesus the author and finisher of our faith; who for the joy that was set before him endured the cross, despising the shame, and is set down at the right hand of the throne of God.

**HEBREWS 12:2**

When they came to the place called the Skull, they crucified him there, along with the criminals—one on his right, the other on his left.

**Luke 23:33 NIV**

But God forbid that I should glory, save in the cross of our Lord Jesus Christ, by whom the world is crucified unto me, and I unto the world.

**Galatians 6:14**

He himself bore our sins in his body on the cross, so that we might die to sins and live for righteousness; by his wounds you have been healed.

**1 Peter 2:24 NIV**

But when people keep on sinning, it shows that they belong to the devil, who has been sinning since the beginning. But the Son of God came to destroy the works of the devil.

**1 John 3:8 NLT**

And he said to them all, If any man will come after me, let him deny himself, and take up his cross daily, and follow me.

**Luke 9:23**

Say to them that are of a fearful heart, Be strong, fear not: behold, your God will come with vengeance, even God with a recompence; he will come and save you.

**Isaiah 35:4**

Therefore, with joy shall ye draw water out of the wells of salvation.

**Isaiah 12:3**

With long life will I satisfy him and shew him my salvation.

**Psalm 91:16**

When he died, he died once to break the power of sin. But now that he lives, he lives for the glory of God.

**Romans 6:10**

Let us draw near with a true heart in full assurance of faith, having our hearts sprinkled from an evil conscience, and our bodies washed with pure water.

**Hebrews 10:22**

But God demonstrates his own love for us in this: While we were still sinners, Christ died for us.

**Romans 5:8 NIV**

Wherefore Jesus also, that he might sanctify the people with his own blood, suffered without the gate.

**Hebrews 13:12**

There is salvation in no one else! God has given no other name under heaven by which we must be saved.

**Acts 4:12 NLT**

Much more then, being now justified by his blood, we shall be saved from wrath through him. For if, when we were enemies, we were reconciled to God by the death of his Son, much more, being reconciled, we shall be saved by his life.

**Romans 5:9–10**

And being made perfect, he became the author of eternal salvation unto all them that obey him.

**Hebrews 5:9**

Neither is there salvation in any other: for there is none other name under heaven given among men, whereby we must be saved.

**Acts 4:12**

He has saved us and called us to a holy life—not because of anything we have done but because of his own purpose and grace. This grace was given us in Christ Jesus before the beginning of time.

**2 Timothy 1:9 niv**

For the grace of God that brings salvation has appeared to all men.

**Titus 2:11 amp**

For with the heart man believeth unto righteousness; and with the mouth confession is made unto salvation.

**Romans 10:10**

For the Son of man is come to seek and to save that which was lost.

**Luke 19:10**

Whoever believes and is baptized will be saved, but whoever does not believe will be condemned.

**Mark 16:16 niv**

Enter through the narrow gate; for wide is the gate and broad is the road that leads to destruction, and many enter through it. But small is the gate and narrow the road that leads to life and only a few find it.

**Matthew 7:13–14**

Wherefore he is able also to save them to the uttermost that come unto God by him, seeing he ever liveth to make intercession for them.

**Hebrews 7:25**

As far as the east is from the west, so far hath he removed our transgressions from us.

**Psalm 103:12**

The thief cometh not, but for to steal, and to kill, and to destroy: I am come that they might have life, and that they might have it more abundantly.

**John 10:10**

For I know that my Redeemer and Vindicator lives and at the last He will take His stand upon the earth.

**Job 19:25 amp**

## *Quotes: The Cross/Salvation*

We are to plunder hell to populate heaven for Calvary's sake. **~Reinhard Bonnke**

God grades on the cross, not on the curve. **~Adrian Rogers**

Jesus Christ did not come into this world to make bad people good, he came to make dead people alive. **~Lee Strobel**

The God of the Garden became the God of Gethsemane, sacrificing everything for our salvation. **~David Jeremiah**

Revival comes from heaven when heroic souls enter the conflict to win. ~**Charles Finney**

There can be no more revival until Mr. Amen and Mr. Wet Eyes are found in the congregation. ~**Charles Finney**

No one else has ever come from such infinite heights of glory to such a shameful death. If there had been another way to rid the world of sin, God would not have required His Beloved Son to endure such a death! The humiliation was temporary. The incarnation was everlasting! ~**John Walvoord**

Not all superheroes wear capes, mine wore a cross! ~**Unknown**

Faith and the cross are inseparable; the cross is the shrine of faith and faith is the light of the cross. ~**Madame Guyon**

The only weapon to fight sin is the spear that pierced Jesus' side that drew his flowing blood and water. His wounds are his glories, his jewels, his ornaments. We see him as the Lily of matchless purity and as rose crimsoned with his own blood. There we see all his beauties perfected, all his attributes developed, all his love drawn out, all his character expressed. Beloved, Christ's wounds are more beautiful than all the splendor and pomp of kings. His thorny crown is greater than an empirical diadem. He was plunged into the depths of sorrow, sin and woe, He who has no equal or rival in agonies! He has redeemed a great multitude no man can number, and his scars are the memorial of that fight! ~**Charles Spurgeon**

God works the miracle of salvation. He immerses us in mercy, he stitches together our shredded souls. ~**Max Lucado**

The glory light of God heals our souls. ~**Katie Souza**

Not once did Christ use his supernatural powers for personal comfort. He who was boundless became bound. ~**Max Lucado**

All my sins have been legally and judicially judged at the cross. ~**Joseph Prince**

He who created us without our help will not save us without our consent. ~**Saint Augustine**

Manna is a prophetic representation of Christ's body and blood. ~**Anonymous**

You can contribute nothing to your salvation except the sin that made it necessary. ~**Jonathan Edwards**

I will not dilute or diminish the mighty power present in the simple message of the cross. Christ is the centerpiece of God's wise plan of salvation. He paid an unbelievable price to ransom our eternal souls! ~**Anonymous**

Only in the cross is there peace for our troubled hearts. ~**Michael Youssef**

My salvation was a free gift. I did not have to work for it and it's better than any gold medal that I have ever won. ~**Betty Cuthbert**

There is nothing more important than your eternal salvation. ~**Kirk Cameron**

No man is excluded from calling upon God, the gate of salvation is set open unto all men; neither is there any other thing which keeps us back from entering in, save only our own unbelief. ~**John Calvin**

The Bible says today is the day of salvation, today is the accepted time, but there will come a time when it will be too late for you. ~**Billy Graham**

One single soul saved shall outlive and outweigh all the kingdoms of the world. ~**J. C. Ryle**

Have you no wish for others to be saved? Then you yourself are not saved, be sure of that. ~**Charles Spurgeon**

A man is not saved against his own will but he is made willing by the operation of the Holy Spirit. ~**Charles Spurgeon**

Salvation comes through a cross and a crucified Christ. ~**Andrew Murray**

When you receive salvation, you get saved not because you deserved it, but simply because you let God rescue you. And because you confessed your own poor sinful state and your inability to save yourself. ~**John R. Rice**

The cross must be carried before the crown can be worn! Do you hope for reward without labor or honor without toil? ~**Charles Spurgeon**

## *Hymn: The Cross/Salvation*

**The Old Rugged Cross**
On a hill far away
stood an old rugged cross,
The emblem of suffering and shame
And I love that old cross,
where the dearest and best
For a world of lost sinners was slain.
So I'll cherish the old rugged cross,
Till my trophies at last I lay down.
I will cling to the old rugged cross
And exchange it someday for a crown
~**George Bennard**, 1913 (public domain)

## *Personalized Weaponry*

The year was 1959. The place was First Baptist Church in Lawton, Oklahoma. As a fourteen-year-old, my primary goal of the moment was pledging a local girls' club named Junior Miss. Wow! I made it down to the last week when, inconveniently, a friend invited me to a large revival at the church. Two brothers from England were touring the States with rousing music and preaching, and I decided to attend.

Since I was a good little Methodist girl—and believe me, denominational lines were very distinct—it was a big deal for me to venture out. My parents had sent me to Catholic school the previous year due to prolonged illness, so my exposure to other groups of faith was larger than most.

It had to be a God-appointed moment for me, since we were required to wear our dresses inside out, makeup on one side of our face and some outlandish hairstyle with ribbons for our little Junior Miss club. Remember at this age, one could barely endure being different from your peers. Sure enough, those Taylor Brothers preached the house down, and I stepped out in the aisle and made my way to the "mourners' bench." The conviction of the Holy Spirit pierced right past the small brown-and-pink ribbon pinned on my dress right above my heart, and, looking like a clown, I turned to face the congregation with my profession of faith.

Oh, yes, I made it into the Junior Miss club, but more importantly, I made it into my Savior's Kingdom.

## Weapon 5

# The Blood

### *Scriptures*

But now in Christ Jesus ye who sometimes were far off are made nigh by the blood of Christ.

**Ephesians 2:13**

With his own blood—not the blood of goats and calves—he entered the Most Holy Place once for all time and secured our redemption forever.

**Hebrews 9:12 NLT**

You shall hide them in the secret place of Your presence from the plots of man; You shall keep them secretly in a pavilion from the strife of tongues.

**Psalm 31:20 NKJV**

And they overcame him by the blood of the Lamb, and by the word of their testimony; and they loved not their lives unto the death.

**Revelation 12:11**

Wherefore Jesus also, that he might sanctify the people with his own blood, suffered without the gate.

**Hebrews 13:12**

For you know that God paid a ransom to save you from the empty life you inherited from your ancestors. And it was not paid with mere gold or silver, which lose their value. It was the precious blood of Christ, the sinless, spotless Lamb of God.

**1 Peter 1:18–19 NLT**

And almost all things are by the law purged with blood; and without shedding of blood is no remission.

**Hebrews 9:22**

Behold, I give unto you power to tread on serpents and scorpions, and over all the power of the enemy: and nothing shall by any means hurt you.

**Luke 10:19**

"But I say to you, I will not drink of this fruit of the vine from now on until that day when I drink it new with you in My Father's kingdom."

**Matthew 26:29 AMP**

And they overcame him by the blood of the Lamb, and by the word of their testimony; and they loved not their lives unto the death.

**Revelation 12:11**

And from Jesus Christ, who is the faithful witness, and the first begotten of the dead, and the prince of the kings of the earth. Unto him that loved us and washed us from our sins in his own blood.

**Revelation 1:5**

And to Jesus the mediator of the new covenant, and to the blood of sprinkling, that speaketh better things than that of Abel.

**Hebrews 12:24**

Knowing this, that the law is not made for a righteous man, but for the lawless and disobedient, for the ungodly and for sinners, for unholy and profane, for murderers of fathers and murderers of mothers, for manslayers.

**1 Timothy 1:9**

But if we walk in the light, as he is in the light, we have fellowship one with another, and the blood of Jesus Christ his Son cleanseth us from all sin.

**1 John 1:7**

For the Lord will pass through to strike the Egyptians; and when He sees the blood on the lintel and on the two doorposts, the Lord will pass over the door and will not allow the destroyer to come into your houses to slay you.

**Exodus 12:23 amp**

And the blood shall be to you for a token upon the houses where ye are: and when I see the blood, I will pass over you, and the plague shall not be upon you to destroy you, when I smite the land of Egypt.

**Exodus 12:13**

For our God is a consuming fire.

**Hebrews 12:29**

And they shall see his face; and his name shall be in their foreheads.

**Revelation 22:4**

My God is an all-consuming Fire, a Jealous God, and He will not permit any other gods to be set up in his place and worshipped, His love for us is so strong that he defends us day and night and wants our full affection and attention to be focused on him. This seems only reasonable, in light of such a glorious God, who loves his children with a fury. The Mighty Ancient of Days, The Rock of Ages, The Day Spring from on high, the God Man Messiah, The Great Lover of our Souls, The Majestic Bridegroom King, The Awesome Lord and Master. How I long to see you face to face and at last never be parted!
~**Anonymous**

## *Quotes: The Blood*

Morality can keep you out of jail, but it takes the blood of Jesus Christ to keep you out of hell. ~**Charles Spurgeon**

Let us honor the blood of Jesus Christ every moment of our lives and we will be sweet in our souls. ~**William Seymour**

Any seeds of destruction planted in my life are uprooted, destroyed and brought to ruination by Christ's blood. ~**Anonymous**

As Christians, we are marked by a covering that no evil force can remove, the blood of Jesus. Under the protection of the blood we find a safe retreat. We can remain steadfast in a position of strength via the blood. ~**Billye Brim**

The blood provides protection; a means of deliverance, it provides the promise of a new day, it provides a witness. ~**Jack Hayford**

The precious blood of Christ not only serves as a foundation for our redemption, but it is also the strongest spiritual weapon against our adversary. ~**Anonymous**

The blood of Jesus Christ and His Mighty Name is an antidote to all the subtle seeds of unbelief that Satan will try to sow in your mind. ~**Smith Wigglesworth**

The blood of Jesus unlocks the treasury of heaven, ~**James Goll**

Many keys fit many locks, but the Master key is the blood and the name of him that died and rose again and ever lives in heaven to save us to the uttermost. ~**Charles Spurgeon**

Satan is drowned in the Red Sea of Christ's blood. He will save and deliver in his own unique way. ~**Robert Morgan**

Christ is my Safe house, my Hiding place, my Impenetrable fortress, my Calming refuge in the storms of life, my High tower of heavenly solitude, my Refreshing rest, my Indwelling peace, my Fierce defender and Steadfast deliverer and Exceeding joy of my salvation. ~**Anonymous**

Understanding Jesus as the Sacrificial Lamb is in effect, to understand the very heart of Christianity. It is his blood that cleanses and that's all. We go to him directly for the cleansing, resulting in our salvation. ~**Zola Levitt**

The righteousness of God no longer terrifies man. It meets him as a friend, with an offer of complete justification. God's countenance beams with pleasure and approval as the penitent sinner draws near to him and he invites him to intimate fellowship. ~**Andrew Murray**

Only the blood of Jesus can cleanse us, yet if we withhold ourselves from that blood, we will be unclean forever. ~**A. W. Tozer**

I find no better cure for depression than to trust in the Lord with all my heart and to realize how fresh the power of the "peace-speaking blood" of Jesus remains. ~**Charles Spurgeon**

Atonement by the blood of Jesus is not an arm of Christian truth; it is the very heart of it. ~**Charles Spurgeon**

There is more power in one drop of the blood of Jesus than in all parts of the kingdom of Satan put together. ~**Derek Prince**

When Jesus Christ shed his blood on the cross, it was not the blood of a martyr or the blood of one man for another; it was the life of God poured out to redeem the world. ~**Oswald Chambers**

## Hymn: The Blood

**Nothing but the Blood**
Oh! precious is the flow
That makes me white as snow.
No other fount I know,
Nothing but the blood of Jesus.
What can wash away my sins?
Nothing but the blood of Jesus
What can make me whole again?
Nothing but the blood of Jesus
~**Robert Lowery**, 1876 (public domain)

## Personalized Weaponry

I recall, as a teenager, overhearing a conversation between my parents and a family friend. The friend said, "Don't talk to me about your slaughterhouse religion."

The blinding ignorance of that statement still shakes me. The bloody, gory, repulsive picture of Calvary's hill should be our dearest reality. Hold it right there. "Without the shedding of blood, there is no forgiveness of sin," according to Hebrews 9:22. This can't be human or animal blood. Only the precious pure, untainted blood of the only Son of God will suffice. Do not be fooled. All other blood is filthy with sin, unfit for the ultimate sacrifice.

Christ's blood is the heaven-sent cleansing agent without which no one will see the gates of glory. I, for one, am eternally grateful for the dark, lonely, and bleeding hill so long ago, which secured the salvation of all who would believe and receive. Far from seeing it as offensive, I embrace the fullness of its ghastly horrors and do not shield my senses from its magnificent wonders. Love survived the torment of the cross.

The work of the cross is a finished and thoroughly completed work. It's our passport from this house of mourning and vale of tears to our mansions on high, but even more, our joyful reunion with the God of our salvation. Because of the cross and the Lord's ascension, we can rightfully be called the children of the resurrection.

## Weapon 6

# Humility

### *Scriptures*

Whosoever therefore shall humble himself as this little child, the same is greatest in the kingdom of heaven.

**Matthew 18:4**

Do nothing out of selfish ambition or vain conceit. Rather, in humility, value others above yourselves.

**Philippians 2:3 niv**

Humble yourselves therefore under the mighty hand of God, that he may exalt you in due time.

**1 Peter 5:6**

He has told you, O man, what is good. What does the Lord require of you, except to be just, and to love kindness, and to walk humbly with your God.

**Micah 6:8 amp**

When pride cometh, then cometh shame: but with the lowly is wisdom.

**Proverbs 11:2**

For the Lord taketh pleasure in his people: he will beautify the meek with salvation.

**Psalm 149:4**

For even the Son of man came not to be ministered unto, but to minister, and to give his life a ransom for many.

**Mark 10:45**

It is better to be humble in spirit with the lowly, than to divide the spoil with the proud

**Proverbs 16:19.**

Humble yourselves therefore under the mighty hand of God, that he may exalt you in due time.

**1 Peter 5:6**

Humble yourselves therefore under the mighty hand of God, that he may exalt you in due time.

**James 4:10**

Put on therefore, as the elect of God, holy and beloved, bowels of mercies, kindness, humbleness of mind, meekness, longsuffering.

**Colossians 3:12**

## *Quotes: Humility*

True humility is not thinking less of yourself: it is thinking of yourself less. ~**C. S. Lewis**

Humility is perfect quietness of heart, a peacefulness in a deep sea of calmness, no matter what is going on around you. ~**Andrew Murray**

Pride must die in you or nothing of heaven can live in you. ~**Andrew Murray**

True humility does not know it is humble. If it did, it would be proud for contemplating such a divine virtue. ~**Martin Luther**

There are two things that men should never weary of; goodness and humility, we never have enough of them in this rough, cold world. ~**Robert Louis Stevenson**

Don't accept your dog's adoration as conclusive evidence that you are wonderful! ~**Ann Landers**

Humility, that low, sweet root, from which all heavenly virtues shoot. ~**Thomas Moore**

True humility is staying teachable, regardless of how much you already know. ~**Unknown**

Nothing sets a person so far out of the devil's reach as humility. ~**Jonathan Edwards**

True greatness is devoting all my energy to becoming a servant and not getting upset when I am treated like one. ~**Bill Gothard**

When you wear the weed of impatience in your heart, instead of the flower of acceptance with joy, you will always find your enemies get an advantage over you. ~**Hannah Hurnard**

Some never get started on their destiny course because they cannot humble themselves to learn, grow, change and have the ability to develop contentment and even common sense. ~**C. S. Lewis**

Christ is the beginning of humility, for he took the form of a servant even though he was equal with the Father in the majesty of his power. ~**Madeleine L'Engle**

Pride is a barrier to all spiritual progress. ~**H. A. Ironside**

It is amazing what you can accomplish if you do not care who gets the credit. ~**Harry S. Truman**

The degree of your anger over correction equals the measure of your pride. ~**John Paul Jackson**

Pride works frequently under a dense mask and will often assume the garb of humility. ~**Adam Clarke**

Humility is the mother of giants. One sees great things from the valley; only small things from the peak. ~**G. K. Chesterton**

Pride is the king of all vices, it is the first of the pallbearers of the soul. Pride destroys all virtues, it secretly fears all competition and dreads all rivals. ~**Fulton Sheen**

## *Hymn: Humility*

**Sweet Humility**
Humility, oh grace so sweet!
Come, dwell within my heart.
Oh, press me to my Savior's feet,
There lowliness impart.
Come softly from thy throne above,
oh, grace so sweet and bare
Come, touch my heart in gentle love,
and scatter meekness there.
~**Charles E. Orr**, 1907 (public domain)

## *Personalized Prayer Weaponry*

The humble, who have been chiseled by trials, stand as monuments to their Lord and Master. They have willingly submitted to his velvet hammer and find themselves transformed beyond recognition. Thank you, Mighty Rock of our Salvation, for molding and making us after your image, for seeing the potential beauty you alone could sculpt. You pursued us with great loving purpose, knowing exactly how to hew and carve to produce masterpieces of Your grace.

## Weapon 7

# Repentance

### *Scriptures*

Repent ye therefore, and be converted, that your sins may be blotted out, when the times of refreshing shall come from the presence of the Lord.

**Acts 3:19**

This is what the Sovereign Lord, the Holy One of Israel, says: "In repentance and rest is your salvation, in quietness and trust is your strength, but you would have none of it."

**Isaiah 30:15 NIV**

But because you are stubborn and refuse to turn from your sin, you are storing up terrible punishment for yourself. For a day of anger is coming, when God's righteous judgment will be revealed.

**Romans 2:5 NLT**

He that covereth his sins shall not prosper but whoso confesseth and forsaketh them shall have mercy.

**Proverbs 28:13**

Bring forth therefore fruits meet for repentance.

**Matthew 3:8**

I came not to call the righteous, but sinners to repentance.

**Luke 5:32**

Remember therefore from whence thou art fallen, and repent, and do the first works; or else I will come unto thee quickly, and will remove thy candlestick out of his place, except thou repent.

**Revelation 2:5**

John did baptize in the wilderness and preach the baptism of repentance for the remission of sins.

**Mark 1:4**

From that time Jesus began to preach, and to say, Repent: for the kingdom of heaven is at hand.

**Matthew 4:17**

Let the wicked forsake his way, and the unrighteous man his thoughts: and let him return unto the Lord, and he will have mercy upon him; and to our God, for he will abundantly pardon.

**Isaiah 55:7**

If you return to the Almighty, you will be restored: If you remove wickedness far from your tent.

**Job 22:23**

I have blotted out, like a thick cloud, your transgressions, And like a cloud, your sins. Return to Me, for I have redeemed you.

**Isaiah 44:22 NKJV**

The Lord is not slack concerning his promise, as some men count slackness; but is longsuffering to us-ward, not willing that any should perish, but that all should come to repentance.
**2 Peter 3:9**

## *Quotes: Repentance*

Repentance may be old-fashioned, but it is not outdated, as long as there is sin. ~**J. C. Macaulay**

God has promised forgiveness for your repentance, but he has not promised tomorrow to your procrastination. ~**Saint Augustine**

God wills to save us and nothing pleases him more than our coming back to him in true repentance. ~**Maximus**

Only through repentance and faith in Christ can anyone be saved. No religious activity will be sufficient, only true faith in Jesus Christ alone. ~**Ravi Zacharias**

Repentance means you change your mind so deeply that it changes you. ~**Bruce Wilkinson**

When we have heartily repented of a wrong, we should let the waves of forgetfulness roll over it and move forward, unburdened to meet the future. ~**Henry Ward Beecher**

There is a difference between remorse and repentance. Remorse is being sorry for being caught; repentance is being sorry enough to stop. ~**Greg Laurie**

The greatest sorrow and burden you can lay on the Father, the greatest unkindness, is not to believe that he loves you. ~**John Owen**

Repent because of discouragement in life's journey. ~**Unknown**

Think not that you shall turn to God when you will, if you will not when you may. ~**Unknown**

Many mourn for their sins that do not truly repent of them, weep bitterly for them and yet continue in love and league with them. ~**Matthew Henry**

The Christian who has stopped repenting has stopped growing. ~**A. W. Pink**

Repentance is more than just sorrow for the past; repentance is a change of heart and mind, a new life denying self and serving the Savior as King in self's place. ~**J. I. Packer**

You cannot repent too soon because you do not know how soon it will be too late. ~**Thomas Fuller**

Repentance, as we know, is basically not moaning or remorse, but turning and changing. ~**J. I. Packer**

People who cover their faults and excuse themselves do not have a repentant spirit. ~**Watchman Nee**

## *Hymn: Repentance*

**Softly and Tenderly**
Softly and tenderly,
Jesus is calling,
Calling for you and for me.
See, on the portals,
he is waiting and watching
Watching for you and for me.
Come home, Come home,
You who are weary, come home.
Earnestly, tenderly, Jesus is calling
Calling "Oh, sinner, come home!"
~**Will L. Thompson**, 1880 (public domain)

## *Personalized Weaponry*

What does *repent* truly mean? It means to turn around and walk in the opposite direction from sinful behavior and/or lifestyle. It's not about simply being sorry or sad for being caught, but rather it involves an *act of your will,* with God's help and power, to stop the sinning. It doesn't occur when you manage to clean yourself or your circumstances up; it can only happen when you turn it all over to Christ. He will do the cleansing, repairing, and much more, as you submit to His will and His Word.

My two younger children, now in their forties, were watching a Billy Graham crusade in our bedroom in the 1980s, when suddenly, the altar call came, and they both chimed in to call the number on the screen. What a tearful joy I felt because I could tell them we could pray right then and there for their salvation to become an election sure and secured. You're never too young or too old to make the decision to follow Christ; however, first humble yourself, repent of your sins, and then freely receive the Lord. Your life should be visibly changed, old habits and haunts falling away, and you should be able to recall a day and time when this transformation began. No true repentance, no true salvation!

We have now become carriers of the sacred fire of God; help us, Lord, to stay on the ancient, proven, good path. Thank You for Your loving correction and Your unparalleled sacrifice. Unleash Your purposes in our lives and blaze an unmistakable path before us moment by moment. Your greater glory be ever surrounding us as we endeavor to further Your Kingdom. Help us to have a glad heart that has a continual feast in Your awesome presence, regardless of the circumstances.

## WEAPON 8

# Truth

### *Scriptures*

Lead me in Your truth and teach me, For You are the God of my salvation; On You I wait all the day.

**PSALM 25:5 NKJV**

Jesus saith unto him, I am the way, the truth, and the life: no man cometh unto the Father, but by me.

**JOHN 14:6**

The Lord is close to all who call on him, yes, to all who call on him in truth.

**PSALM 145:18 NLT**

And ye shall know the truth, and the truth shall make you free.

**JOHN 8:32**

The one whose walk is blameless is kept safe, but the one whose ways are perverse will fall into the pit.

**PROVERBS 28:18 NIV**

A heart that creates wicked plans, feet that run swiftly to evil.

**Proverbs 6:18 AMP**

The integrity of the upright shall guide them: but the perverseness of transgressors shall destroy them.

**Proverbs 11:3**

My little children, let us not love in word, neither in tongue; but in deed and in truth.

**1 John 3:18**

Show me your ways, Lord, teach me your paths.

**Psalm 24:4 NIV**

Lord, you are my God; I will exalt you and praise your name, for in perfect faithfulness you have done wonderful things, things planned long ago.

**Isaiah 25:1 NIV**

Thy righteousness is an everlasting righteousness, and thy law is the truth.

**Psalm 119:142**

Fear not, little flock; for it is your Father's good pleasure to give you the kingdom.

**Luke 12:32**

For the eyes of the Lord run to and fro throughout the whole earth, to show Himself strong on behalf of those whose heart is loyal to Him. In this you have done foolishly; therefore, from now on you shall have wars.

**2 Chronicles 16:9 NKJV**

If we say that we have fellowship with him, and walk in darkness, we lie, and do not the truth.

**1 John 1:6**

But speaking the truth in love, may grow up into him in all things, which is the head, even Christ.

**Ephesians 4:15**

Of His own will He brought us forth by the word of truth, that we might be a kind of first fruits of His creatures.

**James 1:18 NKJV**

These are the things that ye shall do; Speak ye every man the truth to his neighbour; execute the judgment of truth and peace in your gates.

**Zachariah 8:16**

But a time is coming and is already here when the true worshipers will worship the Father in spirit and in truth; for the Father seeks such people to be His worshipers.

**John 4:23 AMP**

And he that sat upon the throne said, Behold, I make all things new. And he said unto me, write, for these words are true and faithful.

**Revelation 21:5**

Do your best to present yourself to God as one approved, a worker who does not need to be ashamed and who correctly handles the word of truth.

**2 Timothy 2:15 NIV**

If you confess with your mouth the Lord Jesus and believe in your heart that God has raised Him from the dead, you will be saved.

**ROMANS 10:9 NKJV**

Then Peter opened his mouth, and said, "Of a truth I perceive that God is not respecter of persons."

**ACTS 10:34**

In whom the god of this world hath blinded the minds of them which believe not, lest the light of the glorious gospel of Christ, who is the image of God, should shine unto them.

**2 CORINTHIANS 4:4**

For I rejoiced greatly, when the brethren came and testified of the truth that is in thee, even as thou walkest in the truth.

**3 JOHN 1:3**

I do not want you to be ignorant of this mystery, brothers and sisters, so that you may not be conceited: Israel has experienced a hardening in part until the full number of the Gentiles has come in.

**ROMANS 11:25 NIV**

## *Quotes: Truth*

If you tell the truth, you don't have to remember anything. ~**Mark Twain**

Truth hurts only once but a lie hurts every time you remember it. ~**Unknown**

Honesty is an expensive gift, don't expect it from cheap people. ~**Unknown**

Honesty is the first chapter in the book of wisdom. ~**Thomas Jefferson**

There is nothing so powerful as truth and often nothing so strange. ~**Daniel Webster**

Honesty and transparency make you vulnerable. Be honest and transparent anyway. ~**Mother Teresa**

Anyone who doesn't take truth seriously in small matters, cannot be trusted in large ones either. ~**Albert Einstein**

Peace, if possible, but truth at any rate. ~**Martin Luther**

God never made a promise too good to be true. ~**D. L. Moody**

Where I find truth, there I find my God, who is the truth himself. ~**Saint Augustine**

This is God's universe and He does things His way. You may have a better way, but you don't have a universe. ~**J. Vernon McGee**

What is in the well of the heart will come up through the bucket of the mouth. ~**J. Vernon McGee**

God was never the wrathful deity of the ancients; He loved us from the very beginning. ~**David Jeremiah**

Hardships often prepare ordinary people for extraordinary destiny. ~**C. S. Lewis**

As goes the pulpit, so goes the pew, as goes the pew, so goes the nation. ~**Michael Youssef**

True beauty is rare and seldom recognized by the one who possesses it. ~**Francine Rivers**

We have grasped the mystery of the atom and rejected the Sermon on the Mount. ~**Omar Bradley**

There is a day coming when there will be a religion without repentance, a salvation without the Holy Spirit, a Heaven without a Hell. ~**William Booth**

In the absence of any other proof, the thumb alone would convince me of God's existence. ~**Isaac Newton**

If you can't stand the heat, get out of the kitchen! ~**Harry S. Truman**

Whenever a nation turns its back on God, or begins to live as if He does not exist, it starts to show up in the citizens' disregard for human life. ~**Tim LaHaye**

We live under the sun but our destiny is beyond its rising and setting. ~**David Jeremiah**

It is better to go bruised to Heaven than sound to Hell. ~**Richard Sibbes**

The problem with the world is it blames problems on things besides sin and identifies salvation with things other than God. ~**Timothy Keller**

The trouble with the most of us is that we would rather be ruined by praise than saved by criticism. ~**Norman Vincent Peale**

Atheism is something strange, not even demons can come to that point. ~**Charles Spurgeon**

There are two great days in a person's life, the day we were born and the day we discover why. ~**William Barclay**

It's hard to beat a person who never gives up. ~**Babe Ruth**

Some people come into our lives as blessings, some come into our lives as lessons! ~**Mother Teresa**

Things that are covered up do not heal well. ~**T. D. Jakes**

Great minds discuss ideas, average minds discuss events; small minds discuss people. ~**T. D. Jakes**

You have a choice about how to react when someone pushes your fear button. You alone control how you think and react. ~**Gary Smalley**

A real Christian is the one who can give his pet parrot to the town gossip. ~**Billy Graham**

True Gospel ministry is not a party but a battle for souls. ~**Perry Stone**

## *Hymn: Truth*

**O God, Our Help in Ages Past**
O God, our help in ages past,
Our hope for years to come,
our shelter from the stormy blast,
And our eternal home.
Under the shadow of thy throne
Thy saints have dealt secure;
sufficient is thine arm alone,
and our defense is sure!
~**Isaac Watts**, 1719 (public domain)

## *Personalized Prayer Weaponry*

We are eternally thankful that Your Truth forever overrides all earthly facts. Whatever crucible we find ourselves in, may we be reminded that as Christians, we have a holy buoyancy available to us to keep our heads above the waters of life. Help us to sing our best songs while caged in life's adversities. Our frail vessels will be tossed on many rough seas, yet we are confident that there is just too much of God in us to utterly fail at any point.

## WEAPON 9

# Holy Spirit

### *Scriptures*

And the Spirit of the Lord came upon him, and he judged Israel, and went out to war: and the Lord delivered Cushan-Rishathaim king of Mesopotamia into his hand; and his hand prevailed against Cushan-Rishathaim.

**JUDGES 3:10**

Wherefore I say unto you, All manner of sin and blasphemy shall be forgiven unto men: but the blasphemy against the Holy Ghost shall not be forgiven unto men.

**MATTHEW 12:31**

That which is born of the flesh is flesh; and that which is born of the Spirit is spirit.

**JOHN 3:6**

For the law of the Spirit of life in Christ Jesus hath made me free from the law of sin and death.

**ROMANS 8:2**

Therefore, if any man be in Christ, he is a new creature: old things are passed away; behold, all things are become new.

**2 Corinthians 5:17**

But truly I am full of power by the spirit of the Lord, and of judgment, and of might, to declare unto Jacob his transgression, and to Israel his sin.

**Micah 3:8**

Others mocking said, These men are full of new wine.

**Acts 2:13**

Quench not the Spirit.

**1 Thessalonians 5:19**

But the manifestation of the Spirit is given to every man to profit withal.

**1 Corinthians 12:7**

But you, beloved, building yourselves up on your most holy faith, praying in the Holy Spirit.

**Jude 1:20 NKJV**

In the same way, the Spirit helps us in our weakness. We do not know what we ought to pray for, but the Spirit himself intercedes for us through wordless groans.

**Romans 8:26 NIV**

I have filled him with the Spirit of God, giving him great wisdom, ability, and expertise in all kinds of crafts.

**Exodus 31:3 NLT**

He who has an ear, let him hear and heed what the Spirit says to the churches. To him who overcomes, I will grant to eat from the tree of life, which is in the Paradise of God.

**Revelation 2:7 amp**

But the fruit of the Spirit is love, joy, peace, longsuffering, gentleness, goodness, faith, meekness, temperance: against such there is no law.

**Galatians 5:22–23**

A new heart also will I give you, and a new spirit will I put within you: and I will take away the stony heart out of your flesh, and I will give you an heart of flesh. And I will put my spirit within you, and cause you to walk in my statutes, and ye shall keep my judgments, and do them.

**Ezekiel 36:26–27**

Where there is no vision, the people perish: but he that keepeth the law, happy is he.

**Proverbs 29:18**

The steps of a good man are ordered by the Lord: and he delighteth in his way.

**Psalm 37:23**

For God hath not given us the spirit of fear; but of power, and of love, and of a sound mind.

**2 Timothy 1:7**

Then he answered and spake unto me, saying, This is the word of the Lord unto Zerubbabel, saying, Not by might, nor by power, but by my spirit, saith the Lord of hosts.

**Zechariah 4:6**

To them it was revealed that, not to themselves, but to us they were ministering the things which now have been reported to you through those who have preached the gospel to you by the Holy Spirit sent from heaven—things which angels desire to look into.

**1 Peter 1:12 NKJV**

You love justice and hate evil. Therefore, O God, your God has anointed you, pouring out the oil of joy on you more than on anyone else.

**Hebrews 1:9 NLT**

But my horn shalt thou exalt like the horn of a unicorn: I shall be anointed with fresh oil.

**Psalm 92:10**

But the Comforter, which is the Holy Ghost, whom the Father will send in my name, he shall teach you all things, and bring all things to your remembrance, whatsoever I have said unto you.

**John 14:26**

But ye shall receive power, after that the Holy Ghost is come upon you: and ye shall be witnesses unto me both in Jerusalem, and in all Judaea, and in Samaria, and unto the uttermost part of the earth.

**Acts 1:8**

And it shall come to pass afterward, that I will pour out my spirit upon all flesh; and your sons and your daughters shall prophesy, your old men shall dream dreams, your young men shall see visions.

**Joel 2:28**

Guard the good deposit that was entrusted to you—guard it with the help of the Holy Spirit who lives in us.

**2 Timothy 1:14 NIV**

## *Quotes: Holy Spirit*

There is not a better evangelist in the world than the Holy Spirit ~**D. L. Moody**

God speaks through a variety of means. In the present, God speaks via the Holy Spirit through prayer, Bible, church and circumstance. ~**Harry Blackaby**

Souls are made sweet by taking the acid out and pouring a great love, the Holy Spirit, in. ~**Henry Drummond**

Works of the Spirit: **1**. Holy Spirit was involved in creation. **2**. Is an awesome gift-giver. **3**. Holy Spirit gives us wisdom. **4**. He lives in us at conversion. **5**. He convicts the world of sin. **6**. He can be grieved, quenched, ignored. **7**. He gives spiritual illumination. **8**. He loves us deeply. **9**. He conforms us to the image of Christ. **10**. He is the Third divine person of the Trinity. When Holy Spirit is absent, our excuses seem right, but in his presence, our excuses fade away. ~**R. T. Kendall**

It is my opinion that the greatest absence in the church today is the fear of God. ~**R. T. Kendall**

Without the Spirit of God, we can do nothing, we are as a ship without direction, we are useless. ~**Charles Spurgeon**

The Christian who neglects the Holy Spirit is like a lamp that is not plugged in. ~**Unknown**

Holy Spirit is our unfailing, unfaltering, faithful life companion who is also our Great Sustainer. May I be drenched in the fuel of the Holy Spirit. Jesus is the match and God is the flame. ~**Unknown**

We need so deep a baptism of Holy Spirit fire that we go out with zeal for the souls of men. ~**Charles Finney**

Not being filled with Holy Spirit fire is like charging hell with a water pistol. ~**Andrew Wommack**

The Holy Spirit and you are a dynamic duo. Without him you will struggle, with him you are an unstoppable force. ~**Unknown**

I survive because the Holy Spirit fire inside me burns brighter than the fire around me. ~**Unknown**

It was the Lord who put into my mind, the fact that it would be possible to sail from Spain to the Indies. The Holy Spirit inspired me with comforting rays of marvelous light from the Holy Scriptures. ~**Christopher Columbus**

Following the light of the sun we left the old world. The air was so soft and fragrant it was delicious to breathe. ~**Christopher Columbus**

The Fruit of the Spirit is clearly evident in our lives. He is pruning, cultivating and adjusting the soil of my soul to produce a bountiful crop as I yield to Him. ~**Anonymous**

Don't allow religion and tradition to keep women locked up in a box. God did not give women the Holy Spirit to sit down, be quiet, be stopped and ignored. ~**John Eckhardt**

Oh, Great Spirit, help us always speak the truth quietly, to listen with an open mind when others speak, and remember the peace found in silence. ~**Cherokee Prayer**

We cannot affectively serve God without the Holy Spirit. ~**Derek Prince**

We recognize that regeneration of the spirit is the paramount need of man. ~**Watchman Nee**

Only the power of the Holy Spirit can transform us, relieve our guilt, and heal our souls. ~**Anonymous**

God calls many of His most valued workers from the unknown multitude. ~**L. B. Cowman**

Ordinary people are seeing things in the glory that only great people saw in days gone by. ~**Ruth Ward Heflin**

Prophesy is the voice of revival. Let your prophetic voice bring revival, you'll save yourself thousands of hours of vain activities. ~**Ruth Ward Heflin**

Revival glory is standing under the cloud and ministering directly to the people. It is seeing into the eternal realm and declaring what you see, it is gathering the harvest using only the tools of the Spirit. ~**Ruth Ward Heflin**

Some days are like that! I want to thank you for being close to me so far this day, Lord, with your help I have not lost my temper, been impatient, been grumpy, judgmental or envious of anyone. but I will be getting out of bed in a minute and I know I will really need your help then! ~**Unknown**

Tears are liquid words that can only be deciphered by the Holy Spirit. Allow the Great Code Talker/Code Breaker to relieve your aching soul. ~**Anonymous**

The Holy Spirit can be: **1**. Resisted **2**. Tempted **3**. Lied to **4**. Grieved **5**. Blasphemed **6**. Insulted **7**. Quenched **8**. Vexed **9**. Quietened and **10**. Fellowshipped. If you do nothing but read your Bible, you will dry up; if you only pray, you will blow up, if you read your Bible and pray you will grow up. ~**R. T. Kendall**

The Holy Spirit was working through me in this film, and I was just directing traffic. ~**Mel Gibson** on *The Passion of the Christ*

A sinner can no more repent and believe without the Holy Spirit's aid than he can create a world. ~**Charles Spurgeon**

The Holy Spirit is a gift to every child of God. His presence within us isn't something we have to earn or acquire. ~**Charles Stanley**

We have been given the privilege to host this Holy presence. The Spirit is in me for my sake but upon me for others sake. ~**Charles Stanley**

Catch on fire with enthusiasm and people will come from miles to watch you burn. ~**John Wesley**

In the miracle of the moment "with the eyes of the spirit," we can see all things. ~**Anonymous**

I celebrate God's great work in my life, by determining to immerse myself in his rhythm, the DNA of the Spirit. ~**Anonymous**

A great calm overpowered and quietened my soul and I contemplated, God is my omnipotent advocate and my undaunted friend! ~**Anonymous**

God has matched our souls for such an hour. ~**Martin Luther**

The Gifts of the Spirit are indispensable in these days and those that lie ahead. ~**Unknown**

As sacred oil, He anoints believers and sets them apart to the priesthood of saints.
As fire, He both purges our dross and sets our consecrated nature ablaze.
As purifying water, He cleanses and sanctifies believers from the power of sin and works the Lord's good pleasure in them.
As the light, He shows people their lost condition and reveals Christ to them.
As heavenly dew, He removes our barrenness and fertilizes our lives.
As the Dove, with wings of peaceful love, He grieves over His Church and the souls of believers.
As the Comforter, He dispels the cares and doubts that mar the peace of His beloved ones.
As the wind, He brings the breath of life.
~**Charles Spurgeon**

## Hymn: Holy Spirit

**Breathe on Me, Breath of God**
Holy Spirit, breathe on me,
Until my heart is clean.
Let sunshine fill its utmost part,
Without a cloud between.
Take my heart and cleanse every part,
Holy Spirit breathe on me.
~**Edwin Hatch**, 1878 (public domain)

## Personalized Weaponry

Who is this mysterious, often maligned, ignored and overlooked third Person of the Holy Trinity? You may be surprised to learn, like Father and Son, he is referred to in the Scriptures as God also—God being a title much like president—yet another name is not revealed to us regarding him, such as Christ, the Son, Jehovah, the Father.

Helper, Teacher, Guide into the deeper things of God. Parakletos, the one called alongside to assist. Lifelong Companion for the believer, trusted Confidante, the ultimate Comforter. The one who woos the unconverted, the Bestower of the blessed gifts, the One who brings all things to our remembrance.

Hovering, like a mother hen over us, searching men's hearts and lives for an opportunity to light the spark of the eternal flame. He is tender, yet fierce, and one who can easily be hurt by our neglect. He is one of the three distinct personalities who are the "three who always agree" constantly working on our behalf. His convicting power is strong but can be resisted. He is mighty and yet gentle. He is firmly relentless in his love, and He disciplines like a pure and loving mother.

Since He burst on the earthly landscape in the second chapter of Acts and has never left, we see him diligently fulfilling his multiple duties and assignments. His perpetual office is that of the Great Promoter of Christ, as well as encourager of the saints and preparer of the soon-coming Bride. All the while, his search for the lost is monumental.

He purges, anoints, breathes life, brings peaceful love, removes barrenness, executes and guides duties, sets our natures ablaze. Get to know Him. What a precious jewel is His friendship—a beloved gift from the Divine Hand that rules all men and nations.

Christ remains at the right hand of the Father, as our Mighty High Priest, forever making intercession for us that our faith would not fail us. He does not leave this designated position.

## WEAPON 10

# Trust/Obedience

### *Scriptures*

For this is the love of God, that we keep his commandments: and his commandments are not grievous.

**1 JOHN 5:3**

For in him we live, and move, and have our being; as certain also of your own poets have said, for we are also his offspring.

**ACTS 17:28**

If only you would prepare your heart and lift up your hands to him in prayer! Get rid of your sins and leave all iniquity behind you. Then your face will brighten with innocence. You will be strong and free of fear.

**JOB 11:13–15 NLT**

Truly my soul silently waits for God; From Him comes my salvation.

**PSALM 62:1 NKJV**

In the multitude of my thoughts within me thy comforts delight my soul.

**Psalm 94:19**

Let not mercy and truth forsake thee: bind them about thy neck; write them upon the table of thine heart.

**Proverbs 3:3**

Jesus answered and said unto him, If a man love me, he will keep my words: and my Father will love him, and we will come unto him, and make our abode with him.

**John 14:23**

Now it shall be, if you diligently listen to and obey the voice of the Lord your God, being careful to do all of His commandments which I am commanding you today, the Lord your God will set you high above all the nations of the earth.

**Deuteronomy 28:1 AMP**

But be ye doers of the word, and not hearers only, deceiving your own selves.

**James 1:22**

Don't copy the behavior and customs of this world, but let God transform you into a new person by changing the way you think. Then you will learn to know God's will for you, which is good and pleasing and perfect.

**Romans 12:2 NLT**

But I say unto you which hear, love your enemies, do good to them which hate you, Bless them that curse you, and pray for them which despitefully use you.

**Luke 6:27–28**

Submit yourselves therefore to God. Resist the devil, and he will flee from you.

**James 4:7**

And he said to them all, If any man will come after me, let him deny himself, and take up his cross daily, and follow me.

**Luke 9:23**

Now therefore, if you will indeed obey My voice and keep My covenant, then you shall be a special treasure to Me above all people; for all the earth is Mine.

**Exodus 19:5 NKJV**

But he said, Yea rather, blessed are they that hear the word of God, and keep it.

**Luke 11:28**

As obedient children, not fashioning yourselves according to the former lusts in your ignorance.

**1 Peter 1:14**

For this is the love of God, that we keep his commandments: and his commandments are not grievous.

**1 John 5:3**

Never be lazy but work hard and serve the Lord enthusiastically.

**Romans 12:11 NLT**

To you, Lord, I call; you are my Rock, do not turn a deaf ear to me. For if you remain silent, I will be like those who go down to the pit.

**Psalm 28:1 NIV**

Neither have I gone back from the commandment of his lips; I have esteemed the words of his mouth more than my necessary food.

**Job 23:12**

Has the Lord great delight in burnt offerings and sacrifices, as in obeying the voice of the Lord? Behold, to obey is better than sacrifice and to heed, than the fat of rams.

**1 Samuel 15:22 NKJV**

Serve the Lord with gladness: come before his presence with singing.

**Psalm 100:2**

## *Quotes: Trust/Obedience*

Trust the past to God's mercy; the present to God's love, and the future to God's providence. ~**Saint Augustine**

May we be sure that if God sends us over rocky paths, he will provide us with sturdy shoes. He will not be sending you on a journey without equipping you as well. ~**Alexander McLaren**

In perplexities, when we do not understand what is going on around us, nor what to do, let us be calmed and steadied and made patient by the thought that what is hidden from us is not hidden from God. ~**Frances Havergal**

Every evening I turn all my worries over to God, He is going to be up anyway! ~**Mary Crowley**

God marks across some of our days, "will explain later." ~**Vance Havner**

God is not looking for gold or silver vessels, he is looking for trusting, willing ones. ~**Katherine Kuhlman**

Holiness is not to love Jesus and do what you want, holiness is to love God and obey what he wants done. ~**Peter Wagner**

The man who is intimate with God is never intimidated by man. ~**Leonard Ravenhill**

Worry and anxiety are sand in the machinery of life. Faith is the oil. ~**E. Stanley Jones**

Being full of fresh oil and new wine makes us vessels fit for the Master's use. ~**Anonymous**

For God to explain our trials would be to destroy their purpose, calling for simple faith and implicit obedience. ~**Alfred Edersheim**

No Christian has ever been known to recant on his deathbed. ~**C. M. Ward**

Patience is idling your motor when you feel like stripping your gears. ~**Bill Gothard**

Have you learned the beautiful art of letting God take care of you and giving you strength to pray for others? ~**A. B. Simpson**

Spiritual maturity isn't about how much we know, it's about how much we obey. ~**Unknown**

God is awesome, he doesn't need you to be awesome, he needs you to be obedient. ~**Matt Chandler**

Pray, then let it go, don't try to manipulate or force the outcome. Simply trust God to open the right doors at the right time. ~**Unknown**

There will be no peace in any soul, until it is willing to obey the voice of God. ~**D. L. Moody**

He who refuses to obey cannot command. ~**Benjamin Franklin**

God's way is not always going to make sense, just obey and trust him anyway. Not relying on other people but listening to that still, small voice of God. He will not lead you in the wrong way! ~**Unknown**

You can see God from anywhere, if your mind is set on loving him and obeying him. ~**A. W. Tozer**

The ship that does not obey the helm will have to obey the rocks. ~**Old Proverb**

Life is a gift given in trust, like a child. ~**Ann Morrow Lindberg**

A child that never learns to obey his parents in the home, will not obey God or man outside the home. ~**Susannah Wesley**

Teach me the glory of my cross; teach me the value of my thorn, show me that my tears have made my rainbow. We conquer by continuing. ~**George Matheson**

All worry is atheism, because it is a want of trust in God. ~**Fulton Sheen**

I choose trust over control; I am wretched in all the ways that matter. ~**Anonymous**

Let us not resent God's timetable, I trust God in the pain. ~**Anonymous**

Trust is letting go and knowing God will catch you. ~**James Dobson**

Worry is the besetting sin that Christians entertain on a daily basis. ~**John Piper**

When we worry, we put the good thing in the wrong place, fretting makes us a slave instead of a master. The slaves of worry wear thorns in their hearts. Lord, save us from over eagerness about the things of life! ~**Mark Guy Pearce**

I'd rather be in the heart of Africa, in the will of God, than on the throne of England, out of the will of God. ~**David Livingston**

Worrying is like sitting in a rocking chair, it gives you something to do, but you get nowhere. ~**Erma Bombeck**

Worrying does not empty tomorrow of its troubles, it empties today of strength. ~**Corrie Ten Boom**

Worrying often gives a small thing a big shadow. **~Swedish Proverb**

Our fatigue is often caused not by work but by worry, frustration and resentment. **~Dale Carnegie**

When birds of worry and care fly over your head, this you cannot change, but if they build nests in your hair, this you can prevent. **~Chinese Proverb**

May our obedience grow from love and gratitude and may it be cheerful, constant, uniform and universal like that obedience that the holy angels pay our Father in heaven. **~George Whitefield**

Dedication is writing your name on the bottom of a blank sheet of paper and handing it to the Lord for him to fill in! **~Rick Renner**

Rest is the ability to totally trust God without living under the stress of the cares of life. **~Perry Stone**

Good is warm blooded, evil is cold blooded, snakes die at high altitudes so keep climbing the mountain of God and that enemy you're facing will die off. **~Anonymous**

## *Hymn: Trust/Obedience*

**Day by Day**
Day by day and
with each passing moment,
Strength I find to meet my trials here.

Trusting in my Father's
wise bestowment,
I have no cause for worry or fear.
He whose heart is kind
beyond all measure,
Gives unto each day
what he deems best.
Lovingly it's part of pain and pleasure,
Mingling toil with peace and rest.
~**Lina Sandell**, 1865 (public domain)

## *Personalized Prayer Weaponry*

We purposely trust you today, Lord, and deny all forms of hesitation and deception that would lure us from this place of obedience. You have gifted us with unique manifestations and enabled us to bring these spiritual possessions to the place of duty. There, we tell what great things God has done for us and through us. Help us not to indulge in selfish stupidity nor quarrel against sound wisdom, but forever seek your blessed will. May our souls sit under the shadow of Your mighty rays of sacred light and find quiet, comforting and uplifting joy. As you inflame our love for you, cause the beautiful freedom of trust and obedience to produce much fruit in our lives.

The Friend of sinners, Precious and Elect in Zion, we trust and obey the delegated authority given us this day. This is the Lord's doing and it is marvelous in our sight. Thank you, that we are easily entreated, as we allow you to stretch us to your designed capacity.

# WEAPON 11

# Faith

## *Scriptures*

Be strong and of a good courage, fear not, nor be afraid of them: for the Lord thy God, he it is that doth go with thee; he will not fail thee, nor forsake thee.

**DEUTERONOMY 31:6**

You will keep in perfect peace all who trust in you, all whose thoughts are fixed on you.

**ISAIAH 26:3 NLT**

So do not fear, for I am with you; do not be dismayed, for I am your God. I will strengthen you and help you; I will uphold you with my righteous right hand.

**ISAIAH 41:10 NIV**

Peace I leave with you, my peace I give unto you: not as the world giveth, give I unto you. Let not your heart be troubled, neither let it be afraid.

**JOHN 14:27**

Trust in the Lord with all thine heart; and lean not unto thine own understanding. In all thy ways acknowledge him, and he shall direct thy paths.

**Proverbs 3:5–6**

The righteous cry, and the Lord heareth, and delivereth them out of all their troubles. The Lord is nigh unto them that are of a broken heart; and saveth such as be of a contrite spirit.

**Psalm 34:17–18**

For ye are all the children of God by faith in Christ Jesus. For as many of you as have been baptized into Christ have put on Christ.

**Galatians 3:26–27**

And Moses said to the people, "Do not be afraid. Stand still, and see the salvation of the Lord, which He will accomplish for you today. For the Egyptians whom you see today, you shall see again no more forever."

**Exodus 14:13 NKJV**

Thus did Noah; according to all that God commanded him, so did he.

**Genesis 6:22**

By faith Noah, being warned of God of things not seen as yet, moved with fear, prepared an ark to the saving of his house; by the which he condemned the world, and became heir of the righteousness which is by faith.

**Hebrews 11:7**

The Lord had said to Abram, "Go from your country, your people and your father's household to the land I will show you."

**GENESIS 12:1 NIV**

Therefore it is of faith, that it might be by grace; to the end the promise might be sure to all the seed; not to that only which is of the law, but to that also which is of the faith of Abraham; who is the father of us all.

**ROMANS 4:16**

But now the Lord my God hath given me rest on every side, so that there is neither adversary nor evil occurrent.

**1 KINGS 5:4**

I am crucified with Christ: nevertheless I live; yet not I, but Christ liveth in me: and the life which I now live in the flesh I live by the faith of the Son of God, who loved me, and gave himself for me.

**GALATIANS 2:20**

So Jesus said to them, "Because of your unbelief; for assuredly, I say to you, if you have faith as a mustard seed, you will say to this mountain, move from here to there, and it will move; and nothing will be impossible for you."

**MATTHEW 17:20 NKJV**

For all things are for your sakes, that the abundant grace might through the thanksgiving of many redound to the glory of God. For which cause we faint not; but though our outward man perish, yet the inward man is renewed day by day. For our light affliction, which is but for a moment, worketh for us a far more exceeding and eternal weight of glory.

**2 Corinthians 4:15–17**

Therefore, I say unto you, What things whosoever ye desire, when ye pray, believe that ye receive them, and ye shall have them.

**Mark 11:24**

Knowing this, that the trying of your faith worketh patience.

**James 1:3**

Him that is weak in the faith receive ye, but not to doubtful disputations.

**Romans 14:1**

For whatsoever is born of God overcometh the world: and this is the victory that overcometh the world, even our faith.

**1 John 5:4**

I have chosen the way of truth; Your judgments I have laid before me.

**Psalm 119:30 NKJV**

For with the heart man believeth unto righteousness; and with the mouth confession is made unto salvation.

**Romans 10:10**

For God so loved the world, that he gave his only begotten Son, that whosoever believeth in him should not perish, but have everlasting life.

**John 3:16**

Watch ye, stand fast in the faith, quit you like men, be strong.

**1 Corinthians 16:13**

In the same way, faith by itself, if it is not accompanied by action, is dead.

**James 2:17 NIV**

For by grace are ye saved through faith; and that not of yourselves: it is the gift of God: Not of works, lest any man should boast.

**Ephesians 2:8–9**

So then faith cometh by hearing, and hearing by the word of God.

**Romans 10:17**

Now godliness with contentment is great gain.

**1 Timothy 6:6 NKJV**

Fight the good fight for the true faith. Hold tightly to the eternal life to which God has called you, which you have declared so well before many witnesses.

**1 Timothy 6:12 NLT**

But now the Lord my God hath given me rest on every side, so that there is neither adversary nor evil occurrent.

**1 Kings 5:4**

Therefore, he is able to save completely those who come to God through him, because he always lives to intercede for them.

**Hebrews 7:25**

Strengthened with all might, according to his glorious power, unto all patience and longsuffering with joyfulness.

**Colossians 1:11**

For therein is the righteousness of God revealed from faith to faith: as it is written, the just shall live by faith.

**Romans 1:17**

The Lord says, "I will give you back what you lost to the swarming locusts, the hopping locusts, the stripping locusts, and the cutting locusts. It was I who sent this great destroying army against you."

**Joel 2:25 NLT**

And now abide faith, hope, love, these three; but the greatest of these is love.

**1 Corinthians 13:13 NKJV**

And he shall be like a tree planted by the rivers of water, that bringeth forth his fruit in his season; his leaf also shall not wither; and whatsoever he doeth shall prosper.

**Psalm 1:3**

For the Lord your God is bringing you into a good land, a land of brooks of water, of fountains and springs, flowing forth in valleys and hills.

**Deuteronomy 8:7 AMP**

For as he thinks in his heart, so is he. "Eat and drink!" he says to you, but his heart is not with you.

**Proverbs 23:7 NKJV**

Now faith is the substance of things hoped for, the evidence of things not seen.

**Hebrews 11:1**

For we walk by faith, not by sight.

**2 Corinthians 5:7**

## *Quotes: Faith*

Great faith is the product of great fights. Great testimonies are the outcome of great minds. Great triumphs can only come out of great trials. ~**Smith Wigglesworth**

Few things are more infectious than a Godly lifestyle. Not preaching, not prudish. Just crackerjack-clean living. Just honest, bone-deep integrity. ~**Chuck Swindoll**

There is no such thing as failure, there is just giving up too soon. ~**Jonas Salk**

Unless we stand for something, we will fall for anything. ~**Peter Marshall**

A noblewoman named Perpetua and her slave, Felicitas, in the year 203 AD, were martyred for being Christian women at the hands of the Romans in the stadium in Carthage. This is one of the earliest accounts of faithful women on church record who were killed by wild beasts and gladiators. ~**Fox's Book of Martyrs**

The power that was released in the Jerusalem tomb fills the earth even now. Apply your faith to anything you need to be raised to life. ~**Mike Hayes**

Something good is going to happen today! God is our source of supply! If you have a need, plant a seed. Use your seed faith and release it on a point of contact. ~**Oral Roberts**

Great faith will not take no for an answer. ~**Oral Roberts**

Faith can be spelled R-I-S-K. ~**Unknown**

Faith is looking at the impossible and knowing God will not fail you. ~**John Hagee**

Faith expects from God what is beyond all expectation. ~**Andrew Murray**

Faith is taking the first step even when you can't see the whole staircase. ~**Martin Luther King Jr.**

God knows how long you have waited. Every second will be worth it in the end. Keep the faith! ~**Unknown**

Never dig up in unbelief what you have sown in faith. ~**Gordon Lindsay**

Through the various degrees of belief, make us powerful responders. ~**Anonymous**

Sometimes God lets you hit rock bottom, so that you will discover, that he is the Rock at the bottom. ~**Tony Evans**

Nothing in the world glorifies God so much as a simple resting of our faith in what God's word says. ~**Smith Wigglesworth**

Faith is like Wi-Fi, it's invisible, but it has the power to connect you to what you need. ~**Unknown**

You don't have any problems at all, all you need is your faith in God. ~**R. W. Schambach**

Have faith, keep praying and be thankful. Remember God's answers are wiser than your prayers. ~**Unknown**

Some people wonder why they can't have faith for healing. They feed their bodies three meals a day and give their spirit one cold snack once a week. ~**F. F. Bosworth**

Christianity helps us face the music even when we don't like the tune. ~**Phillips Brooks**

Oh, people of God, be great believers! Little faith will bring your souls to heaven, but great faith will bring heaven to your souls. ~**Charles Spurgeon**

Trials strengthen and test your faith. They are waves that wash you further up the rock. They are wind that moves your ship swiftly toward the desired haven. ~**Charles Spurgeon**

Christianity has successfully been attacked and marginalized, because those who professed belief were unable to defend the faith from attack, even when the attacker's arguments were deeply flawed. ~**William Wilberforce**

There is no normal life that is free of pain. It's the very wrestling with our problems that can be the impetus for our growth. ~**Mr. Rogers**

God is down in front of us. He is in all the tomorrows. They must pass before him before they get to us. ~**F. B. Meyer**

If you are hearing from God, you can't dream bigger than God can deliver. ~**Robert Morris**

Remove the poisonous thoughts that people project and cut the shoreline of your past. A new day is breaking forth. Be free from fear, step out into my love and you will not sink. You will see my power and faithfulness and cut loose those things which hold you to bondage and fear. ~**Morris Cerullo**

Beware of the maze, deception and distraction of detours and dead ends threatening your faith. Be strong in truth, repentance and the fires of holiness. Refuse false doctrines and teachings eroding your biblical foundations. Do not be comfortable and silent in darkness, push toward the King. ~**Anonymous**

We are now progressing into a time of maximum danger as we conclude the end times. There will be persecution and perilous, fierce events. We must keep our eyes on the prize of Christ. In distant ages yet to come, in the regions beyond, we will travel the universe with Jesus and we will rule and reign with him. No future generation will enjoy the privileges we have as the bride of Christ. ~**Theresa Garcia**

It's always in the weakest moments, when it looks like the true message is about to be defeated, that's when God steps in. ~**William Branham**

It is abnormal for a Christian not to have an appetite for the impossible. It has been written into our spiritual DNA to hunger for the impossibilities around us in the name of Jesus. ~**Anonymous**

I know he tries me only to increase my faith. ~**Hudson Taylor**

Faith never knows where it is being led, but it loves and knows the one who is doing the leading. ~**Oswald Chambers**

The beautiful thing about this adventure called faith is that we can count on him never to lead us astray. ~**Chuck Swindoll**

You cannot have a positive life and a negative mind. ~**Joyce Meyer**

Faith is the radar that sees through the fog. ~**Corrie Ten Boom**

Faith can move mountains, but don't be surprised if God hands you the shovel. ~**Unknown**

When fear knocks on your door, send faith to answer. ~**Joyce Meyer**

Fear is a dark room where negatives are developed. ~**Joyce Meyer**

A faith that cannot be tested cannot be trusted. ~**Warren Wiersbe**

The only way to avoid despair is to place our faith in Jesus Christ, for the salvation God provides. ~**R. C. Sproul**

Faith shines the brightest in the dark! ~**Unknown**

The Grand Old Book and The Dear Old Faith are the rock on which we stand, The Grand Old Book and The Dear Old Faith are the hope of every land. ~**Unknown**

The five fundamentals of faith. **1**. The Deity of Christ. **2**. The Virgin birth. **3**. Blood Atonement for sin. **4**. Bodily Resurrection and return of Christ. **5**. The Inerrancy of Scriptures.

Zeal of Youth and Wisdom of Senior saints combined with unyielding faith produces divine energy. ~**Anonymous**

By faith, the obedient saint claims his full rights in Christ, and boldly asserts his authority. The powers of the air will recognize this and obey. ~**John A. MacMillan**

Strong faith enables the servants of God to look with calm contempt on their most arrogant foes. ~**Charles Spurgeon**

Faith increases in stability, assurance and intensity, the more it is tried! Faith is precious, and its trial is precious! ~**Charles Spurgeon**

## Hymn: Faith

**Great Is Thy Faithfulness**
Great is thy faithfulness,
oh, God my Father,
There is no shadow
of turning with thee.
Thou changes not,
thy compassions, they fail not,
As thou has been,
thou forever will be.
Great is thy faithfulness
Morning by morning
new mercies I see,
All I have needed
your hand has provided
Great is thy faithfulness,
Lord, unto me.
~**Thomas Chisholm**, 1923 (public domain)

## Personalized Weaponry

There have been several times in my life when surgery was necessary, but I must say, I was not prepared for heart surgery. I had, on many occasions, gone to the ER with palpitations. But with no high blood pressure and no elevated heart enzymes during those visits, I simply spent time on the cardiac floor after each incident. Later, my doctor discovered a 90 percent blockage that a stint would not hold, so in 2010, my grim-faced and teary-eyed children watched as I faced this grueling surgery. While being wheeled into the surgical suite, I experienced an unswerving, unflinching calm, unexplainable but so very real. My shield of faith was locked firmly in place with brothers and sisters in the Lord. Yet, after the surgery, I still endured extended hospital stays due to adverse reactions to medication.

Several months later, during a routine checkup, I was informed the bypass had not held. But my heart had formed a new pathway around the blockage to save my life. My Mighty God had performed another miracle in my life!

## *Personalized Prayer Weaponry*

Great God, may we always be powerful contenders for the faith. Let us not imagine, in our own vain conceit, that we know a better way outside your chosen and provable will for our lives. May we not allow the fleeting vapors of this present evil world to dampen our faith-filled assignment. We declare our constant need of You and ask that You grant us the strength to never turn aside from You, not matter how evil the day.

## WEAPON 12

# Covenant/Commitment

### *Scriptures: Covenant*

Have respect unto the covenant: for the dark places of the earth are full of the habitations of cruelty.

**PSALM 74:20**

For I will have respect unto you, and make you fruitful, and multiply you, and establish my covenant with you.

**LEVITICUS 26:9**

I beseech thee, O Lord God of heaven, the great and terrible God, that keepeth covenant and mercy for them that love him and observe his commandments.

**NEHEMIAH 1:5**

But thou shalt remember the Lord thy God: for it is he that giveth thee power to get wealth, that he may establish his covenant which he sware unto thy fathers, as it is this day.

**DEUTERONOMY 8:18**

For the mountains shall depart, and the hills be removed; but my kindness shall not depart from thee, neither shall the covenant of my peace be removed, saith the Lord that hath mercy on thee.

**Isaiah 54:10**

And the bow shall be in the cloud; and I will look upon it, that I may remember the everlasting covenant between God and every living creature of all flesh that is upon the earth.

**Genesis 9:16**

Blessed be the God and Father of our Lord Jesus Christ, who hath blessed us with all spiritual blessings in heavenly places in Christ.

**Ephesians 1:3**

But now Jesus, our High Priest, has been given a ministry that is far superior to the old priesthood, for he is the one who mediates for us a far better covenant with God, based on better promises.

**Hebrews 8:6 NLT**

And he said unto them, This is my blood of the new testament, which is shed for many.

**Mark 14:24**

But thou, O Lord, art a shield for me; my glory, and the lifter up of mine head.

**Psalm 3:3**

God stands in the congregation of the mighty; He judges among the gods.

**Psalm 82:1 NKJV**

For ye are dead, and your life is hidden with Christ in God. When Christ, who is our life, shall appear, then shall ye also appear with him in glory.

**Colossians 3:3–4**

But my God shall supply all your need according to his riches in glory by Christ Jesus.

**Philippians 4:19**

You prepare a table before me in the presence of my enemies; You anoint my head with oil; My cup runs over.

**Psalm 23:5 NKJV**

Even the captives of the mighty man will be taken away, And the tyrant's spoils of war will be rescued; For I will contend with your opponent, And I will save your children.

**Isaiah 49:25 AMP**

The Lord will send rain at the proper time from his rich treasury in the heavens and will bless all the work you do. You will lend to many nations, but you will never need to borrow from them.

**Deuteronomy 28:12 NLT**

My covenant will I not break, nor alter the thing that is gone out of my lips.

**Psalm 89:34**

## *Scriptures: Commitment*

Obey the Lord your God and follow his commands and decrees that I give you today.

**DEUTERONOMY 27:10 NIV**

But thanks be to God that, though you used to be slaves to sin, you have come to obey from your heart the pattern of teaching that has now claimed your allegiance.

**ROMANS 6:17 NIV**

Let your heart therefore be perfect with the Lord our God, to walk in his statutes, and to keep his commandments, as at this day.

**1 KINGS 8:61**

If ye keep my commandments, ye shall abide in my love; even as I have kept my Father's commandments and abide in his love.

**JOHN 15:10**

And thou shalt love the Lord thy God with all thine heart, and with all thy soul, and with all thy might.

**DEUTERONOMY 6:5**

For the eyes of the Lord move to and fro throughout the earth so that He may support those whose heart is completely His. You have acted foolishly in this; therefore, from now on you will have wars.

**2 CHRONICLES 16:9 AMP**

Commit thy works unto the Lord, and thy thoughts shall be established.

**PROVERBS 16:3**

But without faith it is impossible to please him: for he that cometh to God must believe that he is, and that he is a rewarder of them that diligently seek him.

**HEBREWS 11:6**

Repent ye therefore, and be converted, that your sins may be blotted out, when the times of refreshing shall come from the presence of the Lord.

**ACTS 3:19**

Redeeming the time, because the days are evil.

**EPHESIANS 5:16**

When a strong man, fully armed, guards his own palace, his goods are in peace. But when a stronger than he comes upon him and overcomes him, he takes from him all his armor in which he trusted, and divides his spoils. He who is not with Me is against Me, and he who does not gather with Me scatters.

**LUKE 11:21–23 NKJV**

## *Quotes: Covenant*

Keeping covenants protects us, prepares us and empowers us. ~**Anonymous**

The beauty of covenant keeps love between Christ and His church shining brightly when nothing but Christ can sustain it. ~**John Piper**

Because God is a living God, he can hear; because he is a loving God, he will hear; because he is a covenant God, he has bound himself to hear. ~**Charles Spurgeon**

God doesn't want us to have rigid rituals with Him in the new covenant, he is more interested in having a close relationship with us. ~**Joseph Prince**

After the work of Christ on the cross, we have the promise of the new covenant that produces a new heart. ~**John Eldredge**

Our trials need not be spiritually fatal, they need not take us from our covenants or from the household of God. ~**Neil Anderson**

When you choose to make or keep a covenant with God, you choose whether or not you will leave an inheritance of hope to those who might follow your example. ~**Anonymous**

Covenant community is like air, we don't miss it until we need it. ~**Tim Keller**

Really, our problems are not weakness but independence, in covenant we must die to independent living. ~**Kay Arthur**

God has a remnant according to the election of grace. His people are scattered among every kindred, tongue and nation, committed, devoted and covenant bound. ~**Anonymous**

## *Quotes: Commitment*

Commitment is what transfers a promise into a reality. ~**Abraham Lincoln**

Most people fail, not because of lack of desire, but because of a lack of commitment. ~**Vince Lombardi**

Commitment is doing the thing you said you were going to do, long after the mood you said it in has left you. ~**Unknown**

Productivity is never an accident; it is always the result of a commitment to excellence, intelligent planning and focused effort. ~**Paul J. Meyer**

The beautiful statement of commitment is the language of covenant marriage. ~**Gary Chapman**

Commitment in the face of conflict produces character. ~**Unknown**

Commitment is a big word that requires both guts and diligence and change is never easy. ~**Anonymous**

The important thing is to make sure no day passes, without you committing at least half an hour to commune with God. ~**Anonymous**

## *Hymn: Covenant/Commitment*

**Guide Me, O Thou Great Jehovah**
Guide me, O thou Great Jehovah,
Pilgrim through this barren land.
I am weak, but you are mighty,
Hold us with your powerful hand.
Bread of heaven, Bread of heaven,
feed us til we want no more.
~**William Williams**, 1745 (public domain)

## *Personalized Prayer Weaponry*

We seek this very day to enter Your covenant promises and make them a reality in our lives. Our commitment is real and unrelenting with Your help and power. Speak peace to our agitated minds and circumstances and drive out all arrogant pride. You saw our potential beauty, pursued us, and carved us out of the Rock, which is Christ Himself. Grant us, Father, the ability to emulate Your meekness, humility and loving Spirit, and draw us ever closer to Your covenant-making, covenant-keeping presence. We are our Beloved's and our Beloved is ours!

We are blessed with a strong confidence; when we revere and honor the Lord of hosts, and as his children, we will always have a place of very real refuge.

## Weapon 13

# Discipline/Determination

### *Scriptures: Discipline*

Whoever loves discipline loves knowledge, but whoever hates correction is stupid.

**Proverbs 12:1 NIV**

As many as I love, I rebuke and chasten; be zealous therefore, and repent.

**Revelation 3:19**

Those who spare the rod of discipline hate their children. Those who love their children care enough to discipline them.

**Proverbs 13:24 NLT**

No discipline seems pleasant at the time, but painful. Later; however, it produces a harvest of righteousness and peace for those who have been trained by it.

**Hebrews 12:11 NIV**

For the commandment is a lamp; and the law is light; and reproofs of instruction are the way of life.

**Proverbs 6:23**

But refuse profane and old wives' fables and exercise thyself rather unto godliness.

**1 Timothy 4:7**

But I keep my body and bring it into subjection: lest that by any means, when I have preached to others, I myself should be a castaway.

**1 Corinthians 9:27**

Think about it: Just as a parent disciplines a child, the Lord your God disciplines you for your own good. So obey the commands of the Lord your God by walking in his ways and fearing him.

**Deuteronomy 8:5–6 NLT**

The rod and reproof give wisdom: but a child left to himself bringeth his mother to shame.

**Proverbs 29:15**

Behold, happy is the man whom God corrects; therefore do not despise the chastening of the Almighty.

**Job 5:17 NKJV**

Keep thy heart with all diligence; for out of it are the issues of life.

**Proverbs 4:23**

When she speaks, her words are wise, and she gives instructions with kindness.

**Proverbs 31:26 NLT**

Hear; for I will speak of excellent things; and the opening of my lips shall be right things.

**PROVERBS 8:6**

Finally, brethren, whatsoever things are true, whatsoever things are honest, whatsoever things are just, whatsoever things are pure, whatsoever things are lovely, whatsoever things are of good report; if there be any virtue, and if there be any praise, think on these things.

**PHILIPPIANS 4:8**

And do not murmur, as some of them did—and were destroyed by the destroyer.

**1 CORINTHIANS 10:10 AMP**

Yea, they despised the pleasant land, they believed not his word: But murmured in their tent, and hearkened not unto the voice of the Lord. ,therefore he lifted up his hand against them, to overthrow them in the wilderness: To overthrow their seed also among the nations, and to scatter them in the lands.

**PSALM 106:24–27**

## *Scriptures: Determination*

I can do all things through Christ which strengtheneth me.

**PHILIPPIANS 4:13**

I have fought a good fight, I have finished my course, I have kept the faith.

**2 TIMOTHY 4:7**

Behold, the people shall rise up as a great lion, and lift up himself as a young lion: he shall not lie down until he eats of the prey, and drink the blood of the slain.

**Numbers 23:24**

Be ye strong; therefore and let not your hands be weak: for your work shall be rewarded.

**2 Chronicles 15:7**

I seek you with all my heart; do not let me stray from your commands.

**Psalm 119:10**

For the Lord God will help me; therefore, shall I not be confounded: therefore, have I set my face like a flint, and I know that I shall not be ashamed.

**Isaiah 50:7**

For I determined not to know anything among you, save Jesus Christ, and him crucified.

**1 Corinthians 2:2**

The anger of the Lord shall not return, until he has executed, and till he have performed the thoughts of his heart: in the latter days ye shall consider it perfectly.

**Jeremiah 23:20**

And let us not be weary in well doing; for in due season we shall reap, if we faint not.

**Galatians 6:9**

And Jesus said unto him, No man having put his hand to the plough and looking back, is fit for the kingdom of God.

**Luke 9:62**

Do you not know that those who run in a race all run, but one receives the prize? Run in such a way that you may obtain it.

**1 Corinthians 9:24 NKJV**

Finally, my brethren, be strong in the Lord, and in the power of his might.

**Ephesians 6:10**

Confirming the souls of the disciples, and exhorting them to continue in the faith, and that we must through much tribulation enter into the kingdom of God.

**Acts 14:22**

Commit thy works unto the Lord, and thy thoughts shall be established.

**Proverbs 16:3**

Trust in the Lord with all thine heart; and lean not unto thine own understanding. In all thy ways acknowledge him, and he shall direct thy paths.

**Proverbs 3:5–6**

Delight thyself also in the Lord: and he shall give thee the desires of thine heart.

**Psalm 37:4**

There are many devices in a man's heart; nevertheless, the counsel of the Lord, that shall stand.

**Proverbs 19:21**

Before I formed you in the womb I knew you, and before you were born I consecrated you; I have appointed you as a prophet to the nations.

**Jeremiah 1:5 AMP**

Now unto him that is able to do exceeding abundantly above all that we ask or think, according to the power that worketh in us.

**Ephesians 3:20**

## *Quotes: Discipline*

It hurts when God has to pry things out of our hands. **~Corrie Ten Boom**

Discipline, for the Christian, begins with the body; we cannot give our hearts to God, and keep our bodies to ourselves. **~Elizabeth Elliot**

Discipline is choosing between what you want to do now and what you want most. **~Unknown**

It was character that got us out of bed, commitment that moves us into action, and discipline that enables us to follow through. **~Zig Ziglar**

Discipline is the soul of an army, it makes small numbers formidable; procures success for the weak, and esteem to all. **~George Washington**

I believe that through knowledge and discipline, financial peace is possible for all of us. **~Dave Ramsey**

Most people want to avoid pain and discipline is usually painful. ~**John Maxwell**

I relied on the discipline, character and strength that I started to develop as a little girl in my first swimming pool. ~**Esther Williams**

Chastisement is designed for our good, to promote our highest interests. Look beyond the rod to the all-wise hand that wields it. ~**Arthur Pink**

It is clear from the Bible that those who fail to heed the Lord's discipline, whether nations, cities or individuals, suffer devastating consequences. ~**Charles Stanley**

Discipline yourself and others will not need to. ~**John Wooden**

Discipline is just doing the same thing the right way whether anybody is watching or not. ~**Michael J. Fox**

You can judge the quality of a person's faith by the way they behave. Discipline is an index to doctrine. ~**Tertullian**

## *Quotes: Determination*

The world makes way for the man who knows where he is going. ~**Ralph Waldo Emerson**

You may be disappointed if you failed, but you are doomed if you do not try. ~**Beverly Sills**

If one does not know to which port he is sailing, no wind is favorable. ~**Seneca**

Don't give up, for this is just the place and the time, that the tide may well turn. ~**Harriet Beecher Stowe**

The man who can drive himself further, once the effort gets painful, is the man who will win. ~**Roger Bannister**

Wake up with determination, go to bed with satisfaction. ~**Unknown**

A dream does not become a reality through magic; it takes sweat, determination and hard work. ~**Colin Powell**

Determination gives you the resolve to keep going, in spite of the roadblocks that lay before you. ~**Denis Waitley**

If you set goals with all the determination you can muster, your gifts will take you places that will amaze you. ~**Les Brown**

The future belongs to those who believe in the beauty of their dreams. ~**Eleanor Roosevelt**

The world is moved along, not only by the mighty, but by the heroes in the tiny pushes of each honest worker. ~**Unknown**

## *Hymn: Discipline/Determination*

**It Is Well with My Soul**
When peace, like a river,
attendeth my way,
When sorrows like
sea billows roll.
Whatever my lot,
you have taught me to say,
"It is well, it is well with my soul."
~**Horatio Spafford**, 1873 (public domain)

## *Personalized Prayer Weaponry*

Strange words, *discipline* and *determination*, that have faded from the landscape of humanity in this day and age. What? Lord, You are asking us to be disciplined and to deny ourselves much of what this earth screams for us to embrace? No instant gratification? No "right now, I want it"? No "but I deserve it"? We need Your instruction, Your wise counsel to counteract the spirit of slackness, of laziness, of malcontent. Sharpen our skill of waiting to ensure we will experience the greater glory You ordained us to enjoy. You, our Lord and Master, are timeless and yet timely. Help us, according to Isaiah 50:7, to set our face like a flint towards heaven and we shall not be moved or put to shame.

## WEAPON 14

# Forgiveness

Forbearing one another, and forgiving one another, if any man has a quarrel against any: even as Christ forgave you, so also do ye.

**COLOSSIANS 3:13**

For if you forgive men their trespasses, your heavenly Father will also forgive you. But if you do not forgive men their trespasses, neither will your Father forgive your trespasses.

**MATTHEW 6:14–15 NKJV**

If we confess our sins, he is faithful and just to forgive us our sins, and to cleanse us from all unrighteousness.

**1 JOHN 1:9**

In whom we have redemption through his blood, the forgiveness of sins, according to the riches of his grace.

**EPHESIANS 1:7**

To the Lord our God belong mercies and forgiveness, though we have rebelled against him.

**DANIEL 9:9**

He has not dealt with us according to our sins, nor punished us according to our iniquities. For as the heavens are high above the earth, so great is His mercy toward those who fear Him; As far as the east is from the west, So far has He removed our transgressions from us.

**Psalm 103:10–12 NKJV**

And when ye stand praying, forgive, if ye have ought against any: that your Father also which is in heaven may forgive you your trespasses.

**Mark 11:25**

But I say unto you, love your enemies, bless them that curse you, do good to them that hate you, and pray for them which despitefully use you, and persecute you.

**Matthew 5:44**

And be ye kind one to another, tenderhearted, forgiving one another, even as God for Christ's sake hath forgiven you.

**Ephesians 4:32**

But when you are praying, first forgive anyone you are holding a grudge against, so that your Father in heaven will forgive your sins, too.

**Mark 11:25 NLT**

Let all bitterness, and wrath, and anger, and clamour, and evil speaking, be put away from you, with all malice: And be ye kind one to another, tenderhearted, forgiving one another, even as God for Christ's sake hath forgiven you.

**Ephesians 4:31–32**

Confess your faults one to another, and pray one for another, that ye may be healed. The effectual fervent prayer of a righteous man availeth much.

**James 5:16**

Then said Jesus, Father, forgive them; for they know not what they do. And they parted his raiment and cast lots.

**Luke 23:34**

I, only I, am He who wipes out your transgressions for My own sake, And I will not remember your sins.

**Isaiah 43:25 AMP**

Repent ye therefore, and be converted, that your sins may be blotted out, when the times of refreshing shall come from the presence of the Lord.

**Acts 3:19**

Then came Peter to him, and said, Lord, how oft shall my brother sin against me, and I forgive him? till seven times?

**Matthew 18:21**

## *Quotes: Forgiveness*

Forgiveness gives me boundaries because it unhooks me from the hurtful person, and I can act responsibly and wisely. ~**Unknown**

The rattlesnake, if cornered, can become so angry it will bite itself. The harboring of hate and resentment against others is a biting of oneself. Stop holding the spite and stop harming yourself. ~**E. Stanley Jones**

The first to apologize is the bravest. The first to forgive is the strongest. The first to move forward is the happiest. ~**John Eckhardt**

Everyone says forgiveness is a lovely idea until they have someone to forgive! ~**C. S. Lewis**

The greater the sin you forgive them of, the greater the measure of the spirit that will come to you. ~**R. T. Kendall**

Anger dwells only in the bosom of fools. ~**Albert Einstein**

Forgiveness is the fragrance that the violet sheds on the heel of the one that has crushed it. ~**Mark Twain**

The weak can never forgive. Forgiveness is an attribute of the strong. ~**Gandhi**

A happy marriage is the union of two good forgivers. ~**Ruth Graham**

To forgive is the highest, most beautiful form of love. In return, you will receive untold peace and happiness. ~**Robert Mueller**

Forgiveness does not excuse their behavior. Forgiveness prevents their behavior from destroying your heart. ~**Unknown**

Without forgiveness, life is governed by an endless cycle of resentment and retaliation. ~**Unknown**

Sweet forgiveness is nobility's true badge. ~**William Shakespeare**

Christ, in the dying moments of the cross, gives us the greatest illustration of forgiveness possible. **~T. D. Jakes**

The glory of Christianity is to conquer by forgiveness. **~William Blake**

Forgiveness is an act of the will, and the will can function regardless of the temperature of the heart. **~Corrie Ten Boom**

Love is an act of endless forgiveness, a tender look which can become a habit. **~Peter Ustinov**

Forgiveness gives you back the laughter and the lightness of your life. **~Joan Lunden**

Forgiveness is the needle that knows how to mend. **~Jewel**

A lack of forgiveness makes us bitter and hateful, and our lack of compassion makes us hard hearted, keeping us in a constant whirlwind of agitation and self-pity. **~Mother Angelica**

Bitterness is a dangerous drug in any dosage, and your health is at risk, if you stubbornly persist in being unforgiving. **~Lee Strobel**

Forgive others as quickly as you expect God to forgive you. **~Unknown**

Unforgiveness denies the victim the possibility of parole, leaving them stuck in prison and unable to escape the drama and the pain. **~T. D. Jakes**

To be unforgiving is to drink poison and wait for somebody else to die. ~**T. D. Jakes**

Forgiveness is the power to choose how events will affect you. ~**T. D. Jakes**

One of the great healing balms of the Holy Spirit is forgiveness. To forgive is to break the link between you and your past. ~**T. D. Jakes**

Help us to overlook offense and transgressions, without seeking revenge or harboring resentment. ~**Anonymous**

## *Hymn: Forgiveness*

**Weary of Wandering from My God**
Weary of wandering from my God,
And now made willing to return.
I hear and bow me to the rod,
For Thee, not without hope, I mourn.
I have an Advocate above,
A Friend before the throne of love.
~**Charles Wesley**, 1749 (public domain)

## *Personalized Weaponry*

The subject of forgiveness is generally broad but biblically narrow. We have many diverse opportunities to get offended, and not just at people but places and things. There is a subtle progression that can take place if you're uninformed or unaware. The world, the flesh, and the enemy will all gladly escort you down a blind alley marked, "I have a right to hold a grudge. They did me so dirty. My pain is their fault!"

In 2013, I had come to the conclusion that it was time to see a urologist, and I carefully chose what I thought was one of the finest in my area of DFW. Fast-forward to three surgeries and the implanting of a recalled device. This produced months of extreme pain, catheters, and painkillers but no resolution to the problem.

When my daughter began researching to find a qualified doctor to remove the mesh, few were willing or qualified. By God's help and powerful guidance, she found a doctor at UT Southwestern. This wonderful man was able to chisel out a large portion of the embedded implant that was suffocating my bladder. The organ was damaged, so healing was long and arduous.

This was one of the most difficult forgiveness assignments put before me. But I knew that, according to Scripture, if I wanted to continue needing forgiveness, God would require me to forgive this original doctor, who had knowingly inserted/fitted this recalled device in my body. We later found out there are bonuses and trips given to doctors who use expired materials.

Enter now on the scene forgiveness or unforgiveness. This is a command from the Lord and one of the principles of the Kingdom. It should be noted, no matter how difficult to forgive or how justifiable to remain hurt in light of all forms of pain that has been inflicted, without forgiveness from the heart, a looming and severe problem arises. The dark dungeon of unforgiveness will devour your joy and place you in a position where God will not forgive you your sins. On a brighter note, true and honest forgiveness will bring justification, vindication and recompense from sources you would never expect!

**Warning**: Do not trifle with the snake of unforgiveness, thinking it will slither away and not bite you. To forgive others is a direct command from our Heavenly Commander, who willingly died a merciless and excruciating death so that He could forgive us of our manifold sins. His Kingdom revolves around many principles, one of which is that either you forgive all others or he will *not* forgive you. This requires from the heart thorough forgiveness not just lip service. Refuse to be offended! Just in case nobody has ever brought this to your attention, it is in the Bible, the seriousness is real. So let the people out of the prison in your heart, open the gate and clear the slate. Your eternal happiness can depend on this issue. The Kingdom is not a democracy; it is a theocracy ruled by one Sovereign Monarch to which we lovingly answer, whether you like it or not! It is not on our terms but on His that we function under his attentive rule. If you're a believer, then you're a part of His family—a family that has many names, all of which are elevating and deeply personal. Like the willing servants and loyal subjects, the sheep of His pasture, the soon-coming Bride of Christ, brothers and sisters in the Lord, people of the Book, ambassadors of the King, priests and kings unto God, the body of Christ, blood-bought children of the Resurrection, divine instruments, ordained vessels fit for the Master's use, joint heirs with Christ, partakers of the heavenly inheritance, children of the Most High God, precious and elect in Zion, peculiar set-apart ones, a royal priesthood, a holy nation, perpetual witnesses, bright lights in an ever-darkening world, temples of the eternal flame, beacons of hope, redeemed remnant, soul winners, destined rulers, enriched and engrafted, jewels in Christ's crown, and on go the glorious descriptions. Make no mistake, He is the Ruler both now and forever, and His strong right arm is barred on your behalf. Let us bow and gratefully surrender to all He requires of us since it is all motivated by his unsurpassed love. Our names are graven on the palms of his Hands and we are bound to him with mighty cords of love! He is trustworthy and reliable, devoted to his royal cherished saints. Let us gather in submissive wonder around his throne. Humbly pledging our love, our adoration and reverent, godly fear to the one who first loved us and gave Himself *for* us.

# WEAPON 15

# Fellowship/Friendship

## *Scriptures*

The righteous is more excellent than his neighbour: but the way of the wicked seduceth them.

**PROVERBS 12:26**

When a man's ways please the Lord, he maketh even his enemies to be at peace with him.

**PROVERBS 16:7**

Be not deceived: evil communications corrupt good manners.

**1 CORINTHIANS 15:33**

And as ye would that men should do to you, do ye also to them likewise.

**LUKE 6:31**

A man that hath friends must shew himself friendly: and there is a friend that sticketh closer than a brother.

**PROVERBS 18:24**

Open rebuke is better than secret love. Faithful are the wounds of a friend; but the kisses of an enemy are deceitful.

**Proverbs 27:5–6**

Two are better than one; because they have a good reward for their labour. For if they fall, the one will lift up his fellow: but woe to him that is alone when he falleth; for he hath not another to help him up.

**Ecclesiastes 4:9–10**

Greater love has no one than this, than to lay down one's life for his friends. You are My friends if you do whatever I command you.

**John 15:13–14 NKJV**

A friend loveth at all times, and a brother is born for adversity.

**Proverbs 17:17**

My friends scorn me, but I pour out my tears to God. I need someone to mediate between God and me, as a person mediates between friends.

**Job 16:20–21 NLT**

Be kindly affectioned one to another with brotherly love; in honour preferring one another.

**Romans 12:10**

Wherefore comfort yourselves together, and edify one another, even as also ye do.

**1 Thessalonians 5:11**

Then Jonathan and David made a covenant, because he loved him as his own soul.

**1 Samuel 18:3**

But if we walk in the light, as he is in the light, we have fellowship one with another, and the blood of Jesus Christ his Son cleanseth us from all sin.

**1 John 1:7**

For where two or three are gathered together in my name, there am I in the midst of them.

**Matthew 18:20**

Bear ye one another's burdens, and so fulfil the law of Christ.

**Galatians 6:2**

Not giving up meeting together, as some are in the habit of doing, but encouraging one another—and all the more as you see the Day approaching.

**Hebrews 10:25 NIV**

We proclaim to you what we have seen and heard, so that you also may have fellowship with us. And our fellowship is with the Father and with his Son, Jesus Christ. We write this to make our joy complete.

**1 John 1:3–4 NIV**

## *Quotes: Fellowship/Friendship*

Friends, they cherish one another's hopes, they are kind to one another's dreams. ~**Henry David Thoreau**

A real friend is one who walks in when the rest of the world walks out. ~**Walter Winchell**

A friend is a gift you give yourself. ~**Robert Louis Stevenson**

Close friends are truly life's treasures, their presence reminds us we are not alone. ~**Van Gogh**

Share your smile with the world, it's a symbol of friendship and peace. ~**Christie Brinkley**

The worst solitude is to be destitute of sincere friendship. ~**Francis Bacon**

A true friend is someone who sees the pain in your eyes while everyone else believes your smile. ~**Unknown**

Good friends are hard to find, harder to leave, and impossible to forget. ~**Unknown**

More beautiful than all the stars that shine, is the heart of a loving friend. ~**Unknown**

There is nothing on this earth more to be prized than true friendship. ~**Thomas Aquinas**

A friend is one who knows the song in your heart and can sing it back to you when you have forgotten the words. ~**Unknown**

Wishing to be friends is quick work, but real friendship is a slow-ripening fruit. ~**Aristotle**

Sweet is the memory of distant friends! Like the mellow rise of the departing sun, it falls tenderly yet sadly on the heart. **~Washington Irving**

The only way to have a friend is to be one.
**~Ralph Waldo Emerson**

Be mindful of the company you keep. Fellowship with people that aspire to live for God. Always make time to be a friend. **~Unknown**

Three great gifts you can give another person are: your time, a listening ear and your support. **~Unknown**

In a world that screams for attention, seek the quiet voice of God and the fellowship of others doing the same. **~Unknown**

Unless the fellowship of His sufferings touches us, we will never have much power. **~Smith Wigglesworth**

Fellowship, purity, unity, these things reflect a living corporation in which we are being changed from faith to faith. **~Smith Wigglesworth**

Fellowship in the community of believers, is a mutual belonging, that is a thread that ties together all the diverse elements. **~Jerry Bridges**

## Hymn: Fellowship/Friendship

**What a Friend We Have in Jesus**
What a friend we have in Jesus,
All our sins and griefs to bear.
What a privilege to carry,
Everything to God in prayer.
Oh, what peace we often forfeit oh,
what needless pain we bear,
All because we do not carry,
Everything to God in prayer.
~**Joseph Scriven**, 1855 (public domain)

## Personalized Weaponry

Do you have a handful of trusted friends? My grandmother once told me that if in a lifetime you can count on one hand the number of true friends you have, you are indeed a blessed person. Since we're told pure and honest friendship is a gift from God, how do we search out such relationships? Often, they're placed in our lives in strange and mystical ways. Other times they're cultivated over many years and a variety of circumstances. Proverbs 18:24 says, "A man that hath friends must shew himself friendly. There is a friend that sticks closer than a brother." Be interested in others' lives and their joys and sorrows, be available, be kind and thoughtful, be true to form, be comfortable company. We can't chose our biological family, but we can and should choose our friends carefully. Remember, they influence you, and you have the power to influence them, for good or bad.

Isolation is a tactic of the enemy, so search out opportunities to pursue godly friendships. This produces a deeper form of fellowship, where hearts are knit together in the common bond. God's people gathering together and sharing life. John Fawcett's hymn titled "Blest Be the Tie That Binds" expressed these sentiments when he wrote, "the fellowship of kindred minds is like to that above."

## Weapon 16

# Church/Body of Christ

### *Scriptures*

Now ye are the body of Christ, and members in particular.

**1 Corinthians 12:27**

There is one body and one Spirit, just as you were called in one hope of your calling.

**Ephesians 4:4 NKJV**

And he is the head of the body, the church: who is the beginning, the firstborn from the dead; that in all things he might have the preeminence.

**Colossians 1:18**

And are built upon the foundation of the apostles and prophets, Jesus Christ himself being the Chief Cornerstone.

**Ephesians 2:20**

Mortify therefore your members which are upon the earth; fornication, uncleanness, inordinate affection, evil concupiscence, and covetousness, which is idolatry.

**Colossians 3:5**

So that if I am delayed, you will know how people must conduct themselves in the household of God. This is the church of the living God, which is the pillar and foundation of the truth.

**1 Timothy 3:15 NLT**

Remember them that are in bonds, as bound with them; and them which suffer adversity, as being yourselves also in the body.

**Hebrews 13:3**

Blessed is the man who does not walk in the counsel of the wicked, Nor stand in the path of sinners, Nor sit in the seat of scoffers.

**Psalm 1:1 AMP**

Then they that gladly received his word were baptized: and the same day there were added unto them about three thousand souls.

**Acts 2:41**

The glory of this latter house shall be greater than of the former, saith the Lord of hosts: and in this place will I give peace, saith the Lord of hosts.

**Haggai 2:9**

You also, as living stones, are being built up a spiritual house, a holy priesthood, to offer up spiritual sacrifices acceptable to God through Jesus Christ.

**1 Peter 2:5 NKJV**

For as we have many members in one body, and all members have not the same office: So we, being many, are one body in Christ, and every one members one of another.

**Romans 12:4–5**

There is one body, and one Spirit, even as ye are called in one hope of your calling.

**Ephesians 4:4**

Now I beseech you, brethren, by the name of our Lord Jesus Christ, that ye all speak the same thing, and that there be no divisions among you; but that ye be perfectly joined together in the same mind and in the same judgment.

**1 Corinthians 1:10**

Behold, how good and how pleasant it is for brethren to dwell together in unity!

**Psalm 133:1**

Finally, be ye all of one mind, having compassion one of another, love as brethren, be pitiful, be courteous.

**1 Peter 3:8**

For he himself is our peace, who has made the two groups one and has destroyed the barrier, the dividing wall of hostility.

**Ephesians 2:14 NIV**

And he gave some, apostles; and some, prophets; and some, evangelists; and some, pastors and teachers; For the perfecting of the saints, for the work of the ministry, for the edifying of the body of Christ.

**Ephesians 4:11–12**

## *Quotes: Church/Body of Christ*

I believe that if there is one thing that pierces the Master's heart with unutterable grief, it is not the world's sins, but the church's indifferences. ~**F. B. Meyer**

The church is like a great ship being pounded by the waves of life's stresses. Our duty is not to abandon ship but to keep her on her course. ~**Boniface**

The church is not a museum to display perfect people but a hospital for the hurting. ~**John Osteen**

May God use us to bring divine life to dead sinners, to dead churches, and to Christians whose spiritual experience is dead. ~**Christmas Evans**

God is preparing his heroes and when the opportunity comes, he can send them into places and the world will wonder where they came from. ~**A. B. Simpson**

The congregation, not the building is holy. The church is holy because the congregation is the house of God. ~**Edmund Clowney**

I do not think the devil cares how many churches you build, if only you have lukewarm preachers and lukewarm people in them. ~**Charles Spurgeon**

The body of Christ is a multicultural citizenry of another worldly kingdom. ~**David Platt**

The church is her true self only when she exists for humanity. ~**Dietrich Bonhoeffer**

The church is the great lost and found department. ~**Robert Short**

Whenever we see the word of God purely preached and heard; there is a church where God exists, even if it swarms with faults. ~**John Calvin**

I think if the church did what they are supposed to do, we wouldn't have anyone sleeping on the streets. ~**Michael W. Smith**

The church, as the Body of Christ, is a group of people who allow God to be mingled with them and who are mingled with God. ~**Unknown**

Christians have been called to be salt and light but unfortunately, many churches across this fruited plain, have been on a salt-free diet. ~**Todd Starnes**

God is preparing his church to become an invincible, unstoppable, unconquerable, overcoming army of the Lord that subdues everything under Christ's feet. ~**Bill Hamon**

The word of God is always most precious to the man who most lives upon it. ~**Charles Spurgeon**

When we preach Christ crucified, we have no reason to stammer, stutter, apologize or hesitate. ~**Charles Spurgeon**

Whenever God means to make a man great, he always breaks him in pieces first. ~**Charles Spurgeon**

You will never know the fullness of Christ until you know the emptiness of everything else. ~**Charles Spurgeon**

The temple of God is the holy people in Jesus Christ. The body of Christ is the living temple of God and of the new humanity. ~**Dietrich Bonhoeffer**

God gives power to his people so that they might serve those who are powerless. ~**Unknown**

The church is not a select circle of the immaculate but a home where the outcasts may come in. ~**Unknown**

Just going to church doesn't make you a Christian, any more than standing in your garage makes you a car. ~**G. K. Chesterton**

In a world full of idols, cruelties and devilries, if the church does not pray, how can she excuse the neglect? ~**Charles Spurgeon**

## *Hymn: Church/Body of Christ*

**I Stand Amazed in the Presence**
I stand amazed in the presence,
Of Jesus The Nazarene.
And wonder how He could love me,
A sinner condemned and unclean.
Oh, how marvelous,
oh, how wonderful,
My song shall ever be
Oh, how marvelous
oh, how wonderful,
Is my Savior's love for me.
~**Charles Gabriel**, 1905 (public domain)

## *Personalized Weaponry*

Born from His riven side, flowing with blood and water, the Church emerged. She is His new creation, His holy Bride, bought with His own blood, and for her life, He died! His visible body was placed in the earth.

The Church is not just a selection of buildings scattered across the face of the planet, but a living and breathing entity. The mysterious design of the heavenly edifice still baffles even the most learned and devout.

We, the converted, are not left stranded travelers, but have royal fellowship and friendship in the Church body available to assist us. This unusual combination is designed to complement our union, not only with one another, but with the Holy Spirit as well.

We have been uniquely fashioned as "lively stones" by the Master Architect, fitly joined together. The manifold purpose, to strengthen our marriage to Christ, to love one another as he has loved us, to reach out to the lost and perishing with the Good News of salvation. Set apart as a nucleus of prayer, blessing, instruction, praise/worship, hope, power and authority and much, much more—an oasis of rest from the weary world. As His "human beams," forever shining, greatly loved and begotten to a living hope, we are to rejoice in our salvation, remembering we have been preserved as costly monuments of His mercy.

## Weapon 17

# Water Baptism

### *Scriptures*

For as many of you as have been baptized into Christ have put on Christ.

**Galatians 3:27**

I indeed baptize you with water unto repentance. but he that cometh after me is mightier than I, whose shoes I am not worthy to bear: he shall baptize you with the Holy Ghost, and with fire.

**Matthew 3:11**

And now why tarriest thou? arise, and be baptized, and wash away thy sins, calling on the name of the Lord.

**Acts 22:16**

One Lord, one faith, one baptism.

**Ephesians 4:5**

Having been buried with him in baptism, in which you were also raised with him through your faith in the working of God, who raised him from the dead.

**Colossians 2:12 NIV**

John did baptize in the wilderness and preach the baptism of repentance for the remission of sins.

**Mark 1:4**

Go ye therefore, and teach all nations, baptizing them in the name of the Father, and of the Son, and of the Holy Ghost.

**Matthew 28:19**

## *Quotes: Water Baptism*

Water baptism is an outward expression of inward faith. ~**Watchman Nee**

Water baptism separates the tire kickers from the car buyers. ~**Max Lucado**

Just as water ever seeks and falls to the lowest place, so the moment God finds you abased and empty, His glory and His power flow in. ~**Andrew Murray**

God's people should be baptized because God commanded it, not because some church requires it. ~**Unknown**

Water baptism is a sign of dedication to Christ. ~**Dietrich Bonhoeffer**

We ought to regard the sacrament of water baptism with reverence. An ordinance to which the great head of the church himself submitted, ought to be ever honorable in the eyes of professing Christians. ~**J. C. Doyle**

Water baptism is a vow, a sacred vow of the believer to follow Christ. It celebrates the union of the sinner with our Savior. ~**Max Lucado**

Water baptism is a picture of you buried in Christ and coming up out of the water with a new life. ~**Perry Stone**

## *Hymn: Water Baptism*

**Baptized into Thy Name Most Holy**
Baptized into Thy name most holy,
O Father, Son and Holy Ghost.
I claim a place, though weak and lowly,
Among Thy seed, Thy chosen host,
Buried with Christ and dead to sin,
Thy Spirit now shall live within.
~**Johann Rambach**, 1723 (public domain)

## *Personalized Weaponry*

Actually, I was in my late thirties before I had the proper biblical teaching on water baptism. The finest way is at the moment of salvation; the person is taught from the scriptures, to follow the Lord's example in submerged water baptism. The symbolism is this: buried with Christ in death, going under the water, coming up or raised to new life in Him. Many experience a renewed, cleansed feeling and a desire to go forward with the Lord. Often a hallowed hue, an aura of the Holy Spirit, will sweeten the moment, enveloping our very being and continuing to call us to further closeness with our Servant King.

No matter how old you may be, if you have professed Christ as your sole Savior, I encourage you to search out a sacred spot to follow your Lord's instruction. This is one of His dear and blessed actions that produces a tenderness in our hearts that nothing else can replace. It's also just the beginning of a deepening of His revealed love.

## WEAPON 18

# Warfare

**Attention:** Calling all freedom fighter warriors of the cross of Jesus Christ. Muster. Allow no ground to be taken. Carry out your duties. You are a part of an epic task-force. Man your battle stations. Lock and load. Close ranks. Your borders and territories are securely patrolled. Hold your fortified positions, guard your posts, and repel enemy fire. Mobilize and unify around your Sovereign Sabaoth, the Lord of heaven's armies. He is observing your coordinates and dispatching skilled angelic commandos, as well as the armaments of His Word to assist you. The land mines of warfare are being exposed. Your maneuvers are carefully observed and directed by your Heavenly Commander-in-Chief. Lay down the gauntlet of his sacred name and over-come the strongholds for his glory! Be encouraged, pick up your shield, and raise your sword. You are fully equipped and dressed in your God gear to kill! Soldiers of the Cross, do not choose a silken couch or a downy pillow. Rather search out the personal service to Christ as your call to duty. Your sealed orders include a dual assignment: destroy the enemy at all costs and execute the Soul Patrol to populate the Master Recruiter's kingdom! ~**Anonymous**

## *Scriptures*

Yet in all these things we are more than conquerors through Him who loved us.

**Romans 8:37 NKJV**

But thanks be to God, which giveth us the victory through our Lord Jesus Christ.

**1 Corinthians 15:57**

Then he answered and spoke unto me, saying, This is the word of the Lord unto Zerubbabel, saying, Not by might, nor by power, but by my spirit, saith the Lord of hosts.

**Zechariah 4:6**

But the Lord is faithful, who shall stablish you, and keep you from evil.

**2 Thessalonians 3:3**

The Lord will grant that the enemies who rise up against you will be defeated before you. They will come at you from one direction but flee from you in seven.

**Deuteronomy 28:7 NIV**

Have I not commanded you? Be strong and of good courage; do not be afraid, nor be dismayed, for the Lord your God is with you wherever you go.

**Joshua 1:9 NKJV**

God arms me with strength, and he makes my way perfect.

**Psalm 18:32 NLT**

Finally, my brethren, be strong in the Lord, and in the power of his might. Put on the whole armour of God, that ye may be able to stand against the wiles of the devil. For we wrestle not against flesh and blood, but against principalities, against powers, against the rulers of the darkness of this world, against spiritual wickedness in high places. Wherefore take unto you the whole armour of God, that ye may be able to withstand in the evil day, and having done all, to stand. Stand therefore, having your loins girt about with truth, and having on the breastplate of righteousness; And your feet shod with the preparation of the gospel of peace; Above all, taking the shield of faith, wherewith ye shall be able to quench all the fiery darts of the wicked. And take the helmet of salvation, and the sword of the Spirit, which is the word of God: Praying always with all prayer and supplication in the Spirit and watching thereunto with all perseverance and supplication for all saints.

**Ephesians 6:10–18**

For ye shall not go out with haste, nor go by flight: for the Lord will go before you; and the God of Israel will be your reward.

**Isaiah 52:12**

For the weapons of our warfare are not carnal, but mighty through God to the pulling down of strong holds.

**2 Corinthians 10:4**

"No weapon that is formed against you will succeed; And every tongue that rises against you in judgment you will condemn. This is the heritage of the servants of the Lord, And this is their vindication from Me," says the Lord.

**Isaiah 54:17 amp**

Submit yourselves therefore to God. Resist the devil, and he will flee from you.

**JAMES 4:7**

And he shall pass over to his strong hold for fear, and his princes shall be afraid of the ensign, saith the Lord, whose fire is in Zion, and his furnace in Jerusalem.

**ISAIAH 31:9**

So shall they fear the name of the Lord from the west, and his glory from the rising of the sun. When the enemy shall come in like a flood, the Spirit of the Lord shall lift up a standard against him.

**ISAIAH 59:19**

The one who does what is sinful is of the devil, because the devil has been sinning from the beginning. The reason the Son of God appeared was to destroy the devil's work.

**1 JOHN 3:8 NIV**

Behold, I give unto you power to tread on serpents and scorpions, and over all the power of the enemy: and nothing shall by any means hurt you.

**LUKE 10:19**

Blessed be the LORD, who hath not given us as a prey to their teeth.

**PSALM 124:6**

But you will not even need to fight. Take your positions; then stand still and watch the Lord's victory. He is with you, O people of Judah and Jerusalem. Do not be afraid or discouraged. Go out against them tomorrow, for the Lord is with you.

**2 Chronicles 20:17 NLT**

Fight the good fight of faith, lay hold on eternal life, whereunto thou art also called, and hast professed a good profession before many witnesses.

**1 Timothy 6:12**

Wherefore gird up the loins of your mind, be sober, and hope to the end for the grace that is to be brought unto you at the revelation of Jesus Christ.

**1 Peter 1:13**

For the weapons of our warfare are not carnal, but mighty through God to the pulling down of strong holds; Casting down imaginations, and every high thing that exalteth itself against the knowledge of God, and bringing into captivity every thought to the obedience of Christ; And having in a readiness to revenge all disobedience, when your obedience is fulfilled.

**2 Corinthians 10:4–6**

Be shattered, O you peoples, and be broken in pieces! Give ear, all you from far countries. Gird yourselves, but be broken in pieces; Gird yourselves, but be broken in pieces.

**Isaiah 8:9 NKJV**

No one serving as a soldier gets entangled in civilian affairs, but rather tries to please his commanding officer.

**2 Timothy 2:4 NIV**

One man of you shall chase a thousand: for the Lord your God, he it is that fighteth for you, as he hath promised you.

**Joshua 23:10**

And from the days of John the Baptist until now the kingdom of heaven suffers violence, and the violent take it by force.

**Matthew 11:12 NKJV**

O God the Lord, the strength of my salvation, thou hast covered my head in the day of battle.

**Psalm 140:7**

For You, O Lord, bless the righteous man; You surround him with favor as with a shield.

**Psalm 5:12 AMP**

Be sober, be vigilant; because your adversary the devil, as a roaring lion, walketh about, seeking whom he may devour.

**1 Peter 5:8**

For, behold, I have made thee this day a defended city, and an iron pillar, and brazen walls against the whole land, against the kings of Judah, against the princes thereof, against the priests thereof, and against the people of the land.

**Jeremiah 1:18**

It doesn't matter if you're a spiritual boot camp enlistee or a graduate with honors from the War College of the Spirit. You might be wounded, worshipping, weary, winning, or working, in any case your commissioning from the War Room of Heaven requires that you recognize the shout of the King is among us, and our combat missions are won in His victory! He is our Unfaltering Guide, our Forward

Observer, we are the army of God. No AWOLs, no MIAs, and no POWs are allowed. All present and accounted for, Sir. Maintain your rank and file. Memorize your training field manual and keep it close at hand. Maintain your military occupation specialty code (MOS), and do not deviate from its instructions. Help us not to fall by friendly fire but to remain lionhearted in God's army. Stay in close proximity to your battle buddy! Our warfare declaration: no enemy allowed to bring reinforcements, retaliation or transfers of any evilness. Fight on, dear warrior, fight on! ~**Anonymous**

## *Quotes: Warfare*

Strife is food that feeds evil spirits. ~**Perry Stone**

The Lord gets His best soldiers from the highlands of affliction. ~**Charles Spurgeon**

To ignore Satan and his strategies is to commit spiritual suicide, but to become preoccupied with Satan and his kingdom is equally dangerous. ~**Mark Hitchcock**

The Bride of Christ has combat boots under her wedding dress! ~**Bill Hamon**

There is an order of beings, whose iron fists rule the empire of hell. Their cloud of evil darkens nearly every facet of life on earth. To topple this wicked kingdom and prevail victoriously in our warfare, we must discern our enemies and set to flight these hordes of hellish darkness. ~**Francis Frangipane**

As we allow God to polish us and our armor, we will grow to become vessels of honor in the house of the Lord. ~**Cindy Jacobs**

There is no neutral ground in the universe, every square inch, every split second, is claimed by God and counterclaimed by Satan. ~**C. S. Lewis**

God's holy armor of light enables us to resist, restrain and rebuke. ~**Perry Stone**

We will not bow to any form of darkness; we are afraid of no one and nothing at any time, for any reason, by the help and power of God Almighty. ~**Anonymous**

Until you know that life is war, you cannot know what prayer is for. ~**John Piper**

You and I are going to be victorious because God is fighting with us on our behalf. ~**Kurt Schneider**

The battleground of the mind is where life's most precious victories are won or lost. ~**Kenneth Copeland**

The enemy will try to lure you by distraction into some other activity, to get you sidetracked, stay focused on your last marching orders. ~**Mark Pfeifer**

God wants you to have the victory but only if you show up for the battle. ~**James Robison**

We draw our strength from the battle; from our greatest conflicts, come our greatest victories. ~**Rod Parsley**

God can bring pure, holy sweetness out of bitterness and beauty out of shattered chaos from the battlefield. ~**Anonymous**

Do not allow, or be comfortable living with, oppressive forces of fear and worry. They attempt to bind you and destroy Christ's work in you and in the church, making you helpless and useless. ~**Anonymous**

Satan, the master deceiver, works best when he is underestimated, ignored or denied. ~**Mark Hitchcock**

Satan is the great "I am not" and he is never happier than when he has convinced people he does not exist. ~**Mark Hitchcock**

The only true conqueror who shall be crowned in the end, is he who continues until war's trumpet is blown no more. Christian, wear your shield close to your armor and cry earnestly to God, that by His spirit you may endure until the end. ~**Alistair Begg**

It is fatal to enter a war without the will to win. ~**Douglas MacArthur**

You may have to fight a battle more than once to win it. ~**Margaret Thatcher**

Seducing spirits and doctrines of demons are agents of Satan, become a discerning expert at recognizing their covert actions. ~**Anonymous**

We are high-level targets, every battle in life affects your faith, we must keep our faith strong because success in warfare depends on it. ~**Perry Stone**

We don't want to think that something as ugly and brutal as combat can be in any way involved with the spiritual. However, would any practicing Christian, say Calvary's hill was not a sacred battlefield? ~**Karl Marlantes**

Everybody is not going to understand where God has called you, but that is no excuse not to go there. In certain places, it will be spiritual warfare to stay there. ~**CeCe Winans**

In the war upon the powers of darkness, prayer is the primary and the mightiest weapon. ~**Jessie Penn Lewis**

The beauties of nature come after the storm. The rugged beauty of the mountains born in the storm, and the heroes of life are the storm-swept and the battle-scarred. ~**Lettie Cowman**

Persevere and preserve yourself for better circumstances that will come after the fight. ~**Virgil**

Champions have the courage to keep turning the pages, because they know a better chapter lies ahead after each battle. ~**Paula White**

Worry is an attack by Satan on the mind of the believer; one meaning is to torment ourselves with disturbing thoughts, to seize by the throat, to mangle, to harass repeatedly! It is totally useless, do not be drawn into long, costly combat. ~**Joyce Meyer**

The enemy can't stay where God's love is poured out. ~**Ron Phillips**

The battle is a legal one, where we silence the accuser of the brethren, who has built a case against us to hold territory. We take the blood of Jesus and His sacrifice to remove every legal right the devil has to resist us, this is again a legal process in the spirit realm. ~**Robert Henderson**

Right now, you're in training for a trial you are not yet in, public victory comes from private discipline. ~**Levi Lusko**

God never uses anyone greatly until He has tested them deeply. ~**A. W. Tozer**

No calm is deeper than the one that follows the storm, victory banquets are for combat veterans only. ~**Charles Spurgeon**

Expect and avoid strategies of Satan's attacks. Look for them as follows: **1**. After spiritual victory. **2**. When we are alone. **3**. When we are tired. **4**. When we are in church. **5**. When attempting something great for God. ~**Jack Graham**

**Psalm 91** (author's paraphrase): The covenant circle of protection, warfare and healing. I live within the shadow of the Almighty, sheltered by the God who is above all gods. This I declare, that he alone is my refuge. My place of hiding and safety, he is my God and I am trusting Him. For he rescues me from every enemy trap and protects me from the fatal plague. He will shield me with his wings! They will shelter me. His faithful promises are my armor. Now, I do not need to be afraid of the dark anymore, nor fear the dangers of the day, nor dread the plagues of darkness, nor disasters in the morning. Though a thousand fall at my right hand, though ten thousand are dying around me, the evil will not touch me. I will see the wicked punished, but I will not share in it. For Jehovah is my refuge! I choose the God above all gods to shelter me. How, then, can evil overtake me or any plague come near me? For He orders His angels to protect me wherever I go. They will steady me with their hands to help me from stumbling against the rocks on the trail. I can safely meet a lion or step on a poisonous snake yes, even trample them underfoot! For the Lord has said "because you love me, child, I will rescue you, I will make you great because you trust in my name"." When you call to me, I will answer you, I will be with you and honor you. I will satisfy you with long life and show you my salvation."

## *Personalized Prayer Weaponry*

Today as we fight the good fight of faith. We keep our focus on our El Gibhor, the fiery fierce Gallant Warrior God, whose banner over us strikes fear in the hearts of our enemies. Lead Your troops onward, King Eternal, and make us awesome weapons in your mighty victorious hands.
We possess a holy, unshakable confidence that we are the objects of divine delight, and this, in turn, produces sanctified gladness amid spiritual perils.

Trust in God, do good, and *fight on, dear warrior, fight on!*

## *Hymn: Warfare*

**Ever Forward! Up and Onward**
Men of faith and men of courage,
waiting orders from the Lord,
Here's a telegram from heaven,
Onward, forward is the word.
Get you ready for the battle,
press into the hottest fray.
Onward, forward be the watchword,
All along the lines today!
~**Elisha Albright Hoffman**, 1914 (public domain)

**Red Alert**: When you recognize the enemy is closing in, immediately give him no *legal* ground to attack or accuse. Proclaim out loud a barricaded boundary around you and your fire support base. This is accomplished by verbally declaring the "blood of Jesus" strategically on everyone and everything. Release your precision-targeted prayers. Renounce all generational sin, cancel all word curses, ungodly contracts, and unholy vows and covenants. Keep your records clean of known sin. Inspect and evaluate your forgiveness gauge often. Your air space is now cleared to operate in your assigned rank.

All rise. Attention to orders. The Ultimate Warrior goes before you. He who has never lost a battle surveys and calculates your victory. Fight on, dear warrior, in shining splendor!

Consider Revelation 12:11. "We overcome by the Blood of the Lamb and the word of our testimony and do not love our lives so much as to shrink from death."

## Weapon 19

# Victory

### *Scriptures*

For the Lord your God is he that goeth with you, to fight for you against your enemies, to save you.

**Deuteronomy 20:4**

For whatsoever is born of God overcometh the world: and this is the victory that overcometh the world, even our faith.

**1 John 5:4**

The horse is prepared against the day of battle: but safety is of the Lord.

**Proverbs 21:31**

But thanks be to God, which giveth us the victory through our Lord Jesus Christ.

**1 Corinthians 15:57**

Thine, O Lord is the greatness, and the power, and the glory, and the victory, and the majesty: for all that is in the heaven and in the earth is thine; thine is the kingdom, O Lord, and thou art exalted as head above all.

**1 Chronicles 29:11**

For by wise counsel thou shalt make thy war: and in multitude of counsellors there is safety.

**Proverbs 24:6**

And having spoiled principalities and powers, he made a shew of them openly, triumphing over them in it.

**Colossians 2:15**

Put on the whole armour of God, that ye may be able to stand against the wiles of the devil.

**Ephesians 6:11**

So when this corruptible shall have put on incorruption, and this mortal shall have put on immortality, then shall be brought to pass the saying that is written, Death is swallowed up in victory.

**1 Corinthians 15:54**

And I saw as it were a sea of glass mingled with fire: and them that had gotten the victory over the beast, and over his image, and over his mark, and over the number of his name, stand on the sea of glass, having the harps of God.

**Revelation 15:2**

## *Quotes: Victory*

The harder the battle, the sweeter the victory. ~**Unknown**

There is no victory without a battle. ~**Christine Caine**

Embrace the struggle, it will be part of your victory speech. ~**Unknown**

Lasting victory can never be separated from a longstanding position on the foundation of the cross. ~**Watchman Nee**

Embrace the fact that God is on your side and if God is on your side, you are destined for victory. ~**John Hagee**

Accept challenges, so that you may feel the exhilaration of victory. ~**George Patton**

Victory at all costs, victory in spite of all terror, victory however long and hard the road may be, for without victory there is no survival. ~**Winston Churchill**

Every great achievement is the victory of a flaming heart. ~**Ralph Waldo Emerson**

You did not come this far to walk away without victory! ~**Anonymous**

War's very objective is victory, not prolonged indecision. In war there is no substitute for victory. ~**Douglas MacArthur**

## *Hymn: Victory*

**Lead on, O King Eternal**
Lead on, O King Eternal,
Till sin's fierce war shall cease,

And holiness shall whisper
The sweet amen of peace.
For not with swords loud clashing,
Nor roll of stirring drums.
With deeds of love and mercy,
The heavenly kingdom comes.
~**Ernest W. Shurtleff**, 1887 (public domain)

## *Personalized Prayer Weaponry*

Thank You this very day, Lord, that victory is coursing through our veins, that the smell of sweet success is in the air around us. That anything less will not satisfy and will be like stale bread in our mouths. May the greater, glory gateways be opened to us as we pursue and overcome any and all strongholds. Reignite us, re-fire us against every chilling, clandestine attack so that we may be crowned only after we have become conquerors! The greater the mission, the greater the storm. Help us recognize that we are polished arrows in the hand of the Lord.

This is *our* watch, and we will not shirk our duties nor remain silent. Our moment-by-moment dependence on Christ's guidance is a formidable weapon in itself. The power from the courtroom and the throne room of Almighty God is propelling us forward into victory.

Our invisible allies are also continuously by our sides, fighting, guarding, ministering to ensure complete and thorough victory, nothing left undone. To accomplish, to triumph over, to take dominion, to utterly defeat, to ensure mastery and superiority. These terms describe our orders!

## Weapon 20

# Courage/Devotion

### *Scriptures: Courage*

Have I not commanded you? Be strong and of good courage; do not be afraid, nor be dismayed, for the Lord your God is with you wherever you go.

**Joshua 1:9 NKJV**

Finally, my brethren, be strong in the Lord, and in the power of his might.

**Ephesians 6:10**

Be on your guard; stand firm in the faith; be courageous; be strong.

**1 Corinthians 16:13 NIV**

Wait on the Lord: be of good courage, and he shall strengthen thine heart: wait, I say, on the Lord.

**Psalm 27:14**

He shall not be afraid of evil tidings: his heart is fixed, trusting in the Lord.

**Psalm 112:7**

So, my dear brothers and sisters, be strong and immovable. Always work enthusiastically for the Lord, for you know that nothing you do for the Lord is ever useless.

**1 Corinthians 15:58 NLT**

For God hath not given us the spirit of fear; but of power, and of love, and of a sound mind.

**2 Timothy 1:7**

Yea, though I walk through the valley of the shadow of death, I will fear no evil: for thou art with me; thy rod and thy staff they comfort me.

**Psalm 23:4**

I must work the works of him that sent me, while it is day: the night cometh, when no man can work.

**John 9:4**

The fear of man bringeth a snare: but whoso putteth his trust in the Lord shall be safe.

**Proverbs 29:25**

Trust in the Lord with all thine heart; and lean not unto thine own understanding. In all thy ways acknowledge him, and he shall direct thy paths.

**Proverbs 3:5–6**

Be strong and courageous, for you are the one who will lead these people to possess all the land I swore to their ancestors I would give them. Be strong and very courageous. Be careful to obey all the instructions Moses gave you. Do not deviate from them, turning either to the right or to the left. Then you will be successful in everything you do. Study this Book of

Instruction continually. Meditate on it day and night so you will be sure to obey everything written in it. Only then will you prosper and succeed in all you do. This is my command—be strong and courageous! Do not be afraid or discouraged. For the Lord your God is with you wherever you go.

**Joshua 1:6–9 NLT**

Wait on the Lord, be of good courage, and he shall strengthen thine heart: wait, I say, on the Lord.

**Psalm 27:14**

## *Quotes: Courage*

Have courage for the great sorrows of life and patience for the small ones; and when you have accomplished your daily tasks, go to sleep in peace for God is awake. ~**Victor Hugo**

Don't let the fog of life hide God's vision for you. ~**Florence Chadwick**

Success is not final, failure is not fatal, it is the courage to continue that counts. ~**Winston Churchill**

Courage is doing what you are afraid to do; there is no courage unless you are scared. ~**Eddie Rickenbacker**

Courage is being scared and saddling up anyway. ~**John Wayne**

Courage is resistance to fear, mastery of fear, not absence of fear. ~**Mark Twain**

Courage does not always roar, sometimes it is a quiet voice at the end of the day saying, "I will try again tomorrow." **~Mary Radmacher**

I beg you to take courage; the brave soul can mend even disaster. **~Catherine the Great**

Do not limit the limitless God, with Him, face the future unafraid because you are never alone. **~Lettie Cowman**

Courage is contagious. When a brave man takes a stand, the spines of others are often stiffened. **~Billy Graham**

What sets lion-chasers apart isn't the outcome, it's the courage to chase God-sized dreams. **~Unknown**

## *Scriptures: Devotion*

Honor the Lord with your possessions, And with the first fruits of all your increase.

**Proverbs 3:9 NKJV**

Therefore, I urge you, brothers and sisters, by the mercies of God, to present your bodies as a living sacrifice, holy and well-pleasing to God, which is your rational act of worship.

**Romans 12:1 AMP**

Whether therefore ye eat, or drink, or whatsoever ye do, do all to the glory of God.

**1 Corinthians 10:31**

And thou shalt love the Lord thy God with all thine heart, and with all thy soul, and with all thy might.

**DEUTERONOMY 6:5**

Only fear the Lord and serve him in truth with all your heart: for consider how great things he hath done for you.

**1 SAMUEL 12:24**

Delight thyself also in the Lord: and he shall give thee the desires of thine heart.

**PSALM 37:4**

Be not deceived; God is not mocked: for whatsoever a man soweth, that shall he also reap.

**GALATIANS 6:7**

If then you were raised with Christ, seek those things which are above, where Christ is, sitting at the right hand of God.

**COLOSSIANS 3:1 NKJV**

And be ye kind one to another, tenderhearted, forgiving one another, even as God for Christ's sake hath forgiven you.

**EPHESIANS 4:32**

And whoever does not carry their cross and follow me cannot be my disciple.

**LUKE 14:27 NIV**

## *Quotes: Devotion*

To the world you may be one person, but to one person you may be their whole world. ~**Bill Wilson**

Jesus Christ founded His empire upon love, and at this very hour millions of men would die for him. ~**Napoleon**

We ought not to be weary of doing little things for the love of God, who regards not the greatness of the work, but the love with which it is performed. ~**Brother Lawrence**

The discipline of daily devotion to God undergirds our decisions. ~**Ed Cole**

Your devotion to God is illustrated, demonstrated and authenticated by your love for others. ~**Andy Stanley**

To succeed in your mission, you must have single-minded devotion to your goal. ~**Anonymous**

Be sure that you never try to work God into your schedule, but always work your schedule around him. ~**Joyce Meyer**

Don't pray just when you feel like it, have an appointment with God and keep it. ~**Corrie Ten Boom**

Relying on God to begin all over again, as if nothing had ever been accomplished in the first place. ~**C. S. Lewis**

Before there were padded pews and steeples and marble floors; there were circuit riders traveling through storms and heat to hungry souls desiring to hear God's Word. These fearless and devoted preachers of days gone by blazed a trail of righteousness across the land. ~**Anonymous**

## *Hymn: Courage/Devotion*

**Stand Up, Stand Up for Jesus**
Stand up, stand up for Jesus,
Stand in His strength alone.
The arm of flesh will fail you,
You dare not trust your own.
Put on the Gospel armor,
Each piece put on with prayer,
Where duty calls or danger.
Be never wanting there!
~**George Duffield**, 1858 (public domain)

## *Personalized Weaponry*

Willie Jane Sparks, my maternal grandmother, was already in her late seventies when I was born. Since she was almost deaf and required hearing aids, we were both at a disadvantage in forming an expanded relationship. The few stories of her life that I was able to piece together formed an interesting mosaic of courage and devotion, much like the lovely quilts on her bed.

Any way you look at it, life was hard for her in the years following the Civil War. She was one of six children, and she and her siblings worked to send her younger brother to law school, while she was acquiring her own teaching certificate. The one-room schoolhouse she worked in was set in the piney woods of Louisiana and housed grades one through twelve.

At age twenty-three, after a sorrowful time of giving up her baby girl for a needful adoption, she headed, by stage-coach, to Mexia, Texas, where she had been offered a teaching position. After meeting and marrying my grandfather, they decided to venture into the Indian Territory, which later became Oklahoma. Upon arriving, they built a sod house on a small plot of land near Addington, Oklahoma. They tried farming there but were unsuccessful. They, in 1901, then decided to take part in the land rush and procured a quarter acre in a settlement near the Red River. Leaving a tiny grave of their infant son on a lonely hill, they trudged on to the small but bustling railroad town of Waurika, Oklahoma, where they would remain the rest of their lives. Another child was born, years later, in 1913: my mother, Winnie. Finally my grandfather settled on a feed and seed store for his employment.

I still remember my Gaga's long, flowing hair, which never saw a pair of scissors. She kept it in two braids and coiled it on the top of her head. At night, she would take it down and brush the beautiful waves. The pure gold and opal earrings that she bought by selling a bushel of peaches at eighteen, never came out of her pierced ears. She walked everywhere in that tiny town: to church on the hill, to the hospital to visit with her garden-grown flowers, and to Mr. Snider's grocery store.

Sparky, as she was called, was a woman of strength from pioneer stock. One of the faithful founders of the local Methodist church. At a time when women were not in the workforce, she had a great job at the post office. This new fledging settlement placed her as Postmaster for several years, and she earned a gold watch for dutiful service. She was a character in her own right, dipping snuff, chopping her own wood, and having a swig or two of laced chicory coffee now and then. Her large vegetable garden was the envy of the neighborhood, and there were unforgettable moments when Sparky would run across the unpaved street to the dirt cellar of the Helm family when the sky looked like tornadoes were brewing.

She survived breast cancer at the age of seventy-two, but twenty years later, at the ripe old age of ninety-two, after witnessing a lifetime of events and a rapidly changing world, she passed away in her sleep. As a woman to be admired for her iron constitution, her prayers were answered: "Don't let me lose my facilities, and let me go quietly."

# WEAPON 21

# Angels

## *Scriptures*

Likewise, I say unto you, there is joy in the presence of the angels of God over one sinner that repenteth.

**LUKE 15:10**

And I saw another angel fly in the midst of heaven, having the everlasting gospel to preach unto them that dwell on the earth, and to every nation, and kindred, and tongue, and people.

**REVELATION 14:6**

And the angels which kept not their first estate, but left their own habitation, he hath reserved in everlasting chains under darkness unto the judgment of the great day.

**JUDE 1:6**

But ye are come unto mount Sion, and unto the city of the living God, the heavenly Jerusalem, and to an innumerable company of angels.

**HEBREWS 12:22**

For he shall give his angels charge over thee, to keep thee in all thy ways.

**Psalm 91:11**

For the Son of man shall come in the glory of his Father with his angels; and then he shall reward every man according to his works.

**Matthew 16:27**

Be not forgetful to entertain strangers: for thereby some have entertained angels unawares.

**Hebrews 13:2**

The angel of the Lord encamps all around those who fear Him and delivers them.

**Psalm 34:7 NKJV**

And he answered, Fear not: for they that be with us are more than they that be with them.

**2 Kings 6:16**

Praise the Lord, you angels, you mighty ones who carry out his plans, listening for each of his commands.

**Psalm 103:20 NLT**

Behold, I am going to send an Angel before you to keep and guard you on the way and to bring you to the place I have prepared.

**Exodus 23:20 AMP**

And he said, Hear thou the word of the Lord: I saw the Lord sitting on his throne, and all the host of heaven standing by him on his right hand and on his left.

**1 Kings 22:19**

And he dreamed, and behold a ladder set up on the earth, and the top of it reached to heaven: and behold the angels of God ascending and descending on it.

**Genesis 28:12**

And one cried unto another, and said, Holy, holy, holy, is the Lord of hosts: the whole earth is full of his glory.

**Isaiah 6:3**

And he shall send his angels with a great sound of a trumpet, and they shall gather together his elect from the four winds, from one end of heaven to the other.

**Matthew 24:31**

## *Quotes: Angels*

It was pride that changed angels into devils, it is humility that makes men as angels. ~**Saint Augustine**

In prayer, we stand where angels bow with veiled faces. ~**Charles Spurgeon**

Believers, look up, take courage, the angels are nearer than you think. ~**Billy Graham**

The earth has grown old with its burden of care but at Christmas, it is always young. The heart of the jewel burns lustrous and fair and its soul full of music breaks the air, when the song of angels is heard. ~**Phillips Brooks**

May you have heaven in your heart, starlight in your soul and angels all around you. ~**Unknown**

Even when alone, be cheerful, remembering always you are in the sight of angels. ~**Saint Theresa**

God not only sends special angels into our lives but sometimes he sends them back again if we forgot to take notes the first time. ~**Unknown**

Our invisible allies, Heaven's fiery warrior angels, our partners to bring transformation to individuals as well as to entire regions. These fierce, divine fighters help transform our lives and overthrow the powers of darkness. They work with our prayers to release heaven's answers and push breakthroughs forward. They battle in the spirit realm (clashing of the swords) to ensure protection and give assistance, engaging in the collision of kingdoms. ~**Tim Sheets**

Let us not forget the vast array of additional ranks of heavenly hosts: guardian angels, warring angels, ministering angels and the cherubim, seraphim, etc. We must never worship them, only thank the Lord for their faithful assignments carried out on our behalf! ~**Anonymous**

Angels are vastly intelligent reflections of light, that original light which has no beginning. They can illuminate, they can communicate without speech by thought. ~**John of Damascus**

Oh, passing angel, speed me with a song, a melody of heaven to reach my heart and rouse me to the race and make me strong. ~**Christina Rossetti**

An angel can illuminate the thought in the mind of a man by strengthening the powers of vision and by bringing within his reach some truth which the angel himself contemplates. ~**Thomas Aquinas**

An angel is a spirit-being created by God for the service of Christendom and the church. ~**Martin Luther King Jr.**

The angels are the dispensers and administrators of the divine benefits toward us. They regard our safety, undertake our defense, direct our ways, and exercise a constant watch that no evil befalls us. ~**John Calvin**

Angels are not kept from us by storms or hindered by darkness. Their visits will be frequent during nights of fitful tossing. Oh, how I do love my angels! ~**Charles Spurgeon**

Angels form protective circles around the righteous. A single angel can provide better protection than the entire secret service. Angels on assignment are God's relentless protection. They are marveling at the word of God being preached by mortal men. ~**Perry Stone**

How noble a thing, to have the couriers of heaven as bodyguards and border guards! ~**Charles Spurgeon**

Make yourself familiar with the angels and behold them frequently in spirit; for without being seen, they are present with you. ~**Francis de Sales**

Angels of the covenant are attracted to God's word. ~**Unknown**

Angels are operating in the supernatural realm; they are swift in their movements. Angels are strong soldiers and are systematic and organized in rank. They warn, assist, minister, guard, they go before us as life's monitors, fighting for us, bringing messages, journeying toward our promised destiny. They are part of the wonder, mystery and majesty of the Christian experience! They share our allegiances and loyalties, they love and protect us and ours, they face the common enemy, they operate covertly for us in enemy territory. ~**Ron Phillips**

## *Hymn: Angels*

**Blessed Assurance**
Angels descending bring from above,
Echoes of mercy, whispers of love.
Blessed assurance, Jesus is mine,
O what a foretaste of glory divine!
Heir of salvation, purchased of God,
Born of his Spirit, washed in his blood.
~**Fanny Crosby**, 1873 (public domain)

## *Personalized Weaponry*

Oh, I do love to recount these astoundingly unique stories of personal angel appearances. There were two extraordinary incidences where I visibly saw my angels. My car was sitting in an underground parking lot in a major downtown building in Dallas, Texas. To say that my car at that time was a clunker is an understatement. As I hurried to join the commuters slowly circling up the ramps four floors below, to my horror, my old car stopped abruptly on the enclosed incline. There was not room to walk in the tight enclosure. I put my head on the steering wheel and began to pray, "Lord, help me. I'm trapped!"

The people behind me were honking and hollering. That didn't help matters.

Suddenly, I looked up and saw a man with one hand on my car hood and the other waving for the cars to back up, saying in a strong, commanding voice, "Move back." The crowd began grudgingly going in reverse, and the helpful stranger pushed my car back to the level where I was originally parked. Like rats fleeing a sinking ship, not one car was left in that extremely large lot. The stranger walked up to my car and said, "Is there anything else you need?" I turned for one instant to reach for a pen and paper to take his email so I could write him a note of thanks. "No thanks. I'm okay," I muttered. But when I turned back, I found that he'd vanished in the middle of a wide open space with no place to hide. I knew, in that moment, my guardian angel had let himself be seen.

My second encounter happened several years later, when I was in a fierce battle of fear, which had assaulted me with a vise-grip unlike anything I had ever experienced. Anywhere and everywhere, methodically, this demon would bombard my mind relentlessly. The Holy Spirit had prompted me to purchase 3x5 cards and write out scriptures for handy access to quote out loud to combat my fear. I began retaliating against the attack with the Word unmercifully. It was a season of intense spiritual training, and I was honing my weapons of offense and defense. One especially wearing day, I looked up to see, for a snapshot moment, into that other dimension. Two angels, about the size of young teens, were rushing toward my bedside. Their long hair was blowing in the glorious splendor of that other heavenly domain. I knew they had been sent, as the mighty messengers of light to encourage and minister and replenish me from my weariness. A time of reprieve gave me rest and newfound strength in God's promises.

The heavenly order is as follows: angels, archangels, principalities, powers, virtues, dominions, thrones, cherubim, and seraphim. They take a deep interest in and love for the royal children of God.

Charles Spurgeon once said, "The chosen are elevated to high dignity when angels of heaven become our willing servants."

## Weapon 22

# Fasting

### *Scriptures*

And when they had ordained them elders in every church, and had prayed with fasting, they commended them to the Lord, on whom they believed.

**Acts 14:23**

I ate no pleasant food, no meat or wine came into my mouth, nor did I anoint myself at all, till three whole weeks were fulfilled.

**Daniel 10:3 NKJV**

Go, gather together all the Jews that are present in Shushan, and fast ye for me, and neither eat nor drink three days, night or day: I also and my maidens will fast likewise; and so will I go in unto the king, which is not according to the law: and if I perish, I perish.

**Esther 4:16**

Therefore, also now, saith the Lord, turn ye even to me with all your heart, and with fasting, and with weeping, and with mourning.

**Joel 2:12**

Being forty days tempted of the devil. And in those days he did eat nothing: and when they were ended, he afterward hungered.

**Luke 4:2**

Moreover, when you fast, do not be like the hypocrites, with a sad countenance. For they disfigure their faces that they may appear to men to be fasting. Assuredly, I say to you, they have their reward. But you, when you fast, anoint your head and wash your face, so that you do not appear to men to be fasting, but to your Father who is in the secret place; and your Father who sees in secret will reward you openly.

**Matthew 6:16–18 NKJV**

Is not this the fast that I have chosen? to lose the bands of wickedness, to undo the heavy burdens, and to let the oppressed go free, and that ye break every yoke?

**Isaiah 58:6**

And it came to pass, when I heard these words, that I sat down and wept, and mourned certain days, and fasted, and prayed before the God of heaven.

**Nehemiah 1:4**

And he said unto them, This kind can come forth by nothing, but by prayer and fasting.

**Mark 9:29**

## *Quotes: Fasting*

The best of all medicines is resting and fasting, health and healing will follow quickly. ~**Ben Franklin**

The discipline of fasting breaks you out of the world's routine. ~**Jentezen Franklin**

The man who never fasts is no more in the way of heaven than the man who never prays. ~**John Wesley**

A diet changes the way you look, a fast changes the way you see, it burns out ego, pride and sin. ~**Lisa Bevere**

Perhaps the greatest hindrance to our work is our own imagined strength, in fasting we learn what poor weak creatures we really are. ~**Hudson Taylor**

Fasting is what prepares you for a new anointing, you regain your edge, recapture your dream, recover your passion and restore your joy. ~**Jentezen Franklin**

The giving up of self for God's glory. Fasting is not about fame. It is about faith. It leads to the "breaking of chains" and a breaking through. ~**Unknown**

Fasting detaches you from this world, prayer reattaches you to the next world. ~**Fulton Sheen**

A fast is not a hunger strike. Fasting submits to God's commands. A hunger strike desires God submit to our demands. ~**Ed Cole**

If you say, "I will fast when God lays it on my heart," you never will. You are too cold and indifferent to take that yolk upon yourself. ~**Dwight L. Moody**

Fasting is abstaining from anything that hinders prayers. ~**Andrew Bonar**

Fasting helps express, deepens, and confirms the resolution that we are ready to sacrifice anything, even ourselves, to obtain what we seek for the kingdom of God. ~**Andrew Murray**

Fasting is a grace that significantly increases our receptivity to the Lord's voice and to his Word. ~**Mike Bickle**

Let the mouth also fast from disgraceful speeches and wailings. The evil speaker eats the flesh of his brother and bites the body of his neighbor. ~**John Chrysostom**

## *Hymn: Fasting*

**Untitled**
The fast which is the Lord's delight,
But tis to mortify our sin.
To be sincere and pure within,
To break the mourning captive's chain,
The proud oppressor to restrain.
To clothe the naked, feed the poor
And bring the friendless to thy door.
~**Unknown**, 1850

**In Fasting We Approach Thee**
In fasting we approach thee here
And pray thy Spirit from above
Will cleanse our hearts, cast out our fear
And fill our hunger with thy love.
Thru this small sacrifice may we
Recall that strength and life each day
Are sacred blessings sent from thee
Fill us with gratitude, we pray.
~**Clay Christiansen**, 1949 (public domain)

## *Personalized Prayer Weaponry*

Blessed Holy Spirit, do not allow our hearts to grow cold, starved and shriveled from lack of denying our selfishness. Help us to feed our souls rather than our flesh with Your empowering presence, by setting aside all worldly temptations. Help us to seek Your face rather than only Your hand. Our Father is greater than all. He knows what is best for us, and His care never falters. We need You above all else and all others to train us in Your ways, O, Lord. Cause us to prohibit the world, flesh, and the devil to burrow into our flesh by fasting regularly as a holy venture pleasing to You!

## Weapon 23

# Agreement/Unity/Influence

### *Scriptures*

o not be deceived, bad company corrupts good morals.

**1 Corinthians 15:33**

I will speak of the glorious honour of thy majesty, and of thy wondrous works.

**Psalm 145:5**

Finally, brethren, whatsoever things are true, whatsoever things are honest, whatsoever things are just, whatsoever things are pure, whatsoever things are lovely, whatsoever things are of good report; if there be any virtue, and if there be any praise, think on these things.

**Philippians 4:8**

But take heed lest by any means this liberty of yours become a stumbling block to them that are weak.

**1 Corinthians 8:9**

Don't team up with those who are unbelievers. How can righteousness be a partner with wickedness? How can light live with darkness?

**2 Corinthians 6:14** NLT

Submit yourselves therefore to God. Resist the devil, and he will flee from you.

**James 4:7**

Of these things put them in remembrance, charging them before the Lord that they strive not about words to no profit, but to the subverting of the hearers.

**2 Timothy 2:14**

Your boasting is not good. Don't you know that a little yeast leavens the whole batch of dough?

**1 Corinthians 5:6** NIV

A good name is rather to be chosen than great riches, and loving favour rather than silver and gold.

**Proverbs 22:1**

Salt is good: but if the salt has lost his saltiness, wherewith will ye season it? Have salt in yourselves and have peace one with another.

**Mark 9:50**

I appeal to you, dear brothers and sisters, by the authority of our Lord Jesus Christ, to live in harmony with each other. Let there be no divisions in the church. Rather, be of one mind, united in thought and purpose.

**1 Corinthians 1:10** NLT

Behold, how good and how pleasant it is for brethren to dwell together in unity.

**Psalm 133:1**

Finally, be ye all of one mind, having compassion one of another, love as brethren, be pitiful, be courteous.

**1 Peter 3:8**

Endeavor to keep the unity of the Spirit in the bond of peace.

**Ephesians 4:3**

Fulfill my joy by being like-minded, having the same love, being of one accord, of one mind.

**Philippians 2:2 NKJV**

Can two walk together, except they be agreed?

**Amos 3:3**

And above all these things put on charity, which is the bond of perfectness.

**Colossians 3:14**

Again, I say unto you, that if two of you shall agree on earth as touching anything that they shall ask, it shall be done for them of my Father which is in heaven.

**Matthew 18:19**

Remember ye not the former things, neither consider the things of old. Behold, I will do a new thing; now it shall spring forth; shall ye not know it? I will even make a way in the wilderness, and rivers in the desert.

**Isaiah 43:18–19**

By long forbearing is a prince persuaded, and a soft tongue breaketh the bone.

**Proverbs 25:15**

And be not conformed to this world: but be ye transformed by the renewing of your mind, that ye may prove what is that good, and acceptable, and perfect, will of God.

**Romans 12:2**

As iron sharpens iron, so one person sharpens another.

**Proverbs 27:17 niv**

He that walketh with wise men shall be wise: but a companion of fools shall be destroyed.

**Proverbs 13:20**

A soft answer turneth away wrath: but grievous words stir up anger.

**Proverbs 15:1**

## *Quotes: Agreement/Unity/Influence*

United we stand, divided we fall. ~**Aesop**

We must learn to live together as brothers or perish together as fools. ~**Martin Luther King Jr.**

On the essentials, unity. On the nonessentials, liberty. In everything charity or love. ~**Jack Hyles**

Unity without the Gospel is worthless. It is, in essence, the very unity of hell. ~**J. C. Ryle**

I have never yet known the spirit of God to work where the Lord's people were divided. ~**Dwight Moody**

The true secret of union is for us to look upon God and in the act of looking past ourselves to Him, we become unconsciously united. ~**A. B. Simpson**

Be united with other Christians. A wall with loose bricks is not good. The bricks must be cemented together. ~**Corrie Ten Boom**

Christ's love creates unity in the midst of adversity. ~**Unknown**

Things that happen in the power of agreement—**1**: There is victory. **2**: There is escape from temptation. **3**: We make the right decision. **4**: There is a sudden move of God. **5**: Miracles are brought forth. **6:** Great power is bestowed. **7**: There is no lack. **8**: Release is manifested. **9**: Deliverance is attained. **10**: Boldness is brought forth. **11**: Doors are opened. **12**: The Word is freed. **13**: Your abilities are greatly increased. ~**Anonymous**

Don't find fault, find a remedy. ~**Henry Ford**

Everything in life that truly matters boils down to relationships. ~**Gary Smalley**

The power of agreement, our righteous alignment, sent up with intensity and great velocity thunders through the heavens, to find its holy destination at the celestial throne of God. ~**Anonymous**

Get a good idea and stay with it. Dog it and work at it until it's done and done right. ~**Walt Disney**

The buck stops here. ~**Harry S. Truman**

You cannot warm the hearts of people with God's love if they have an empty stomach and cold feet. ~**William Booth**

If you want to go quickly, go alone; if you want to go far, go together. ~**African Proverb**

I can do things you cannot, you can do things I cannot; together we can do great things. ~**Mother Teresa**

We are all a little broken, but last time I checked, broken crayons still color the same. ~**Unknown**

Unity is strength, when there is teamwork and collaboration, wonderful things can be achieved. ~**Unknown**

Blessed is the influence of one true, loving soul on others. ~**George Elliott**

Heavy influence is not about elevating yourself, but about lifting up others. ~**Anonymous**

Example is not the main thing in influencing others, it is the only thing. ~**Albert Schweitzer**

One of the best ways to influence people is to make them feel important, it is one of the deepest human desires. ~**Anonymous**

The people who influence you are the people who believe in you. ~**Henry Drummond**

Never underestimate the power of dreams and the influence of the human spirit, the potential for greatness lives in each one of us. ~**Wilma Rudolph**

Our enemy, the devil, wants to control us and his target is our will. The main way he tries to influence our will is by lying to us. ~**Joyce Meyer**

Leadership is not about titles, positions or flowcharts, it is about one life influencing another. ~**John Maxwell**

Only God himself fully appreciates the influence of a Christian mother in the molding of character in her children. ~**Billy Graham**

The hour is desperately dark; your flame is desperately needed. ~**Lettie Cowman**

When we pray, we are petitioning God, but when we confess, we are agreeing in unity with God. ~**Perry Stone**

## *Hymn: Agreement/Unity/Influence*

**Blest Be the Tie That Binds**
Blest be that tie that binds,
Our hearts in Christian love.
The fellowship of kindred minds,
Is like to that above.
~**John Fawcett**, 1782 (public domain)

## *Personalized Prayer Weaponry*

There is powerful influence in reigning grace, it reaches far above and beyond our mortal endeavors to impress the world around us. Because we live in a "voice-activated kingdom," our words hold a massive ability to enrich or trample everything around us. They can gnaw with torment or drench with lavish affirmations, uplifting us or trodding us underfoot. Let us choose this day to pursue a place of unity by agreement and influence. May the light of heaven brighten our eyes today so that others will desire to know and follow that light.

## WEAPON 24

# Power/Authority

### *Scriptures*

Be sober, be vigilant; because your adversary the devil, as a roaring lion, walketh about, seeking whom he may devour.

**1 PETER 5:8**

Heal the sick, cleanse the lepers, raise the dead, cast out devils: freely ye have received, freely give.

**MATTHEW 10:8**

Submit yourselves therefore to God. Resist the devil, and he will flee from you.

**JAMES 4:7**

And the God of peace shall bruise Satan under your feet shortly. The grace of our Lord Jesus Christ be with you. Amen.

**ROMANS 16:20**

I'm not asking you to take them out of the world, but to keep them safe from the evil one.

**JOHN 17:15 NLT**

And what is the exceeding greatness of his power to us-ward who believe, according to the working of his mighty power.

**EPHESIANS 1:19**

You, dear children, are from God and have overcome them, because the one who is in you is greater than the one who is in the world.

**1 JOHN 4:4 NIV**

For though we walk in the flesh, we do not war after the flesh: For the weapons of our warfare are not carnal, but mighty through God to the pulling down of strong holds; Casting down imaginations, and every high thing that exalteth itself against the knowledge of God, and bringing into captivity every thought to the obedience of Christ.

**2 CORINTHIANS 10:3–5**

The Lord will cause your enemies who rise against you to be defeated before your face; they shall come out against you one way and flee before you seven ways.

**DEUTERONOMY 28:7 NKJV**

And all this assembly shall know that the Lord saveth not with sword and spear: for the battle is the Lord's, and he will give you into our hands.

**1 SAMUEL 17:47**

But ye shall receive power, after that the Holy Ghost is come upon you: and ye shall be witnesses unto me both in Jerusalem, and in all Judaea, and in Samaria, and unto the uttermost part of the earth.

**ACTS 1:8**

For he hath made him to be sin for us, who knew no sin; that we might be made the righteousness of God in him.

**2 Corinthians 5:21**

That he would grant unto us, that we being delivered out of the hand of our enemies might serve him without fear, In holiness and righteousness before him, all the days of our life.

**Luke 1:74–75**

So take a new grip with your tired hands and strengthen your weak knees. Mark out a straight path for your feet so that those who are weak and lame will not fall but become strong.

**Hebrews 12:12–13 NLT**

Finally, my brethren, be strong in the Lord, and in the power of his might.

**Ephesians 6:10**

But if the Spirit of him that raised up Jesus from the dead dwell in you, he that raised up Christ from the dead shall also quicken your mortal bodies by his Spirit that dwelleth in you.

**ROMANS 8:11**

Behold, I give unto you power to tread on serpents and scorpions, and over all the power of the enemy: and nothing shall by any means hurt you.

**Luke 10:19**

For I know that my redeemer liveth, and that he shall stand at the latter day upon the earth.

**Job 19:25**

You are the salt of the earth; but if the salt loses its flavor, how shall it be seasoned? It is then good for nothing but to be thrown out and trampled underfoot by men. You are the light of the world. A city that is set on a hill cannot be hidden. Nor do they light a lamp and put it under a basket, but on a lampstand, and it gives light to all who are in the house. Let your light so shine before men, that they may see your good works and glorify your Father in heaven.

**Matthew 5:13–16 NKJV**

After these things the word of the Lord came unto Abram in a vision, saying, Fear not, Abram: I am thy shield, and thy exceeding great reward.

**Genesis 15:1**

Let both grow together until the harvest: and in the time of harvest I will say to the reapers, gather ye together first the tares, and bind them in bundles to burn them: but gather the wheat into my barn.

**Matthew 13:30**

There is no fear in love. But perfect love drives out fear, because fear has to do with punishment. The one who fears is not made perfect in love.

**1 John 4:18 NIV**

He giveth power to the faint; and to them that have no might he increaseth strength.

**Isaiah 40:29**

And hath raised us up together and made us sit together in heavenly places in Christ Jesus.

**Ephesians 2:6**

## *Quotes: Power/Authority*

Ancient soul wounds handed down through the generations can be destroyed by Dunamis and Exocia power. ~**Katie Souza**

A leader is one who knows the way, goes the way, and shows the way. ~**John Maxwell**

God has given us power over darkness, power to overcome our sinful nature, power to move mountains in the name of Jesus. ~**Unknown**

The territory of the uncrucified thought life is the beachhead of satanic assault. We must be renewed in the spirit of our minds. ~**Francis Frangipane**

Pulling down strongholds is the demolition and removal of your old ways of thinking, so that the actual presence of God can be manifested in us. ~**Francis Frangipane**

A spiritual law few recognize is that our confession rules us. It is what we confess with our lips that really dominates our inner being. ~**F. F. Bosworth**

Other birds fly in groups, only eagles fly alone. ~**Francine Rivers**

We may be a small group but a midget on a mountain can see further than a giant in a valley. ~**Kim Clement**

Nearly all men can stand adversity, but if you want to test his character, give him power. ~**Abraham Lincoln**

Do not be blinded by Satan's cunning and brutal deceptions. He is an ancient, treacherous foe seeking your destruction yet perhaps cloaking himself in comfort and indifference. ~**Anonymous**

Never yield to force; never yield to the apparently overwhelming might of the enemy. ~**Winston Churchill**

You have enemies. Good! That means you stood up for something sometime in your life; never, never give up. ~**Winston Churchill**

Do all the good you can, by all the means you can, in all the ways you can, in all the places you can, in all the times and to all the people you can, as long as you ever can. ~**John Wesley**

The words you speak become the house you live in! ~**Unknown**

Words are the most powerful thing in the universe. Words are containers. They contain faith or fear and they produce after their own kind. ~**Charles Capps**

Lying in the hospital, thinking about all those women going for cancer checkups because of me, I've come to recognize the power of the woman in the White House. Not my power, but the power of the position, an influence that can be used to help others. That's why we are put on this earth. ~**Betty Ford**

No reserves. No retreats. No regrets. ~**William Borden**

"His kingdom will never end" or an old Moravian version says, "His kingdom shall have no frontier." ~**Henry Van Dyke**

The only way to flow in power and authority of God is through compassion. ~**Unknown**

Being powerful is like being a lady, if you have to tell people you are, you are not. ~**Margaret Thatcher**

Champions are a rare breed, they see beyond the dangers, the risks, the obstacles and the hardships. ~**Lester Sumrall**

What sets lion-chasers apart isn't the outcome, it's the courage to chase God-sized dreams. ~**Mark Batterson**

The word of God conceived in the heart, formed by the tongue and spoken out of the mouth is creative power. ~**Charles Capps**

The world does not need cool Christians, who are culturally saturated. It needs exiles with a scent of heaven and the aroma of Christ. ~**John Piper**

We herd sheep, we drive cattle, we lead people. Follow me, lead me or get out of the way. ~**George Patton**

We are reigning as kings in this life, take authority and enforce dominion. ~**Anonymous**

The price of constant victory is constant watchfulness. ~**Billye Brim**

You are expected not to just be a spectator, you are supposed to be ruling and reigning through Christ's power and authority given to you. ~**Billye Brim**

You have a ministry to rule and reign (dominate and dictate) over Satan during the time you are in your earth's suit, it's part of your ministry. ~**John A. MacMillan**

The master of all guards his servants with his own power and entrusts them with authority to command. ~**John A. MacMillan**

By faith the obedient saint claims his throne rights in Christ and boldly asserts his power, the authorities of the air will recognize and obey. ~**John A. MacMillan**

Whatever is stealing your peace and rocking your boat, whatever is taking your smile away, reach down, pick it up and throw it overboard. ~**Jentezen Franklin**

Power is a gift from God, this spiritual authority is the fruit of a relationship with Him. ~**John Paul Jackson**

As believers, we have every right as well as responsibility, to enact and enforce the power twins of Dunamis and Exocia, "power and authority." ~**Katie Souza**

Sin and trauma wound our souls and allow a place for enemies to badger us! Speak dunamis power to cleanse and make our souls excellent, healing wounds, forgiving offenses and preparing for restoration in every area of our lives. ~**Katie Souza**

Destroy and dethrone the strong man and all underlings with him will fall and flee. ~**Fred and Ida May Hammond**

## *Hymn: Power/Authority*

**All Hail the Power of Jesus' Name**
All hail the power of Jesus's name!
Let angels prostrate fall.
Bring forth the royal diadem,
And crown him Lord of all.
Let every kindred, every tribe,
On this terrestrial ball,
To him all majesty and power ascribe,
And crown him Lord of all.
~**Edward Perronet**, 1780 (public domain)

**O Worship the King**
Oh, worship the King,
All glorious above,
And gratefully sing of
His wonderful love.
Our Shield and Defender,
The Ancient of Days,
Pavilioned in splendor
and girded with praise.
~**Robert Grant**, 1779 (public domain)

## *Personalized Weaponry*

One bright, sunny morning a year ago, my son-in-law came through the front door, and seeing me, he said, "Momma Dobbs, where is your car?" I promptly told him it was parked in front of our house, to which he replied, "No, it isn't!"

Sensing something was wrong, I rushed outside, and my car was nowhere to be found! After calling the police and being informed our sleepy little country neighborhood had several similar complaints, I began prayer in my God-given power and authority mode.

Taking authority over the situation and commanding the evil to desist their operations, I then began to call on powerful angelic help to recue my car. I had always wanted a red car, and this one was perfect for a still-active grandma.

Two days later, I received a call from the local police saying they had found my car about two miles away, parked in the back of a local thrift shop that I frequented. What? One of my favorite little shops, the Helping Hands, whose outdoor cameras were being replaced, was harboring my little lost car?

When one of my sons and I went to look at the car after the police sent it to the wrecking yard, we found a series of surprises. The seat was in the same position, up close to the steering wheel, the mirrors were in my preferred position, nothing was rummaged through, nothing was missing, there was no forced entry, no scratched glass, no extra mileage, and the mystery went on. Even the worker said he had never seen anything like it.

My car was definitely locked, so in the early morning, without any neighbors noticing any activity, how was my car stolen or moved to a favorite shopping spot? It was remotely possible that someone went to the dealership and had a key made, but that has become difficult without identification and is also fairly costly unless one was going to actually steal the car for keeps.

We continued to thank the Lord in our amazement, and personally, I am convinced the Lord sent his angels on a mission to show me nothing is impossible for Him. If he can move mountains, why not a car to prove his loving involvement in our everyday lives? Works for me!

# Weapon 25

### *Scriptures*

And this is the confidence that we have in him, that, if we ask any thing according to his will, he heareth us.

**1 John 5:14**

Seek the Lord and his strength, seek his face continually.

**1 Chronicles 16:11**

And they that were vexed with unclean spirits: and they were healed.

**Luke 6:18**

Then you will call on me and come and pray to me, and I will listen to you.

**Jeremiah 29:12 NIV**

But I say unto you, love your enemies, bless them that curse you, do good to them that hate you, and pray for them which despitefully use you, and persecute you.

**Matthew 5:44**

Watch and pray, that ye enter not into temptation: the spirit indeed is willing, but the flesh is weak.

**Matthew 26:41**

The sacrifice of the wicked is an abomination to the Lord: but the prayer of the upright is his delight.

**Proverbs 15:8**

Rejoicing in hope; patient in tribulation; continuing instant in prayer.

**Romans 12:12**

Then Jesus told his disciples a parable to show them that they should always pray and not give up.

**Luke 18:1 NIV**

If my people, which are called by my name, shall humble themselves, and pray, and seek my face, and turn from their wicked ways; then will I hear from heaven, and will forgive their sin, and will heal their land.

**2 Chronicles 7:14**

Continue in prayer and watch in the same with thanksgiving.

**Colossians 4:2**

I exhort therefore, that, first of all, supplications, prayers, intercessions, and giving of thanks, be made for all men; For kings, and for all that are in authority; that we may lead a quiet and peaceable life in all godliness and honesty.

**1 Timothy 2:1–2**

O, my God, incline thine ear, and hear; open thine eyes, and behold our desolations, and the city which is called by thy name: for we do not present our supplications before thee for our righteousness but for thy great mercies.

**Daniel 9:18**

Call unto me, and I will answer thee, and show thee great and mighty things, which thou knowest not.

**Jeremiah 33:3**

But the end of all things is at hand; be ye therefore sober watching unto prayer.

**1 Peter 4:7**

Beloved, I wish above all things that thou mayest prosper and be in health, even as thy soul prospereth.

**3 John 1:2**

If ye then, being evil, know how to give good gifts unto your children: how much more shall your heavenly Father give the Holy Spirit to them that ask him?

**Luke 11:13**

Bear ye one another's burdens, and so fulfil the law of Christ.

**Galatians 6:2**

Confess your faults one to another, and pray one for another, that ye may be healed. The effectual fervent prayer of a righteous man availeth much.

**James 5:16**

I sought the Lord, and he heard me, and delivered me from all my fears.

**Psalm 34:4**

Arise, shine; for thy light is come, and the glory of the Lord is risen upon thee.

**Isaiah 60:1**

Pray for the peace of Jerusalem: they shall prosper that love thee. Peace be within thy walls, and prosperity within thy palaces.

**Psalm 122:6–7**

May the Lord cause you to flourish, both you and your children. May you be blessed by the Lord, the Maker of heaven and earth.

**Psalm 115:14–15 NIV**

For I, saith the Lord, will be unto her a wall of fire round about, and will be the glory in the midst of her.

**Zechariah 2:5**

My voice You shall hear in the morning, O Lord; In the morning I will direct it to You, And I will look up.

**Psalm 5:3 NKJV**

O satisfy us early with thy mercy; that we may rejoice and be glad all our days.

**Psalm 90:14**

Thy kingdom come, thy will be done in earth, as it is in heaven.

**Matthew 6:10**

He was the one who prayed to the God of Israel, "Oh, that you would bless me and expand my territory! Please be with me in all that I do and keep me from all trouble and pain!" And God granted him his request.

**1 Chronicles 4:10 NLT**

Though hand join in hand, the wicked shall not be unpunished: but the seed of the righteous shall be delivered.

**Proverbs 11:21**

Be anxious for nothing, but in everything by prayer and supplication, with thanksgiving, let your requests be made known to God; 7 and the peace of God, which surpasses all understanding, will guard your hearts and minds through Christ Jesus.

**Philippians 4:6–7 NKJV**

Being confident of this very thing, that he which hath begun a good work in you will perform it until the day of Jesus Christ.

**Philippians 1:6**

You number my wanderings; put my tears into your bottle; are they not in Your book?

**Psalm 56:8 NKJV**

Stablish thy word unto thy servant, who is devoted to thy fear.

**Psalm 119:38**

I will lift up mine eyes unto the hills, from whence cometh my help. My help cometh from the Lord, which made heaven and earth.

**Psalm 121:1–2**

Who satisfieth thy mouth with good things; so that thy youth is renewed like the eagle's.

**Psalm 103:5**

## *Scriptures: Morning Prayers*

For a thousand years in thy sight are but as yesterday when it is past, and as a watch in the night.

**Psalm 90:4**

My voice shalt thou hear in the morning, O Lord; in the morning will I direct my prayer unto thee and will look up.

**Psalm 5:3**

O, God, you are my God; early will I seek You; my soul thirsts for You; my flesh longs for You in a dry and thirsty land where there is no water.

**Psalm 63:1**

And be ready in the morning, and come up in the morning unto mount Sinai, and present thyself there to me on the top of the mount.

**Exodus 34:2**

Let the morning bring me word of your unfailing love, for I have put my trust in you. Show me the way I should go, for to you I entrust my life.

**Psalm 143:8 niv**

The first fresh hour of every morning should be dedicated to the Lord, whose mercy gladdens it with golden light. **~Charles Spurgeon**

Wash your face every morning in a bath of praise.
**~Charles Spurgeon**

## *Scriptures: Evening Prayers*

I will bless the Lord, who hath given me counsel: my reins also instruct me in the night seasons.

**Psalm 16:7**

For You have been my help and in the shadow of Your wings I sing for joy. My soul clings to You; Your right hand upholds me.

**Psalm 63:7–8 amp**

Let my prayer be set forth before thee as incense; and the lifting up of my hands as the evening sacrifice.

**Psalm 141:2**

For thou art my lamp, O Lord: and the Lord will lighten my darkness.

**2 Samuel 22:29**

I will both lay me down in peace, and sleep: for thou, Lord, only makest me dwell in safety.

**Psalm 4:8**

Be ye angry, and sin not: let not the sun go down upon your wrath.

**Ephesians 4:26**

For his anger endureth but a moment; in his favour is life: weeping may endure for a night but joy cometh in the morning.

**Psalm 30:5**

I laid me down and slept; I awaked; for the Lord sustained me.

**Psalm 3:5**

God is with us through all the lonely hours. He is an Almighty Watcher, a Sleepless Guardian, a Faithful Friend. ~**Charles Spurgeon**

## *Quotes: Prayer*

Boldness is a great virtue, but it does not begin on the battlefield or in the midst of great conflict. Our boldness must begin in our prayer life. ~**J. Lee Grady**

I had rather stand against the cannons of the wicked than against the prayers of the righteous. ~**Thomas Lye**

Burden is the secret of prayer. If you are not touched inwardly, you cannot pray. ~**Watchman Nee**

No work of God can become established unless it goes through the fire. ~**Rees Howell**

The path of the intercessor is the way of the cross. ~**Rees Howell**

Warfare prayers, faith-fueled, is not for the faint of heart; it is an act of worship, it is hard work and it is outright war. We struggle and agonize and wrestle in prayer. ~**Jack Graham**

It is only when we pray that we set Satan back on his heels. ~**Samuel Chadwick**

Do not see the face of man until you have seen the face of God. Before you enter the day with its temptations, look up into his face and hide his word in your heart. ~**Unknown**

Prayer is the key discipline whereby all spiritual work is done. ~**Chuck Pierce**

Open to us through prayer, Lord, the revelation of the sacred tongue of scripture. The ardent prayers of the generations that came before us are spilling out in ways never before known and never before experienced. ~**Unknown**

The prayer closet is the arena which produces the overcomer. ~**Paul Billheimer**

Intercession is the most unselfish thing anyone can do. ~**Paul Billheimer**

God designed the program of prayer as an apprenticeship for eternal sovereignty with Christ. ~**Paul Billheimer**

Prayer will carry us into the presence of our Royal brother, our Advocate with the father, Jesus Christ the Righteous. ~**Charles Spurgeon**

Bold prayers honor God and God honors bold prayers. If your prayers aren't impossible to you, they are insulting to God. ~**Mark Batterson**

Under the prayer covering, let the spirit of repentance and revival be birthed. ~**Anonymous**

Prayer brings order out of chaos, pulls peace out of confusion and brings joy in the midst of sorrow. ~**Cindy Jacobs**

The enemy is not afraid of how long we shout but how deeply we pray. ~**Jentezen Franklin**

When God is about to do a new thing, he always sets his people to praying. ~**Jonathan Edwards**

We tend to use prayer as a last resort, but God wants it to be our first line of defense. ~**Oswald Chambers**

Redeem your wilderness times by blazing a trail of prayer straight to the mountain of the Lord. ~**Anonymous**

Ordain our days to anoint, to grow, to encounter and to reach our destiny. ~**Jonathan Cahn**

Never underestimate the ability of prevailing prayer to affect reality in the final end of any matter. ~**Joel Richardson**

God desires us to actually wrestle with him in prayer, not only for own souls but those of our families and also for the very nations we live in and call home. ~**Joel Richardson**

If we are going to walk in the power of prayer, there has to be a revelation that it is not all about us. ~**Robert Morris**

They who pray not, know nothing of God and know nothing of the state of their own souls. ~**Adam Clarke**

Intercessory prayer, our ministry in the heavenlies. ~**Unknown**

We are too busy to pray so we are too busy to have great power. ~**R. A. Torrey**

Set up a memorial for your children and grandchildren by speaking this ninefold blessing out loud: **1**. Pray for their salvation **2**. Serve God **3**. They will be healthy in body, soul and spirit **4**. They will be prosperous **5**. They will walk in wholeness **6**. They will be free from disease/plagues **7**. They will be protected against perversion **8**.They will be protected from kidnapping/terrorism **9**. They will be protected from accidents. ~**R. W. Schambach**

One of the best aids to freedom is to ask God for help all the time. ~**Joyce Meyer**

Satan will aggressively fight against the renewal of your mind, but it is vital that you press on and continue to pray and study in this area until you gain measurable victory. ~**Joyce Meyer**

God insists that we ask, not because he needs to know our situation, but because we need the spiritual discipline of asking. ~**Catherine Marshall**

Pray that God molds your heart into that of a willing servant. ~**Michael Youssef**

My prayers are strategic and impactful in the unseen realm. ~**Anonymous**

Go to your place of prayer not only to enjoy spiritual delights but simply to please the Father. ~**Madame Guyon**

My earnest prayer is to paint in true colors the goodness of God to meet the depth of my own ingratitude. ~**Madame Guyon**

God is looking within each family for one intercessor who will stand in the gap and put up a hedge for the entire family. ~**Germaine Copeland**

It is not just saying prayers that gets results, but it is spending time with the Lord, learning his wisdom, drawing on his strength, being filled with his quietness and basking in his love that brings results to our prayers. ~**Germaine Copeland**

Yank some of the groans out of your prayers and shove in some shouts. ~**Billy Sunday**

Lord, keep us out of the hands and out of the way of wicked, evil people and wicked evil circumstances. Remember our names are graven on the palms of your hands and we are bound to you with mighty chords of love. ~**Anonymous**

I do not pray for a lighter load but for a stronger back. ~**Phillips Brooks**

The sigh, the groan of a broken heart, will soon go through the ceiling up to the heavens, yes, into the very bosom of God. ~**Charles Simeon**

Groanings which cannot be uttered are often prayers which cannot be refused. ~**Charles Spurgeon**

Prayer is the autograph of the Holy Spirit upon the renewed heart. ~**Charles Spurgeon**

I've heard enough, read enough, know enough, would to God that I lived it! I wish to stick to Christ as a bur sticks to a topcoat. ~**Katharina von Bora Luther**

A prayer warrior has a heart of compassion for suffering people in bad situations and desires to do something to make a difference. ~**Stormie Omartian**

The truth is there are such things as Christian tears, and too few of us ever weep them. ~**John Stott**

All other efforts are in vain without the sticks of prayer and Bible reading rubbed together to ignite a fire. ~**Beth Moore**

Tucked like rubies in the embers of our flames is the reward of prayer and Bible study. ~**Beth Moore**

Prayer is both communication and a weapon of spiritual warfare. ~**Anonymous**

Nothing lies beyond the reach of prayer except those things outside the will of God. ~**Unknown**

Pray against a web of elected witchcraft that is descending on mankind in every nation. ~**Lance Wallnau**

Prayer should be the key of the day and the lock of the night. ~**George Herbert**

God often brings us into a hard place that He may bring us to our knees. ~**Matthew Henry**

The people who really rule the world know how to pray. ~**Derek Prince**

Prayer that is secret, fervent and believing lies at the root of all personal godliness, oh, the sweet duty of intercession. ~**William Cary**

It is impossible to lose your footing when you are on your knees. ~**Fulton Sheen**

Prayer is our greatest need, our highest activity, our finest habit, and our holiest use of time. ~**David Jeremiah**

The church is looking for better methods; God is looking for better men, men mighty in prayer. ~**E. M. Bounds**

Preaching never edifies a prayerless soul. ~**E. M. Bounds**

Go to the throne, not to the phone! The people on the other end aren't qualified to fix your problems, they can't even fix their own! ~**Joyce Meyer**

Let me say from conviction that tears are the outlet of the heart. ~**Watchman Nee**

Prayer is the greatest of all forces, because it honors God and brings him into active aid. ~**E. M. Bounds**

The prayer closet is the battlefield of the church, its citadel, the scene of heroes and unearthly conflicts. ~**E. M. Bounds**

When prayer fails, the world prevails. ~**E. M. Bounds**

I can touch the world from where I am through prayer. ~**Unknown**

God is usually more anxious to talk to us than we are to listen to him. ~**Bill Hamon**

Worry, why worry, what can worry do? It can never keep a problem from overtaking you. It gives you indigestion and sleepless hours at night and fills with gloom the day however fair and bright. It puts a grumble in your tone, it makes you unfit to live with others and unfit to live alone. Pray, why pray, what can praying do? It can stop a problem from overwhelming you. It's great for indigestion and gives perfect sleep at night. It cheers up every day with all its golden light. Pray, why pray, what can praying do? It can bring God down from heaven to live and work through you. It puts a love note in your tone. It makes you fit to live with others and fit to live alone! ~**Unknown**

Keep the golden altar of your private prayers burning. Secret devotion is the essence, evidence and barometer of Christianity. Let your closeted prayer seasons be regular, frequent and undisturbed. Many foes will attempt to extinguish it but if the unseen Hand pours the sacred oil, the fire will blaze brighter and higher. ~**Charles Spurgeon**

Prayer tears are the golden chain that bind Jesus to His people. If you navigate only the little streams and shallow creeks, you will know nothing of the God of the Storms! ~**Charles Spurgeon**

Pray often, for prayer is a shield to the soul, a sacrifice to God and a scourge to Satan. ~**John Bunyan**

We acquire energy for the great race of life by the hallowed labor of prayer. Prayer girds the loins of God's warriors and sends them into combat with sinews braced and muscles firmed. ~**Charles Spurgeon**

Beautiful in God's sight is tearful, agonizing, unconquerable insistence in prayer. It should be perfumed and saturated with love, love for our fellow saints and for Christ. ~**Charles Spurgeon**

Do not neglect to pray for all those in the Lord's service; that being pastors, apostles, prophets, evangelists and missionaries plus teachers of the Gospel. Their work is solemnly momentous. They are here on God's eternal business with heavy responsibility weighing on their shoulders.

As Officers in the Lord's Army, they are the special target of both saints and devils. They preach, teach, instruct, counsel, pray until the wee hours, all the while yearning for wayward souls and lost humanity. They are bombarded as few men and women are, misunderstood and often at wits' end to fulfill their sacred calling. At times they are frayed and fragmented, longing only to see their assignment successfully completed. Pray for these dear ones, they greatly need the aid of your constant interceding. ~**Anonymous**

## Hymns: Prayer

**Sweet Hour of Prayer**
Sweet hour of prayer,
That calls me from a world of care,
And bids me at my Father's throne,
Make all my wants and wishes known.
In seasons of distress and grief,
My soul has often found relief,
And oft escaped the tempter's snare,
By thy return, sweet hour of prayer.
~**William Walford**, 1845 (public domain)

**In the Garden (I Come to the Garden Alone)**
I come to the garden alone,
While the dew is still on the roses,
And the voice I hear falling on my ear
The son of God discloses.
And he walks with me and he talks with me,
And he tells me I am his own,
And the joy we share as we tarry there,
None other has ever known.
~**C. Austin Miles**, 1912 (public domain)

## Personalized Weaponry

I was front and center during the turbulent sixties, cramming a lot of living into that decade. High school, college, marriage, baby, JFK and MLK assassinations, college riots, the Beatles, two unaccompanied tours to Korea and Vietnam for my former husband, flag burning, radical feminist movement, and heading toward a choice assignment in Europe.

The Vietnam War was raging and 1968 to 1969 found me and my three-year-old son in El Paso, Texas, in a heavily treed apartment community just a few blocks from the dry, dusty desert. I had determined to live surrounded by a group of other military wives waiting for their husbands to return. We kept ourselves busy with shopping, trips to Mexico, fondue dinners, as well as rounding up kids, some babies, and other preschoolers and watching the rivalry between Glen Campbell and Tom Jones on the evening TV.

*Star Trek* was a favorite with some. In fact, one gal wouldn't answer her door when it was showing. Of course, the man on the moon had everyone glued to their sets, along with whatever war coverage we were able to see or hear.

As I look back on how super-shallow I was at twenty-three, I think it was amazing. The lives of the other eight gals was pretty chaotic, as some were not military "lifer" wives and the strain was pretty apparent, even for those of us who were. The courtyard atmosphere provided a small amount of comfort and safety in numbers while we wiled away the hours and days with picnics, games with the children, cookouts, and evenings sitting on the porches. Not to mention, hours spent at the pool working on our golden tans in preparation for our R and R in Hawaii, where we would be meeting up with our husbands. We lived for visits from the mailman, delivering letters with that familiar APO return address and occasionally packages with goodies from the BX catalog when we had told our husbands what to buy. The best treat would be a dozen red roses for a special birthday or anniversary. The Sony reel-to-reel tape recorder was one of the latest gadgets. You could record for an hour or so all that was going on at home and send it to the guys and the process would begin again.

One late afternoon, I looked out my bedroom window only to see an army officer in dress blues, whom I recognized as a Casualty Notification Officer, walk up the sidewalk toward my doorway. My heart sank, because I knew this might be notice that my then-husband had been wounded or killed. I was still a "baby Christian" but at that moment, I knew I had not prayed enough for my husband's safety, since he was not a believer. Thankfully, the officer passed by my door, but a somber and sobering presence came over me. I realized later, the seeds of intercession were planted in my soul and spirit that pivotal day so long ago.

## Weapon 26

# Endurance/Perseverance

### *Scriptures*

You need to persevere so that when you have done the will of God, you will receive what he has promised.

**Hebrews 10:36 NIV**

Now the God of patience and consolation grant you to be likeminded one toward another according to Christ Jesus.

**Romans 15:5**

For if any be a hearer of the word, and not a doer, he is like unto a man beholding his natural face in a glass.

**James 1:23**

And let us not be weary in well doing: for in due season we shall reap, if we faint not.

**Galatians 6:9**

If we suffer, we shall also reign with him: if we deny him, he also will deny us.

**2 Timothy 2:12**

Beareth all things, believeth all things, hopeth all things, endureth all things.

**1 Corinthians 13:7**

I have set the Lord always before me: because he is at my right hand, I shall not be moved.

**Psalm 16:8**

Wherefore seeing we also are compassed about with so great a cloud of witnesses, let us lay aside every weight, and the sin which doth so easily beset us, and let us run with patience the race that is set before us, Looking unto Jesus the author and finisher of our faith; who for the joy that was set before him endured the cross, despising the shame, and is set down at the right hand of the throne of God..

**Hebrews 12:1–2**

I had fainted, unless I had believed to see the goodness of the Lord in the land of the living.

**Psalm 27:13**

In the body of his flesh through death, to present you holy and unblameable and unreproveable in his sight: If ye continue in the faith grounded and settled, and be not moved away from the hope of the gospel, which ye have heard, and which was preached to every creature which is under heaven; whereof I Paul am made a minister.

**Colossians 1:22–23**

And I sent messengers unto them, saying, I am doing a great work, so that I cannot come down: why should the work cease, whilst I leave it, and come down to you?

**Nehemiah 6:3**

I have set watchmen upon thy walls, O Jerusalem, which shall never hold their peace day nor night: ye that make mention of the Lord, keep not silence,

**Isaiah 62:6**

And not only so, but we glory in tribulations also: knowing that tribulation worketh patience ;and patience, experience; and experience, hope.

**Romans 5:3–4**

Strengthened with all might, according to his glorious power, unto all patience and longsuffering with joyfulness; Giving thanks unto the Father, which hath made us meet to be partakers of the inheritance of the saints in light.

**Colossians 1:11–12**

Blessed is the man that endureth temptation: for when he is tried, he shall receive the crown of life, which the Lord hath promised to them that love him.

**James 1:12**

I can do all things through Christ which strengtheneth me.

**Philippians 4:13**

But he that shall endure unto the end, the same shall be saved.

**Matthew 24:13**

Praying always with all prayer and supplication in the Spirit and watching thereunto with all perseverance and supplication for all saints.

**Ephesians 6:18**

But ye, brethren, be not weary in well doing.

**2 Thessalonians 3:13**

He that hath an ear, let him hear what the Spirit saith unto the churches.

**Revelation 3:13**

And Jesus said unto him, No man, having put his hand to the plough, and looking back, is fit for the kingdom of God.

**Luke 9:62**

I have fought a good fight, I have finished my course, I have kept the faith.

**2 Timothy 4:7**

Seek the Lord and his strength, seek his face continually.

**1 Chronicles 16:11**

But the path of the just is as the shining light, that shineth more and more unto the perfect day.

**Proverbs 4:18**

Therefore, turn thou to thy God: keep mercy and judgment and wait on thy God continually.

**Hosea 12:6**

## *Quotes: Endurance/Perseverance*

To learn strong faith is to endure great trials. I have learned faith by standing firm amidst severe testings. ~**George Mueller**

Endurance is not just the ability to bear a hard thing, but to turn it into glory. ~**Phillip Yancey**

That which is bitter to endure may be sweet to remember. ~**Thomas Fuller**

I care not what I have to endure that souls may be saved. When I sleep, I dream of them; when I awake, they are my first thoughts. ~**David Brainerd**

Let me tell you the secret to achieving my goal, it lies solely in my perseverance. ~**Louis Pasteur**

Brave and loyal followers! Long ago we resolved to serve no other than God himself, who alone is the true and just Lord of all mankind. ~**Unknown**

Through hard work, perseverance and strong faith in God, you can live out your dreams. ~**Ben Carson**

In the dust of defeat, as well as the laurels of victory, there is a glory to be found if one has done his best. ~**Eric Liddell**

The school of suffering graduate exceptional scholars. ~**Unknown**

It is not whether you get knocked down, it's whether you get back up. ~**Vince Lombardi**

Face the giants in your life; slay them and move on, do not be daunted by the mistakes and failures of your life. ~**T. D. Jakes**

The greater the anointing, the greater the isolation. ~**Unknown**

Stay put in the hard places and you will eventually rest on the mountaintop. ~**Kenneth Hagin**

My chicken recipe was rejected 1,009 times before a restaurant accepted it. ~**Colonel Sanders**

Concentrate all your thoughts on the work at hand, the sun's rays do not burn until brought to focus! ~**Alexander Graham Bell**

I just say the moral of my life is, don't quit, at age sixty-five maybe your ship hasn't come in yet, mine had not until then. ~**Colonel Sanders**

Many of life's failures are people who did not realize how close they were to success when they gave up. ~**Thomas A. Edison**

Even if I knew that tomorrow the world would go to pieces, I would still plant my apple trees. ~**Martin Luther**

When things go wrong, don't go along with them. ~**Elvis Presley**

Once you learn to quit, it becomes a habit. ~**Vince Lombardi**

Soft water can wear away hard rock, it just takes great patience, perseverance and endurance, so do not give up. ~**Anonymous**

Great works are performed not by strength, but by perseverance. ~**Samuel Johnson**

If at first you don't succeed, try, try again. ~**Unknown**

Perseverance is the hard work you do after you get tired of doing the hard work you already did. ~**Newt Gingrich**

Even the snail, by effort, made it to the ark. ~**Charles Spurgeon**

You must pay the price if you wish to secure the blessings. ~**Andrew Jackson**

I attributed my success to this; I never gave or took an excuse. ~**Florence Nightingale**

If Joan of Arc could turn the tide of an entire war before her eighteenth birthday, get out of bed and get something accomplished for God. ~**Anonymous**

Now is not the time to give up, the end is going to be better than the beginning. ~**Joni Lamb**

If I aim at nothing, I will hit it every time. ~**Zig Ziglar**

When we long for life without difficulty, remind us that great oaks grow stronger under the contrary winds and diamonds are made under extreme pressure. ~**Catherine Marshall**

The most difficult thing is the decision to act, the rest is mere tenacity. ~**Amelia Earhart**

The higher the hill, the stronger the wind; the loftier the life, the stronger the enemy's temptation. ~**John Wycliffe**

If we can know the beauty God is forming in us, we can bear the pain he allows into our lives. ~**James Robison**

If a man hasn't discovered something he will die for, he isn't fit to live. ~**Martin Luther King Jr.**

When you come to the end of your rope, tie a knot in it and hang on. ~**Franklin D. Roosevelt**

Courage is fear that said its prayers and decided to go forward anyway. ~**Joyce Meyer**

Trouble never comes to test what you are doing, it comes to test who you are! ~**Chuck Pierce**

Oh, how rare the Christian who speaks with a tender heart and has a theological backbone of steel. ~**John Piper**

Patience is not the ability to wait, but the ability to keep a good attitude while waiting. ~**Joyce Meyer**

Live long, live strong! ~**Gloria Copeland**

A tried and true saint, like a well-cut diamond, glitters greatly in the King's crown. Nothing reflects honor like a protracted and severe trial that ends in triumphant endurance. We are God's workers and He will be glorified in our afflictions. It is for the glory of Jesus that we endure the trials of our faith with sacred joy! ~**Charles Spurgeon**

## *Hymn: Endurance/Perseverance*

**Jesus Calls Us**
Jesus calls us o'er the tumult
Of our lives wild, restless sea;
Day by day His sweet voice soundeth,
Saying, "Christian, follow Me!"
~**Cecil Francis Alexander**, 1852 (public domain)

## *Personalized Weaponry*

Born in 1912, my dad was the third of five children of Bob and Louella Brigham. His father was the editor of the *Norman Transcript* newspaper in Norman, Oklahoma, and his mother was a tiny, dark-haired beauty at four foot eleven who had a blossoming career as a milliner. This was an industry that was booming for many years—that of making the big, gorgeous, ornate hats that ladies wore at that time with large jeweled hatpins to hold them in place.

His parents divorced when he was seven, and by the time he was twelve, he had experienced more death and heartache than the average adult. One older brother drowned in a local pond and another infant brother died of dehydration. The scourge of a single-mother household was a stinging reality. My grandmother was living on $75 a month, attempting to hold her little family together when, in 1924, her brood all came down with the flu. They had survived WWI, the Great Influenza of 1918, and the twenties were definitely roaring, but this sickness took her life at forty-two. On her sickbed, without hospice or any form of relief, she breathed her last. But before she left, she gave two important messages to her loved ones: "Never give up your faith in God, and get an education. Nobody can take these from you!"

Thrust into a midnight of despair, my dad and his siblings, along with an older aunt, laid his mother to rest during those days when the roadside workers stood with their hats over their hearts as the hearse drove by. The children were left without their dear mother or an involved father.

There was, planted in my dad, a type of resolve to endure and persevere that would be with him throughout his lifetime. It would fortify him during the Depression, his college years, and WWII. He made the choice to not cave in and retreat into nothingness but to push and press on toward goals he had set for himself.

My dad's life was a testimony to hard work, determination, and discipline. His love of God was passed on to me, a legacy to be treasured, honored, and respected. The divine transfer of generational faith was safely secured. As long as you have breath, you have influence.

## Weapon 27

# Mercy/Grace

### *Scriptures Mercy/Grace*

Open thy mouth, judge righteously, and plead the cause of the poor and needy.

**Proverbs 31:9**

It is of the Lord's mercies that we are not consumed, because his compassions fail not.

**Lamentations 3:22**

And he said unto me, My grace is sufficient for thee: for my strength is made perfect in weakness. Most gladly; therefore, will I rather glory in my infirmities, that the power of Christ may rest upon me.

**2 Corinthians 12:9**

But unto every one of us is given grace according to the measure of the gift of Christ.

**Ephesians 4:7**

For sin shall not have dominion over you: for ye are not under the law, but under grace.

**Romans 6:14**

For all have sinned and come short of the glory of God.

**Romans 3:23**

The Lord is good to all: and his tender mercies are over all his works.

**Psalm 145:9**

Blessed are the merciful: for they shall obtain mercy.

**Matthew 5:7**

Who satisfies your years with good things, so that your youth is renewed like the eagles.

**Psalm 103:5 AMP**

For by grace you have been saved through faith, and that not of yourselves; it is the gift of God, not of works, lest anyone should boast.

**Ephesians 2:8–9 NKJV**

And of Benjamin he said, The beloved of the Lord shall dwell in safety by him; and the Lord shall cover him all the day long, and he shall dwell between his shoulders.

**Deuteronomy 33:12**

Let us therefore come boldly unto the throne of grace, that we may obtain mercy, and find grace to help in time of need.

**Hebrews 4:16**

He has not dealt with us according to our sins, Nor punished us according to our iniquities. For as the heavens are high above the earth, So great is His mercy toward those who fear Him; As far as the east is from the west, So far has He removed our transgressions from us. As a father pities his children, So the Lord pities those who fear Him. For He knows our frame; He remembers that we are dust.

**Psalm 103:10–14 NKJV**

They wandered in the wilderness in a solitary way; they found no city to dwell in. Hungry and thirsty, their soul fainted in them. Then they cried unto the Lord in their trouble, and he delivered them out of their distresses. And he led them forth by the right way, that they might go to a city of habitation.

**Psalm 107:4–7**

David said to Gad, "I am in deep distress. Let us fall into the hands of the Lord, for his mercy is great; but do not let me fall into human hands."

**2 Samuel 24:14 NIV**

Not by works of righteousness which we have done, but according to his mercy he saved us, by the washing of regeneration, and renewing of the Holy Ghost.

**Titus 3:5**

Grace and peace be multiplied unto you through the knowledge of God, and of Jesus our Lord.

**2 Peter 1:2**

But go ye and learn what that meaneth, I will have mercy, and not sacrifice: for I am not come to call the righteous, but sinners to repentance.

**Matthew 9:13**

Have mercy upon me, O God, according to thy loving kindness: according unto the multitude of thy tender mercies blot out my transgressions.

**Psalm 51:1**

Who is a God like you, who pardons sin and forgives the transgression of the remnant of his inheritance? You do not stay angry forever but delight to show mercy.

**Micah 7:18 NIV**

## *Quotes: Mercy/Grace*

God does not waste an ounce of our pain or a drop of our tears. He takes our bumps and bruises and shapes them into something beautiful. ~**Frank Peretti**

We must combine the toughness of a servant and the softness of a dove, a tough mind and a tender heart. ~**Martin Luther King Jr.**

Grace is when God gives us what we don't deserve, and mercy is when God doesn't give us what we do deserve. ~**Unknown**

Grace collides with and demolishes exasperation, frustration and procrastination. ~**Anonymous**

The providence of God will not place you where His grace cannot keep you. ~**Mark Buntain**

Christ has enriched the entirety of our lives, giving us every grace and blessing and gift and power for doing His will, plus a full understanding of the truth of the Gospel and the ability to proclaim it to others. ~**Anonymous**

The cross was heavy, the blood was real, the price was extravagant. It would have bankrupted you or me, so He paid it for us. Call it simple, call it a gift. But don't call it easy, call it what it is, Grace. ~**Max Lucado**

Empathetic listening is an awesome medication for the hurting heart. ~**Unknown**

Maybe it's those who have made such chaos of their lives who can understand the heights and the depths of God's mercy. ~**Francine Rivers**

Stretch yourself out in the hammock of grace. You can rest now. ~**Max Lucado**

To be saved by grace, is to be saved by Jesus, not by an idea, doctrine, creed or church membership. But by Jesus himself, who will sweep into heaven anyone who so much as gives him a nod. ~**Max Lucado**

Grace is only an impersonal stained-glass word, until it happens to you. ~**David Jeremiah**

Many have highjacked grace and stretched its benefits far past God's intentions. Just because He loves you unconditionally, doesn't mean we can stomp all over his kindness. ~**Steve Hill**

God is glorified through healing and deliverance, not through sickness and suffering. ~**Kenneth Hagin**

God dispenses His goodness, not with an eyedropper, but with a fire hydrant. Your heart is a Dixie cup and his grace the Mediterranean Sea. You simply cannot contain it all. ~**Max Lucado**

God offers second chances, like a soup kitchen offers meals, to everyone who asks. ~**Max Lucado**

The quality of mercy is not strained. It drops as the gentle rain from heaven upon the place beneath. It is twice blessed; it blesses him that gives and him that takes. ~**William Shakespeare**

Mercy forgave the thief on the cross, grace escorted him to paradise. ~**Max Lucado**

The depths of our misery can never fall below the depths of his mercy. ~**Richard Sibbes**

The first requirement of a hospital is that it should do the sick no harm. Wash your hands often, open the windows and let sunshine pour in and be clean in your surrounds, very clean. Be devoted to your patients and always kind. ~**Florence Nightingale**

God's grace is more than a blessing; it is an actual formidable power within you, that when exercised will strengthen you to overcome any enemy. ~**Morris Cerullo**

When you wear the weed of impatience in your heart instead of the flower of acceptance with joy, you will always find your enemies getting an advantage over you. ~**Hannah Hurnard**

The trust we put in God honors him much and draws down great graces. ~**Brother Lawrence**

The Lord's presence is never so sweet as in moments of appalling difficulty. ~**Unknown**

## *Hymns: Mercy/Grace*

**Come Thou Fount of Every Blessing**
Come, thou Fount of every blessing,
Tune my heart to sing Thy grace.
Streams of mercy, never ceasing,
Call for songs of loudest praise.
Teach me some melodious sonnet,
Sung by flaming tongues above.
Praise the Mount! I am fixed upon it,
Mount of Thy redeeming love.
~**Robert Robison**, 1757 (public domain)

**Amazing Grace**
Amazing grace! how sweet the sound,
That saved a wretch like me!
I once was lost, but now am found,
Was blind, but now I see.
~**John Newton**, 1779 (public domain)

## *Personalized Weaponry*

January 1970 found my former husband and myself and young son landing on a snowy, icy runway in Frankfurt, Germany, in the middle of the night. We were greeted by our sponsor, who drove us to Wiesbaden, where the picturesque Von Steuben Hotel welcomed us weary travelers. This was the same hotel where vendors would bring their wares from the various shops and warehouses, much to the joy of us American shoppers. At Christmas the mezzanine would be glistening with a wonderland of gorgeous decorations and treasures not to be found anywhere else.

Our old French housing was nestled in a German community not far from the Rhine River, which explained why the fog was so thick for three months. For months, the faint streetlights never went off, because the sun didn't come out. But I didn't care. This was a dream assignment to me, full of travel, sights and sounds, food experiences, and extraordinary shopping. Lofty castles, with all their mysterious allure and breathtaking beauty, were scattered up and down the Rhine. I loved the massive, awe-inspiring, Gothic cathedrals rising like monuments in their baroque splendor, cultural exchanges, and the esprit de corps of our military unit. In later years, I would remind myself often of the blessing of living in this beautiful setting, with real hardwood floors, double casement windows with the rouladen wooden shades, and the radiator steam heat generated by the coal in our basement. The lovely flower gardens and immaculate cobblestone streets surrounding the German neighborhood, encircling our twenty huge stone quarters housed four families each. I remember fondly the gasthaus, where Germans would bring their large dogs to sit under the dining tables. To my amazement, the dogs were more well-trained than most people's children. We were within walking distance of the historic, quaint and picturesque town of Mainz-Gonsenheim, where it was not unusual to see a herd of sheep being driven along. We were also fortunate to have a third-floor live-in neighbor, Ingrid, who was a student at the University of Mainz. She was allowed an area in exchange for being our live-in babysitter. She could often be seen on her little black moped, rain or shine, with my six-year-old son begging her for a ride. Once a week, the coal man would back up his truck and dump a load in and shovel the furnace to capacity. What a different time and a different world! All this beyond amazing environment could have had a tragic ending if not for the protection of Almighty God on my behalf.

Preparing for the move, I was advised to take my braided rugs, living room furniture, and as much as I could for that homey feel. I also took my Coppertone Kenmore washer, which would operate on a large transformer. The dryer had to stay behind due to the electrical current difference.

The basement had two large storage rooms in addition to the coal room, and clothes lines had been strung for drying. I would go down a flight of stairs carrying my wet clothes, careful not to drop them in the coal dust that had settled on the floors. The men were out in the field several months out of each year, which left the wives fairly vulnerable. One horrifying day, as I was gathering up my dried clothes, I discovered that it all had been slashed with a knife or box cutter in strategic places. I immediately ran upstairs, noticing footprints in the dust leading to the other room. I called the military police and my then-husband. An investigation resulted in apprehension of a teenage boy from down the street, whose father was a colonel. The boy was sent back to the States for evaluation. The eerie thing was I never noticed or had a moment of discernment about this kid lurking around, no awareness of being stalked, or even realization of who he was. For the most part, this military community had young children, and any healthy teenager would have been highly visible. Like some kind of evil phantom, he was hiding and unrecognizable. Honestly, apprehending him was a stealth operation also, and I was never given any additional details.

The mercy of the Lord and His blood covering was sheltering me from a deadly situation that still gives me the shivers. To this day, I still thank Him for His protection. How many times has the Lord spared us all? We will only know in heaven!

## Weapon 28

# Praise/Worship

### *Scriptures*

Sing unto the Lord, all the earth; shew forth from day to day his salvation. Declare his glory among the heathen; his marvellous works among all nations. For great is the Lord, and greatly to be praised: he also is to be feared above all gods.

**1 Chronicles 16:23–25**

But the hour cometh, and now is, when the true worshippers shall worship the Father in spirit and in truth: for the Father seeketh such to worship him.

**John 4:23**

Let them praise thy great and terrible name; for it is holy. The king's strength also loveth judgment; thou dost establish equity, thou execute judgment and righteousness in Jacob.

**Psalm 99:3–4**

Give unto the Lord the glory due unto his name; worship the Lord in the beauty of holiness.

**Psalm 29:2**

And so, dear brothers and sisters, I plead with you to give your bodies to God because of all he has done for you. Let them be a living and holy sacrifice—the kind he will find acceptable. This is truly the way to worship him.

**Romans 12:1 NLT**

Wherefore, we are receiving a kingdom which cannot be moved, let us have grace, whereby we may serve God acceptably with reverence and godly fear: For our God is a consuming fire.

**Hebrews 12:28–29**

O come, let us sing unto the Lord: let us make a joyful noise to the rock of our salvation.

**Psalm 95:1**

Speaking to yourselves in psalms and hymns and spiritual songs, singing and making melody in your heart to the Lord.

**Ephesians 5:19**

O come, let us worship and bow down: let us kneel before the Lord our maker.

**Psalm 95:6**

Daniel answered and said, Blessed be the name of God for ever and ever: for wisdom and might are his.

**Daniel 2:20**

Blessed be the Lord, that hath given rest unto his people Israel, according to all that he promised: there hath not failed one word of all his good promise, which he promised by the hand of Moses his servant.

**1 Kings 8:56**

He is your praise, and He is your God, who has done for you these great and awesome things which your eyes have seen.

**Deuteronomy 10:21 NKJV**

Let the high praises of God be in their mouth, and a two-edged sword in their hand.

**Psalm 149:6**

Then if my people who are called by my name will humble themselves and pray and seek my face and turn from their wicked ways, I will hear from heaven and will forgive their sins and restore their land. My eyes will be open and my ears attentive to every prayer made in this place. For I have chosen this Temple and set it apart to be holy—a place where my name will be honored forever. I will always watch over it, for it is dear to my heart.

**2 Chronicles 7:14–16 NLT**

By him therefore let us offer the sacrifice of praise to God continually, that is, the fruit of our lips giving thanks to his name.

**Hebrews 13:15**

I will sing of the mercies of the Lord forever: with my mouth will I make known thy faithfulness to all generations.

**Psalm 89:1**

For the gifts and calling of God are without repentance.

**Romans 11:29**

## *Quotes: Praise/Worship*

Worship helps us get rid of many of life's frustrations. God is refining our understanding of true worship from the heart of love and adoration to the Lord. ~**Ruth Ward Heflin**

Worship is adoring contemplation of God. ~**R. A. Torrey**

Praise is a decree set to music. ~**Unknown**

We, the people of God, will take the earth by forceful worship. Violent worship overcomes violence in the natural, because the atmosphere around us has to shift. ~**Chuck Pierce**

When we were children, we were grateful to those who filled our stockings at Christmas. Why are we not grateful to God who filled our stockings with legs?! ~**G. K. Chesterton**

Only in the act of praise and worship can a person learn to believe in the goodness and the greatness of God. ~**C. S. Lewis**

All of my life, in every season, you are still God. I have a reason to sing, I have a reason to worship. ~**Unknown**

I need to worship, because without it, I lose a sense of wonderment and gratitude. I plod through life with blinders on. ~**John Ortberg**

Worship equals bragging on God for who He is. Praise equals thanking God for what he has done. ~**Unknown**

When you enter God's presence with praise, He enters your circumstances with power. ~**Unknown**

Worship is an inward feeling and an outward action that reflects the worth of Almighty God. ~**John Piper**

Worship is simply giving God his breathe back! ~**Lou Giglio**

Go to church once a week and nobody pays attention, worship God seven days a week and you become strange! ~**A. W. Tozer**

If someone doesn't have much use for praising God now, it is foolish to think that they are ready for heaven. ~**Matt Chandler**

Lord, you are our exceeding great reward. The sunshine of our souls, the very light of life itself. ~**Charles Spurgeon**

Carpet the king's way with the lilies of your love and the roses of your gratitude. ~**Charles Spurgeon**

No one can engage in warfare, who is not first a worshipper of God. ~**Francis Frangipane**

The ultimate goal of Satan is to stop all praises to God from His children. Prayer is warfare, praise is a victory. He will use all his strength to stop all our praising. ~**Watchman Nee**

Your problems aren't too big, perhaps your worship is too small. ~**Tommy Tenney**

God made and governs the world invisibly and has commanded us to love and worship him and no other God. ~**Isaac Newton**

When we are filled with panic, that's the time to praise; when we are filled with worry, that is the time to worship. **~David Jeremiah**

Worship is the response to the holiness of God. **~Derek Prince**

A survey of church history will prove that it was those who were yearning worshippers, who also became the great workers. **~A. W. Tozer**

This life is a warm-up session for eternal praise and worship to God. **~John Hagee**

## *Hymn: Praise/Worship*

**O Worship the King**
O worship the King,
all glorious above,
And gratefully sing
His wonderful love.
Our Shield and Defender,
the Ancient of Days,
Pavilioned in splendor
and girded with praise.
~**Robert Grant**, 1833 (public domain)

**We're Marching to Zion**
Come, we that love the Lord
and let our joys be known,
Join in a song with sweet accord
and thus surround the throne.
We're marching to Zion,
beautiful, beautiful Zion.
We're marching upward to Zion,
The beautiful city of God.
~**Isaac Watts**, 1707 (public domain)

## *Personalized Weaponry*

Many years before church services had massive screens and technology overload, there were the hymnals tucked neatly into their holders on the backs of the wooden pews, along with offering envelopes for the collection plates and tiny pencils for the congregants to use to write on the prayer cards or offering envelopes.

In those days, perhaps I was frequently glancing around the sanctuary for the familiar faces of teenage friends, but the overpowering words of those tried and true old hymns, with their endearing and inspiring words, were finding a lodging place, a private, exclusive vault, in my heart to be revisited later.

Down through the ages, singing these hymns has brought joy and strength to countless lives. Believers have cherished their ability to endure. I fear for the last few generations, who have not been so privileged, and have actually been cheated of their power to sustain the body, soul, and spirit.

How often have the words come up in my spirit to calm and reassure me and to direct my days and nights. Even humming them brings an indefinable peace.

We didn't have praise and worship teams when I was young, only a small choir perched in a loft behind the pulpit, comprising a faithful few, many of whom were not musically inclined. But what a sweet time it was while those hymns were sung. The gracious presence of the Lord would descend and envelop that hundred-plus-year-old edifice with its creaking wooden floors and bending balcony.

I later came to understand that praise usually precedes worship. There can be a depth of experience that honors the Lord when we open ourselves to him in praise. We are recounting all He has done for us.

All day, every day, we should be exclaiming our appreciation to our God, joyfully, uninhibitedly, unendingly! Worship comes from a different place in our being. It can be defined as losing ourselves in adoring our Maker. It's usually quieter, more introspective. It's a moment in which a humble heart bows reverently before our most illustrious King!

In these moments of devotion, we create a secret place in our hearts, a type of Holy of Holies, where our devotion can become sublime. Whereas; we may sing God's praises with the fires of fervent love, in worship we are blissfully alone with our beautiful Bridegroom King!

## Weapon 29

# Thankfulness/Gratitude

### *Scriptures*

Isaiah also cries out concerning Israel: "Though the number of the children of Israel be as the sand of the sea, the remnant will be saved."

**Romans 9:27 NKJV**

Who is a God like you, who pardons sin and forgives the transgression of the remnant of his inheritance? You do not stay angry forever but delight to show mercy. You will again have compassion on us; you will tread our sins underfoot and hurl all our iniquities into the depths of the sea.

**Micah 7:18–19 NIV**

The remnant of Israel shall not do iniquity, nor speak lies; neither shall a deceitful tongue be found in their mouth: for they shall feed and lie down, and none shall make them afraid.

**Zephaniah 3:13**

And I will restore to you the years that the locust hath eaten, the cankerworm, and the caterpillar, and the palmerworm, my great army which I sent among you. And ye shall eat in plenty, and be satisfied, and praise the name of the Lord your God, that hath dealt wondrously with you: and my people shall never be ashamed.

**Joel 2:25–26**

Now thanks be unto God, which always causeth us to triumph in Christ, and maketh manifest the savour of his knowledge by us in every place.

**2 Corinthians 2:14**

The Lord is gracious, and full of compassion; slow to anger, and of great mercy.

**Psalm 145:8**

As you therefore have received Christ Jesus the Lord, so walk in Him, rooted and built up in Him and established in the faith, as you have been taught, abounding in it with thanksgiving.

**Colossians 2:6–7**

Enter into his gates with thanksgiving, and into his courts with praise; be thankful unto him, and bless his name.

**Psalm 100:4**

Do all things without murmurings and disputing. That ye may be blameless and harmless, the sons of God, without rebuke, in the midst of a crooked and perverse nation, among whom ye shine as lights in the world.

**Philippians 2:14–15**

But he was wounded for our transgressions, he was bruised for our iniquities: the chastisement of our peace was upon him; and with his stripes we are healed.

**Isaiah 53:5**

O give thanks unto the Lord; for he is good; for his mercy endureth forever.

**1 Chronicles 16:34**

In everything give thanks: for this is the will of God in Christ Jesus concerning you.

**1 Thessalonians 5:18**

I will bless the Lord at all times; his praise shall continually be in my mouth.

**Psalm 34:1**

Enter into his gates with thanksgiving, and into his courts with praise; be thankful unto him, and bless his name.

**Psalm 100:4**

Wherefore, we receiving a kingdom which cannot be moved; let us have grace whereby we may serve God acceptably with reverence and godly fear: For our God is a consuming fire.

**Hebrews 12:28–29**

Be careful for nothing; but in everything by prayer and supplication with thanksgiving let your requests be made known unto God.

**Philippians 4:6**

Thanks be unto God for his unspeakable gift.

**2 Corinthians 9:15**

The foolishness of a man twists his way, And his heart frets against the Lord.

**Proverbs 19:3 NKJV**

You grumbled in your tents and said, "The Lord hates us; so he brought us out of Egypt to deliver us into the hands of the Amorites to destroy us."

**Deuteronomy 1:27 NIV**

Do all things without murmurings and disputing.

**Philippians 2:14**

And don't grumble as some of them did, and then were destroyed by the angel of death.

**1 Corinthians 10:10**

Use hospitality one to another without grudging.

**1 Peter 4:9**

These are murmurers, complainers, walking after their own lusts; and their mouth speaketh great swelling words, having men's persons in admiration because of advantage.

**Jude 1:16**

Be not deceived; God is not mocked: for whatsoever a man soweth, that shall he also reap.

**Galatians 6:7**

## *Quotes: Thankfulness/Gratitude*

People will not have time for you if you are constantly angry or complaining. ~**Stephen Hawking**

Complaining about a problem without posing a solution is called whining. ~**Teddy Roosevelt**

If you can't be positive, at least be quiet. ~**Joel Osteen**

We must take time to stop and thank the people who make a difference in our lives. ~**John F. Kennedy**

Gratitude is not only the greatest of virtues, but the parent of all others. ~**Cicero**

Be grateful for what you have, work hard for what you don't have, stop complaining, stop wishing, start working. ~**Unknown**

Things you take for granted are things someone else is praying for. ~**Unknown**

I hated the fact I had no shoes until I met a man who had no feet. ~**Persian Proverb**

When you feel like criticizing someone, just remember many of the people in this world haven't had all the advantages you have had. ~**F. Scott Fitzgerald**

It is only with gratitude and thankfulness that life becomes rich. ~**Dietrich Bonhoeffer**

When we choose thankful prayer over wallowing in anxiety and worry, we are demonstrating unwavering trust in God. ~**Priscilla Shirer**

Gratitude produces deep, abiding joy because we know that God is working in us, even through difficulties. ~**Charles Stanley**

When it comes to life, the critical thing, is whether you take things for granted or you take them with gratitude. ~**G. K. Chesterton**

A spirit of thankfulness is one of the most distinctive marks of a Christian whose heart is tuned to the Lord. ~**Billy Graham**

The Mighty Endless Reservoir of Wisdom and Knowledge, the Preeminent One, The Originator of Creation, The Cohesive Force of the Universe and the Great Reconciler, praise be to the Glorious Benevolent King of our Salvation. ~**Anonymous**

I imagine that it saddens the heart of God when we murmur and complain, instead of being thankful for all He has done for us. ~**Joyce Meyer**

It is such a comfort to drop the tangles of life into God's hands and leave them there. ~**Lettie Cowman**

When you go through enough dark places, you don't complain about the little stuff. You have been through too much to become sour. ~**Joel Osteen**

Learn to recognize God in the smallest and most ordinary things and your life will be amazingly exciting. ~**Joyce Meyer**

We would worry less if we praised more. Thanksgiving is the enemy of discontent and dissatisfaction. ~**H. A. Ironside**

If you enjoy something in the world without saying a blessing, it is as if you stole it. ~**The Talmud**

Talent is God given, be humble. Fame is man given, be careful. Conceit is self-given, be more careful. ~**John Eckhardt**

May we all fall asleep with grateful hearts having seen another sunset. ~**Unknown**

May the warm winds of heaven blow softly upon your house. May the Great Spirit bless all who enter there. May your moccasins make happy tracks in many snows and may the rainbow always touch your shoulder. ~**Cherokee Blessing**

## *Hymn: Thankfulness/Gratitude*

**For the Beauty of the Earth**
For the beauty of the earth
For the glory of the skies,
For the love which from our birth
Over and around us lies.
Christ, our Lord, to you we raise
This our hymn of grateful praise.
For the joy of human love
Brother, sister, parent, child
For friends on earth
And friends above
For gentle thoughts and mild.
Lord of all to thee we raise
This our hymn of grateful praise.
~**Folliet Pierpoint** 1862 (public domain)

## *Personalized Weaponry*

Does anyone else remember a time when people were more thankful? Have good manners and respect been replaced with entitlement and pushiness in our world?

To be grateful or thankful goes much deeper than a polite nod or a friendly smile. In essence it goes even deeper than caring about others. An unthankful heart is really irritating to God. An unthankful person is much like a spoiled child, who constantly wants but never shows any kind of appreciation. I saw that child at Walmart the other day, did you?

Thankfulness was a trait I insisted my children were taught, and I can confidently report that, with the same enthusiasm, they instill the same attitude in my grandchildren. We carry on the tradition and make sure it does not fade away. Mind your manners is a nice way to sum it up!

Being thankful will definitely open doors for you that no amount of shoving can budge. One can also defuse a situation with a heavy dose of gratitude and humility mixed thoroughly together. When you closely examine an ungrateful or unthankful person, you'll discover selfishness and self-centeredness, and they are generally void of any kind of respect. They dry up and dry out easily when life doesn't go their way. Let the old saying "cultivate an attitude of gratitude" be not only your motto but your lifestyle. Additionally, you'll find the Lord is greatly pleased when you recognize His goodness working in your life. Determine not to be part of an ungrateful or unholy generation filled with corrupt and toxic communication. Rather be a joy-maker wherever you go, handing out your *pleases* and *thank-yous* abundantly to hungry recipients. Often, a polite *excuse me* is needful also.

Train yourself to first be thankful to God. Recognize and rehearse out loud the blessings, from the smallest to the largest, that come to you and yours from His generous and gracious heart. Acknowledge those ordinary moments in life's journey when you stop and ponder what great things the Lord has done.

Let's look at some meanings of *thankful* and *grateful*: agreeable, satisfied, contented, responsive, glad, appreciative, optimistic. "The world does not owe you a living" was a common slogan in bygone days. If you ponder it, you'll see it has a deep meaning. Thankful people will get out there and make things happen; they embrace setbacks and count their blessings, producing greater self-esteem. You will find these people connecting with others more readily. Friendships are dearer to them. Lastly, they've found these identical twins of thankfulness and gratitude to be stress-busters and wellness-boosters, as well as harvesters of happiness and peace.

## WEAPON 30

# Holy Communion

### *Scriptures*

And Jesus said unto them, I am the bread of life: he that cometh to me shall never hunger; and he that believeth on me shall never thirst.

**JOHN 6:35**

For Christ also hath once suffered for sins, the just for the unjust, that he might bring us to God, being put to death in the flesh, but quickened by the Spirit.

**1 PETER 3:18**

But I say unto you, I will not drink henceforth of this fruit of the vine, until that day when I drink it new with you in my Father's kingdom.

**MATTHEW 26:29**

Let us draw near with a true heart in full assurance of faith, having our hearts sprinkled from an evil conscience, and our bodies washed with pure water.

**HEBREWS 10:22**

So He humbled you, allowed you to hunger, and fed you with manna which you did not know nor did your fathers know, that He might make you know that man shall not live by bread alone; but man lives by every word that proceeds from the mouth of the Lord.

**Deuteronomy 8:3 NKJV**

The cup of blessing which we bless, is it not the communion of the blood of Christ? The bread which we break, is it not the communion of the body of Christ?

**1 Corinthians 10:16**

You prepare a table before me in the presence of my enemies. You anoint my head with oil; my cup overflows.

**Psalm 23:5 NIV**

But he was wounded for our transgressions, he was bruised for our iniquities: the chastisement of our peace was upon him; and with his stripes we are healed.

**Isaiah 53:5**

Therefore, whoever eats this bread or drinks this cup of the Lord in an unworthy manner will be guilty of the body and blood of the Lord. But let a man examine himself, and so let him eat of the bread and drink of the cup. For he who eats and drinks in an unworthy manner eats and drinks judgment to himself, not discerning the Lord's body.

**1 Corinthians 11:27–29 NKJV**

And they continued steadfastly in the apostles' doctrine and fellowship, and in breaking of bread, and in prayers.

**Acts 2:42**

But among you it will be different. Those who are the greatest among you should take the lowest rank, and the leader should be like a servant.

**LUKE 22:26 NLT**

For the bread of God is he which cometh down from heaven, and giveth life unto the world.

**JOHN 6:33**

But let a man examine himself, and so let him eat of that bread, and drink of that cup.

**1 CORINTHIANS 11:28**

For as often as you eat this bread and drink this cup, you proclaim the Lord's death till He comes.

**1 CORINTHIANS 11:26 NKJV**

## *Quotes: Holy Communion*

Jesus has made himself the bread of life to give us life. Night and day, He is there, if you really want to grow in love, come back to Holy Communion. ~**Mother Teresa**

This supernatural bread and this consecrated vessel of wine are for the health and salvation of mankind. ~**Cyprian**

Have a great love for Jesus in his divine sacrament of love; this is the divine oasis in the desert. It is the heavenly Manna of the traveler; it is the Holy Ark, the life and the paradise of love on earth. Receive communion often and Christ will change you to be like unto himself. ~**Peter Eymard**

When you approach the table, remember He has been waiting for you for twenty centuries. ~**Josemaría Escriva**

We should come to the Lord's table with the confident expectation of meeting Christ there, of receiving there a blessing. ~**Charles A. Savage**

The table of communion fire sustained the early church, as they broke bread together daily, so it is for us today, the time of divine encounter with Christ. ~**Anonymous**

When we receive Holy Communion, we receive something extraordinary, a joy, a fragrance, a well-being that thrills us; whereby we receive much happiness. ~**John Vianney**

When you proclaim the Lord's death through Holy Communion or partaking of the bread and wine, you declare to all the powers of darkness great victories in Him. You will see your enemies scattered because Jesus was judged and punished for our sins, we are now victorious in Him. The enemies of Christ suffered a humiliating defeat at the cross. ~**Joseph Prince**

The table of remembrance reminds us of Christ's glories and the sacrificial victory over death, hell and the grave, as well as our old sins crucified with Him! ~**Anonymous**

When I find myself in the cellar of affliction, I always look for the bread and the wine. ~**Samuel Rutherford**

The elements of bread and fruit of the vine are reminders of Christ's finished work on the cross, they help us to celebrate the promise of Christ's return. ~**Perry Stone**

Receiving communion is an act of faith and obedience, it identifies you as an intimate believer in Christ. It is powerful because it is based on God's covenant with us. ~**Perry Stone**

All love craves unity, so the highest unity in the divine order, is the unity of the soul and Christ in communion. ~**Fulton Sheen**

The greatest love story of all time is contained in the tiny cup and small wafer of the communion table of remembrance. ~**Fulton Sheen**

The muddy rivers of this world's pleasures and the stale bread of this world's joys will not satisfy our souls, after we have eaten the "bread of angels." ~**Charles Spurgeon**

## *Hymn: Holy Communion*

**Guide Me, O Thou Great Jehovah**
Guide me, O thou great Jehovah,
Pilgrim through this barren land.
I am weak, but thou art mighty.
Hold me with thy powerful hand.
Bread of heaven, bread of heaven,
Feed me till I want no more.
~**William Williams**, 1745 (public domain)

**Bread of the World in Mercy Broken**
Bread of the world in mercy broken,
Wine of the soul in mercy shed,
By whom the words of life were spoken,
And in whose death our sins are dead.
~**Reginald Heber**, 1827 (public domain)

## *Personalized Prayer Weaponry*

Call us to Your holy table as often as You desire, O Lord, that we may humbly partake of Your blessed sacraments—the wine representing Your blood, the wafer, Your body. Cause us to realize what wondrous nourishment is embodied in so doing. Reveal Your river of consolation that flows to every part and parcel of our being. When we honor Your death, burial, and resurrection on a regular basis, we are pleasing You and drinking from the fountain that will never run dry. Each time we partake, we are refreshed with a boundless wellspring of life-giving power. How You have left nothing undone or unfinished in Your dealings with us, Lord, is beyond grateful comprehension.

When we recognize our withered, barren state, spark us with a holy desire to receive a fresh renewal. Remind us to come to the altar, where You meet us with Your life-strengthening presence.

# WEAPON 31

# Attitude

## *Scriptures*

It is the Spirit who gives life; the flesh conveys no benefit. The words I have spoken to you are spirit and life.

**JOHN 6:63 AMP**

Trust in the Lord with all thine heart; and lean not unto thine own understanding.

**PROVERBS 3:5**

And be renewed in the spirit of your mind.

**EPHESIANS 4:23**

And have put on the new man, which is renewed in knowledge after the image of him that created him.

**COLOSSIANS 3:10**

And whatsoever ye do, do it heartily, as to the Lord, and not unto men.

**COLOSSIANS 3:23**

Do all things without murmurings and disputing. That ye may be blameless and harmless, the sons of God, without rebuke, in the midst of a crooked and perverse nation, among whom ye shine as lights in the world.

**PHILIPPIANS 2:14–15**

Blessed are the poor in spirit: for theirs is the kingdom of heaven.

**MATTHEW 5:3**

And be not conformed to this world: but be ye transformed by the renewing of your mind, that ye may prove what is that good, and acceptable, and perfect, will of God.

**ROMANS 12:2**

A proud look, a lying tongue, and hands that shed innocent blood.

**PROVERBS 6:17**

But godliness with contentment is great gain.

**1 TIMOTHY 6:6**

Search me, O God, and know my heart: try me, and know my thoughts: And see if there be any wicked way in me and lead me in the way everlasting.

**PSALM 139:23–24**

## *Quotes: Attitude*

Attitude is a little thing that makes a big difference. **~Winston Churchill**

The greatest part of our happiness or misery depends upon our disposition, not our circumstances. **~Martha Washington**

I love those who can smile in the midst of trouble. **~Leonardo Da Vinci**

Life is 10 percent what you make it and 90 percent how you take it. **~Irving Berlin**

The last of human freedoms, to choose one's attitude in any given set of circumstances, is the greatest thing. **~Viktor Frankl**

People may hear your words, but they feel your attitude. **~John Maxwell**

Weakness of attitude becomes weakness of character. **~Albert Einstein**

A healthy attitude is contagious, but don't wait to catch it from others, be a carrier. **~Tom Stoppard**

Your attitude, not your aptitude, will determine your altitude. **~Zig Ziglar**

Things turn out best for the people who make the best of the way things turn out. **~John Wooden**

A bad attitude is like a flat tire, you can't go anywhere until you change it. ~**Unknown**

Always look at what you have left, never look at what you have lost. ~**Robert Schuller**

The only difference between a good day and a bad day is your attitude. ~**Dennis Brown**

Some cause happiness wherever they go; others whenever they leave. ~**Oscar Wilde**

The best way to destroy an enemy is to make him a friend. ~**Abe Lincoln**

The secret of genius is to carry the spirit of a child into old age, which means never losing your enthusiasm. ~**Anonymous**

Watch out for the joy stealers; gossip, criticism, complaining, fault finding and a negative, judgmental attitude. ~**Joyce Meyer**

Smile and stop complaining about things you can't change. Time keeps ticking whether you are happy or sad. ~**Unknown**

The waters are rising, but so am I. I'm not going under, I'm going over. ~**Catherine Booth**

## *Hymn: Attitude*

**All Things Bright and Beautiful**
All things bright and beautiful,
All creatures great and small,
All things wise and wonderful,
The Lord God made them all.
God gave us eyes to see them,
And lips that we might tell,
How great is God Almighty,
Who has made all things well.
~**Cecil Frances Alexander**, 1848 (public domain)

## *Personalized Prayer Weaponry*

The ancient saints were not exempted from sin and infirmities and the trials of life. They too had to make a daily decision to look at life through the lens of holiness and not circumstance. Their narrative is not that much different from ours; the determining factor is how we approach what is before us. The victories they fought for and attained were not just some quaint stories in history. The same kind of perspective is attainable for us today. We are called by the same Voice that summoned those saints of old to a higher vocation. Thank You, Lord, that our perspective, our posture, our inclination is forever bent toward You. It is our duty to push forward happily, as the same light and the same grace is accessible to us.

## Weapon 32

# Hope

### *Scriptures*

Blessed be the God and Father of our Lord Jesus Christ, which according to his abundant mercy hath begotten us again unto a lively hope by the resurrection of Jesus Christ from the dead, To an inheritance incorruptible, and undefiled, and that fadeth not away, reserved in heaven for you.

**1 Peter 1:3–4**

So the poor hath hope, and iniquity stoppeth her mouth.

**Job 5:16**

And thou shalt be secure, because there is hope; yea, thou shalt dig about thee, and thou shalt take thy rest in safety. Also thou shalt lie down, and none shall make thee afraid; yea, many shall make suit unto thee.

**Job 11:18–19**

The Lord taketh pleasure in them that fear him, in those that hope in his mercy.

**Psalm 147:11**

Hope deferred makes the heart sick but when the desire comes, it is a tree of life.

**Proverbs 13:12 NKJV**

And hope maketh not ashamed; because the love of God is shed abroad in our hearts by the Holy Ghost which is given unto us.

**Romans 5:5**

But they that wait upon the Lord shall renew their strength; they shall mount up with wings as eagles; they shall run, and not be weary; and they shall walk, and not faint.

**Isaiah 40:31**

The name of the Lord is a strong tower: the righteous run into it and is safe.

**Proverbs 18:10**

She makes linen garments and sells them and supplies sashes for the merchants.

**Proverbs 31:24 NKJV**

Thou art my hiding place and my shield: I hope in thy word.

**Psalm 119:114**

Rejoicing in hope; patient in tribulation; continuing instant in prayer.

**Romans 12:12**

The Lord is my portion, saith my soul; therefore, will I hope in him.

**Lamentations 3:24**

But they shall sit every man under his vine and under his fig tree; and none shall make them afraid: for the mouth of the Lord of hosts hath spoken it.

**Micah 4:4**

But as it is written, Eye hath not seen, nor ear heard, neither have entered into the heart of man, the things which God hath prepared for them that love him.

**1 Corinthians 2:9**

That being justified by his grace, we should be made heirs according to the hope of eternal life.

**Titus 3:7**

The Lord thy God in the midst of thee is mighty; he will save, he will rejoice over thee with joy; he will rest in his love, he will joy over thee with singing.

**Zephaniah 3:17**

Now faith is the substance of things hoped for, the evidence of things not seen.

**Hebrews 11:1**

To whom God would make known what is the riches of the glory of this mystery among the Gentiles; which is Christ in you, the hope of glory.

**Colossians 1:27**

The Lord Jesus has a good plan, a pathway of life for me, not for destruction or calamity, but for a hope and a future.

**Jeremiah 29:11 NIV**

## *Quotes: Hope*

Every area of thinking that glistens with hope in God, is an area that is liberated by Christ. Hopelessness is darkness of thought. ~**Francis Frangipane**

If we never had any storms, we would not appreciate the sunshine. ~**Dale Evans**

Happy trails to you, until we meet again. Some trails are happy ones, others are blue, it is the way you ride the trail that counts. Here's wishing a happy one for you. ~**Dale Evans**

Oh, hope! Dazzling, radiant hope. What a change you bring to the hopeless, brightening the darkened path and sharing the lonely way. ~**Aimee Semple McPherson**

The weaker we feel, the harder we lean on God. The harder we lean, the stronger we grow. ~**Joni Eareckson Tada**

Heartache forces us to embrace God out of desperate, urgent need. God is never closer than when your heart is breaking. ~**Joni Eareckson Tada**

The presence of hope, in the invincible Sovereignty of God, drives out fear. ~**John Piper**

Let me assert the firm belief that the only thing we have to fear, is fear itself. ~**Franklin D. Roosevelt**

I am waiting on you, Lord, to open the way. ~**Hudson Taylor**

May the stars carry your sadness away, may the flowers fill your heart with beauty. May hope forever wipe away your tears and may silence make you strong. ~**Chief Dan George**

Everyone has inside of him a piece of good news. The good news is that you don't know how great you can be! ~**Anne Frank**

Today hope is the sunshine God pipes down from heaven into our darkened world. ~**David Jeremiah**

You've got to accentuate the positive, eliminate the negative, latch on to the affirmative, don't mess with Mister in-between. ~ **Johnny Mercer** (lyrics from the song "Ac-Cent-Tchu-Ate the Positive")

Our living hope is a person, not a condition of wishful thinking; therefore, biblical hope is medicine for the soul. ~**David Jeremiah**

Our indestructible hope is based on an imperishable Savior. ~**Unknown**

Faith goes up the stairs love has built. It looks out the window which hope has opened. ~**Charles Spurgeon**

All that I am or ever hope to be, I owe to my angel Mother. ~**Abraham Lincoln**

Of course, you will encounter trouble, but behold a God of power, who can take any evil and turn it into a door of hope. ~**Catherine Marshall**

God can take something little, don't despise it, he will expand it and explode it. ~**Paul Crouch Jr.**

God's book is as full of hope as the sky is full of blue. ~**David Jeremiah**

What oxygen is to the lungs, hope is to our survival in this world. ~**Levi Lusko**

I have reached the point of greatest strength once I have learned to wait for hope. ~**Unknown**

Make no small plans here. ~**Oral Roberts**

Do not be cast down by what happens in this poor, fleeting state of time, for our hope is above the sky, in that third glorious heaven. Rejoice in the God of your salvation! ~**Unknown**

## *Hymn: Hope*

**He Lives**
He lives! He lives!
Christ Jesus lives today!
He walks with me
and talks with me
along life's narrow way.
He lives! He lives!
Salvation to impart!
You ask me how I know He lives?
He lives within my heart!
~**Alfred Ackley**, 1933 (public domain)

## Personalized Weaponry

I truly do love the word *hope*; it opens up new worlds to be submerged in and adventures to be embarked upon. In 1 Corinthians 13:13, hope is sandwiched in between faith and love as a kind of glue, and there is a good reason for this.

I found myself having to deal with the practical application of this concept in 1972, after coming back from Germany. My oldest son, John Brandon, was seven, and for some reason, I hadn't been able to have any more children. I started investigating my options and checking on my health, and I discovered I was lacking in some hormones necessary for pregnancy.

After one procedure and treatment, I found myself joyfully pregnant, and in 1973, I became the mother of a second son, Robert Ashley, whose name means "a young man of excellence dwelling in a peaceful woodland." What a joy, after all those years, to find myself once again in baby land, with all its diapers, bottles, and fitful nights. When my baby became sick, with symptoms that included projectile vomiting, I sought medical help. The doctor's diagnosis was that Ashley had webbing of the intestine. The remedy required that he undergo surgery at the tender age of eight months. As soon as he recovered from the surgery, he began to thrive. He was into everything and curious to boot.

Still, much illness followed. At one point he needed rabies shots after being bitten by a stray dog. Then, just after his dad had returned from Korea, the enemy attempted to stop our son's destiny with an acute case of aggravated chicken pox. The doctors contacted the Centers for Disease Control, fearing the solid black crusting on his body was due to some strange disease. They took pictures for the *American Journal of Medicine*, with our permission. We all survived the trauma, all older and much wiser.

The years that followed revealed a young child full of mischief mixed with much intelligence and musical talent. He also had much interest in many of his older brother's activities.

God had granted me the ability to hope and pray for another child and uniquely endowed him with traits and abilities that would later help his family. Ashley was and is a blessing to me and his siblings, though there have been some rough roads along the way. Today, he is hardworking and full of insight the rest of us don't possess—bright to astonishing extremes sometimes. He's also an excellent, involved father of two and a sincerely devoted man of God, always ready to help others. He is loyal, generous, and handyman extraordinaire. He's thoroughly organized, trustworthy, and well-rounded, in addition to being a great cook and a true neatnik.

All my children and grandchildren are involved in each other's lives and in close proximity, so we're able to celebrate milestones with each other. Thank you, God, because my children all love each other and are devoted to me. They are all practical, full of common sense, yet dreamers and sailors on unchartered waters. What a tremendous blessing! A handpicked crew for this life's journey, to be sure. Many battles have been fought and won with the Lord's help and power. When we're in tight places, we like to say, "God was with us in the trenches!"

It's definitely true that parent/child roles reverse at a certain point. Just as I labored over them in their sickbeds and growing-up crises, one has slept in chairs next to my hospital beds, and all have been engaged in my heartaches and triumphs. They cared for me in times of sickness and momentarily painful despair. We have held to the helm of this ship that God has entrusted to us, our little family, and found great joy in doing so!

## WEAPON 33

# Joy/Happiness

### *Scriptures*

My brethren, count it all joy when ye fall into divers temptations; Knowing this, that the trying of your faith worketh patience.

**JAMES 1:2–3**

Go eat your bread with joy and drink your wine with a merry heart; For God has already accepted your works.

**ECCLESIASTES 9:7 NKJV**

The hope of the righteous shall be gladness: but the expectation of the wicked shall perish.

**PROVERBS 10:28**

Cry out and shout, thou inhabitant of Zion: for great is the Holy One of Israel in the midst of thee.

**ISAIAH 12:6**

When doubts filled my mind, your comfort gave me renewed hope and cheer.

**PSALM 94:19 NLT**

O clap your hands, all ye people; shout unto God with the voice of triumph.

**PSALM 47:1**

May the God of hope fill you with all joy and peace as you trust in him, so that you may overflow with hope by the power of the Holy Spirit.

**ROMANS 15:13 NIV**

For we have great joy and consolation in thy love, because the bowels of the saints are refreshed by thee, brother.

**PHILEMON 1:7**

I have no greater joy than to hear that my children walk in truth.

**3 JOHN 1:4**

Glory and honour are in his presence; strength and gladness are in his place.

**1 CHRONICLES 16:27**

Then he said unto them, Go your way, eat the fat, and drink the sweet, and send portions unto them for whom nothing is prepared: for this day is holy unto our Lord: neither be ye sorry; for the joy of the Lord is your strength.

**NEHEMIAH 8:10**

You will show me the way of life, granting me the joy of your presence and the pleasures of living with you forever.

**PSALM 16:11 NLT**

Do not remember the sins of my youth, nor my transgressions; According to Your mercy remember me, For Your goodness' sake, O Lord.

**Psalm 25:7 NKJV**

When you go through deep waters, I will be with you. When you go through rivers of difficulty, you will not drown. When you walk through the fire of oppression, you will not be burned up; the flames will not consume you. For I am the Lord, your God, the Holy One of Israel, your Savior. I gave Egypt as a ransom for your freedom; I gave Ethiopia and Seba in your place. Others were given in exchange for you. I traded their lives for yours because you are precious to me. You are honored and I love you.

**Isaiah 43:2–4 NLT**

For those God foreknew he also predestined to be conformed to the image of his Son, that he might be the firstborn among many brothers and sisters.

**Romans 8:29 NIV**

Then he said unto them, Go your way, eat the fat, and drink the sweet, and send portions unto them for whom nothing is prepared: for this day is holy unto our Lord: neither be ye sorry; for the joy of the Lord is your strength.

**Nehemiah 8:10**

How shall we escape, if we neglect so great salvation; which at the first began to be spoken by the Lord, and was confirmed unto us by them that heard him.

**Hebrews 2:3**

Happy are thy men, and happy are these thy servants, which stand continually before thee, and hear thy wisdom.

**2 Chronicles 9:7**

And the second is like it: 'You shall love your neighbor as yourself.

**Matthew 22:39 NKJV**

But he said, Yea rather, blessed are they that hear the word of God, and keep it.

**Luke 11:28**

I have shown you in every way, by laboring like this, that you must support the weak. And remember the words of the Lord Jesus, that He said, "It is more blessed to give than to receive."

**Acts 20:35 NKJV**

Happy is that people, that is in such a case: yea, happy is that people, whose God is the Lord.

**Psalm 144:15**

The lines are fallen unto me in pleasant places; yea, I have a goodly heritage.

**Psalm 16:6**

O, taste and see that the Lord is good: blessed is the man that trusteth in him.

**Psalm 34:8**

A merry heart maketh a cheerful countenance: but by sorrow of the heart the spirit is broken.

**Proverbs 15:13**

## *Quotes: Joy/Happiness*

Happy the soul that has been awed by a view of God's majesty. ~**A. W. Pink**

It is not how much we have, but how much we enjoy, that makes for happiness. ~**Charles Spurgeon**

Don't cry because it's over, be happy and smile because it happened! ~**Dr. Seuss**

Happiness is an inside job. Do not assign anyone else that much power over your life. ~**Unknown**

There are so many beautiful reasons to be happy today! ~**Unknown**

Be unselfish. That is the first and final commandment for those who would be useful and happy in their usefulness. ~**George Elliott**

Do not waste a minute being unhappy; if one window closes, run to the next window or break down a door. ~**Unknown**

Happiness is good health and a bad memory. ~**Ingrid Bergman**

A life of sacrifice is the pinnacle that is full of true joy. ~**Gandhi**

True joy comes when you inspire, encourage and guide someone on a path that benefits them. ~**Zig Ziglar**

Joy is the infallible sign of the presence of God. ~**Pierre Teilhard de Chardin**

Find ecstasy in life; the mere sense of living produces joy. ~**Emily Dickinson**

The commands of God are given not to rob you of joy, but it is to lead you into the fullness of joy. ~**Matt Chandler**

Give happiness and joy to others, there is nothing better or greater than that. ~**Beethoven**

There is no sport equal to that which aviators enjoy, while being carried away on great white wings. ~**The Wright Brothers**

It is only through service and surrender that we find true joy, happiness and freedom in Christ. ~**Nicky Cruz**

We are told to let our light shine, and if it does, we don't need to tell anybody. Lighthouses don't fire cannons to call attention to their shining, they just shine. ~**Dwight L. Moody**

Enjoyment is an incredible energizer to the human spirit. ~**John Maxwell**

Think of all the beauty still left around you and be happy. ~**Anne Frank**

Happiness must be grown in one's own garden. ~**Mary Engelbreit**

Joy is the birthright and privilege of every Christian. ~**Ron Phillips**

Most people are about as happy as they make up their minds to be. ~**Abraham Lincoln**

If you lack joy, your Christianity must be leaking somewhere. ~**Billy Sunday**

Do something wonderful, people may try to imitate you. ~**Albert Schweitzer**

Believers have joy and comfort; that joy that angels cannot give and devils cannot take. ~**Christopher Fowler**

We make a God out of whatever we find most joy in. So find your joy in God and be done with idolatry. ~**John Piper**

## *Hymn: Joy/Happiness*

**Joyful, Joyful, We Adore You**
Joyful, joyful we adore you,
God of glory, Lord of love.
Hearts unfold like flowers before you,
Opening to the son above.
Melt the clouds of sin and sadness,
Drive the dark of doubt away.
Giver of immortal gladness,
Fill us with the light of day!
~**Henry Van Dyke**, 1907 (public domain)

## *Personalized Prayer Weaponry*

There seems to be an inordinate amount of emphasis on joy and happiness these days, as if you should be examining the scales in your own life to see if you measure up. God forbid you should find you're not laden to capacity with a staggering amount of joy and happiness. Exactly what is the difference and who decided the measurements?

Some would have us believe that if we're not oozing with perks, benefits, and rewards of gleeful happiness, we're missing the boat and should therefore be highly unhappy and unfulfilled. Or should we be lightly doused on occasion with these heavenly commodities?

And furthermore, is it possible we have control over the dosage of these precious products of a life well-intentioned? Should we actually be enriching others who will in turn bless us?

Happiness is contingent on our surroundings, our little corner of the world and what's pressing in on us. On the other hand, joy is quietly nesting deeply in our souls and can be brought to the surface in our lives when all around us is crumbling. It is to be reveled in and embraced at times when observing our circumstances would ordinarily make us question our sanity. That's the beauty of embedded joy; it's indomitable, stalwart, a welcome friend. Happiness, on the other hand, is fickle, elusive, and may or may not be present longer than a flitting sparrow. It loves to evaporate at the first sign of trouble.

Life can flow more smoothly and productively when you purposely watch for opportunities to make someone else's life happier and more enriched. Proceed to use shovels, not teaspoons, to dish out help in their direction, and make it what they like and need, not what you think they like and need. Wonder of wonders, when you do this, your mind is off yourself, and that refocus has brought you abundant joy and served multiple kingdom purposes.

Awaken us, Lord, to the teeming crowds or the singular sadness right in our own backyard. Send us forth as ambassadors to reap a harvest for others and discover the realization that we ourselves are massively blessed.

## Weapon 34

# Tongues of Fire/Holy Spirit Baptism

### *Scriptures*

And suddenly there came a sound from heaven as of a rushing mighty wind, and it filled all the house where they were sitting. And there appeared unto them cloven tongues like as of fire, and it sat upon each of them. And they were all filled with the Holy Ghost, and began to speak with other tongues, as the Spirit gave them utterance.

**Acts 2:2–4**

That in everything ye are enriched by him, in all utterance, and in all knowledge.

**1 Corinthians 1:5**

And they were all filled with the Holy Ghost, and began to speak with other tongues, as the Spirit gave them utterance.

**Acts 2:4**

But ye, beloved, building up yourselves on your most holy faith, praying in the Holy Ghost.

**Jude 1:20**

Praying always with all prayer and supplication in the Spirit and watching thereunto with all perseverance and supplication for all saints.

**Ephesians 6:18**

Pray in the Spirit and in understanding, oh, magnify the Lord.

**Acts 2:47**

I thank my God that I speak with tongues more than ye all.

**1 Corinthians 14:18**

Wherefore tongues are for a sign, not to them that believe, but to them that believe not: but prophesying serveth not for them that believe not, but for them which believe.

**1 Corinthians 14:22**

Likewise, the Spirit also helps our infirmities: for we know not what we should pray for as we ought: but the Spirit itself maketh intercession for us with groanings which cannot be uttered.

**Romans 8:26**

Now He who searches the hearts knows what the mind of the Spirit is, because He makes intercession for the saints according to the will of God.

**Romans 8:27 NKJV**

Wherefore I put thee in remembrance that thou stir up the gift of God, which is in thee by the putting on of my hands.

**2 Timothy 1:6**

John answered their questions by saying, "I baptize you with water; but someone is coming soon who is greater than I am—so much greater that I'm not even worthy to be his slave and untie the straps of his sandals. He will baptize you with the Holy Spirit and with fire. He is ready to separate the chaff from the wheat with his winnowing fork. Then he will clean up the threshing area, gathering the wheat into his barn but burning the chaff with never-ending fire."

**Luke 3:16–17 NLT**

Then I said, I will not make mention of him, nor speak any more in his name. But his word was in mine heart as a burning fire shut up in my bones, and I was weary with forbearing, and I could not stay.

**Jeremiah 20:9**

And I will pour upon the house of David, and upon the inhabitants of Jerusalem, the spirit of grace and of supplications: and they shall look upon me whom they have pierced, and they shall mourn for him, as one mourneth for his only son, and shall be in bitterness for him, as one that is in bitterness for his firstborn.

**Zechariah 12:10**

## *Quotes: Tongues of Fire/Holy Spirit Baptism*

Glossolia: Greek for divine heavenly language. God has ordained this speaking in an unknown tongue unto himself as a wonderful, supernatural means of communication by the Spirit. ~**Smith Wigglesworth**

The Holy Spirit is the seal, the foretaste, the engagement ring, the earnest and the pledge. He designates us as God's own and guarantees our inheritance. Conforming us unto the Son, He stamps his image on our hearts. ~**Anonymous**

God's washcloth for your brain is the prayer language of the Holy Spirit. ~**Perry Stone**

The Holy Spirit baptism builds your faith, while you are speaking great mysteries, as you are tapping into the will of God. It is also acting as a release valve. ~**Unknown**

We desperately need the explosive power of praying in tongues in this end time battle. It is a proven weapon of victory and enrichment. ~**John G. Lake**

This heavenly language opens up a door into the Father's presence, which is the only place we can receive deep revelations from his mouth. ~**John G. Lake**

Tongues has been the making of my ministry, that peculiar communication with God, when he reveals the truth I need day to day. ~**John G. Lake**

The blessing of tongues has transformed me and brought miracles, boldness and the supernatural to my life. ~**John G. Lake**

The baptism of the Holy Spirit will do for you what a phone booth did for Clark Kent, it will change you into a different person. ~**Rod Parsley**

Soak us in the fire to remove all the dross, then smear us down with the oil of the Spirit daily. ~**Anonymous**

All-consuming fire, living flame of love, my heart's desire, come baptize us once again. ~**Anonymous**

The miracle of tongues are signs, not for the believer, but to them who believe not. ~**Thomas Aquinas**

Speaking in tongues increases mental health and emotional stability. ~**Caroline Leaf**

The Holy Spirit Himself is a marvelous gift, His baptism is also a marvelous gift. If you do not want this glorious gift, you can reject it but oh, the great loss you will experience! ~**Anonymous**

Tongues is the most misunderstood of all the spiritual gifts. There is no gift in the entire world that receives so explosive a reaction as the gift of tongues! Because the devil is afraid of it, he gets everybody fighting over it. If tongues did not cause him trouble, he would ignore it, but speaking in tongues is dynamite! It will change a person's life, so Satan fights it with every force he can muster! ~**Lester Sumrall**

## *Hymn: Tongues of Fire/Holy Spirit Baptism*

**Baptism of the Holy Spirit**
Let cloven tongues of holy fire,
Baptize each soul with power.
Come, blessed Spirit, sanctify,
With Jesus' blood this hour.
~**Barney Warren**, 1903 (public domain)

## *Personalized Weaponry*

Jesus Chapel, in El Paso, Texas, was a wonderful spiritual oasis for me, which I discovered in 1977. After years as a military wife, attending post services, I longed for more fulfillment in my walk with the Lord, and I knew something was missing. I heard about this marvelous nondenominational church and ventured out of my cloistered, dry current church experiences. Meanwhile, my oldest son, Brandon, had discovered Oral Roberts on TV and encouraged me to watch, since my two younger ones, Ashley and Christie Greer, were sick, and this frequently prevented us from attending church. My yearning soul was so fed that the Oral Roberts program became a beacon of refreshment from that moment forward.

As for Jesus Chapel, what a warm and inviting fellowship greeted us there! Never had I seen such glowing, sunshine-filled faces in a church, with hands raised in willing worship. The praise choir and the preaching overwhelmed and nourished me in a manner that was strange but glorious. One Sunday, as we were being drenched in the presence of the Lord, my twelve-year-old, Brandon, stepped out in the aisle at the beckoning of the altar call and received his Savior firsthand.

I must have slept through the early seventies, when the Jesus movement was in full swing, when masses of Catholics, Methodists, and other mainliners were swept into the Holy Spirit baptism by fire. Even Ivy League college groups and many unsuspecting pilgrims in the faith were overwhelmed by His movement. Thankfully, no deep fear or resentment had been taught to me or handed down through denominational doctrines concerning this phenomenon.

I would hear the gentle reverberations of congregants praying in the Spirit. Not only did it awe me, it thrilled me to the core of my being. I deeply longed to have this experience of speaking in heavenly tongues that came as a result of being baptized in the Holy Spirit. It would be a few more years (remember, waiting is a war tactic too) before earnest prayer and persistence propelled me to attend a Holy Spirit Seminar at Oral Roberts University in Tulsa, Oklahoma.

In such surroundings, a mighty surge of power was tangible as I stepped on the campus grounds. I had a definite assurance that I would not leave without this precious gift. Sure enough, at one remarkable, unforgettable moment, I was impacted and forever changed. I returned home glowing with my long-desired gift intact, and my life has been eternally enriched because of the heavenly language.

In an attempt to inform on the subject, I will add the following: the Spirit baptism with the evidence of speaking in other tongues is not a sideshow or a back alley occurrence for ignorant persons to sneer or jeer at. It is a holy gift from a Holy God to be graciously and gratefully received and utilized for the remainder of your life.

It should be noted in simple language, you can be a strong Christian with the infilling of the Spirit at the moment of salvation. Holy Spirit baptism with the evidence of speaking in tongues is another step, if you desire, but it is not necessary for salvation. You could say this is an extra available benefit. But remember, you shouldn't denigrate it if you don't want the gift, or be willfully ignorant of it, since this can border on blasphemy of the Spirit.

The baptism of the Holy Spirit empowers Christians to supernaturally speak in an unknown language, unlike our earthly one, that is not learned but bestowed. However, similar somewhat to natural speaking, it can mature and expand depending on the amount of usage.

An additional huge benefit is that the kingdom of darkness, with all its minions of demons, can't understand one syllable of these dialects. Don't worry though, just as you're not forced to receive any earthly gift, Holy Spirit will *not* force His supernatural presence on anyone. It must be lovingly, and at times, steadfastly sought after. When this occurs, He becomes our trusted coach and loyal mentor, illuminating, igniting, and revealing the Word to us, always pointing to Christ and the work of the cross and resurrection. He brings empowering, extraordinary advantages to those yoked up with Christ, and He places us in perfect alignment to grow day by day under His tutelage. It should be noted that there is "personal edification" and "public edification" of the saints and by the saints. The interpretation should come immediately in a service or in intimate times spent with the Spirit, even through our sanctified thoughts or Bible reading and prayer time. Our wavelengths or frequencies of the Spirit can be trained to hear. We're built up and strengthened on our most Holy faith by praying in the Holy Ghost.

Some interesting stats: According to the World Christian Database, at least one quarter of the world's two billion Christians adhere to the Pentecostal preferences which is not exactly a fringe element. The Barna Group reports that in America, 36 percent claimed Pentecostal moorings. That equals eighty million adults! The Pew Forum reports one in three Pentecostals speaks in tongues.

**Warning**: Blasphemy of or against the Holy Spirit is dangerous. Jesus declared, in Mark 3:28–30 NIV: "Truly I tell you, people can be forgiven all their sins and every slander they utter, but whoever blasphemes against the Holy Spirit will never be forgiven; they are guilty of an eternal sin."

In basic terms, this can mean attributing or stating the miracles done by Jesus came by the power of Satan. It can also include slandering or speaking injury to the good name of the Lord, not out of ignorance or lack of solid teaching, but by knowingly and willingly pouring contempt on the works of the Holy Spirit as coming from Satan. This is a deliberate berating of a power you know nothing about. Therein lies the danger.

## Weapon 35

# Anointing/Zeal

### *Scriptures: Anointing*

But you have an anointing from the Holy One, and you know all things.

**1 John 2:20 NKJV**

And it shall come to pass in that day, that his burden shall be taken away from off thy shoulder, and his yoke from off thy neck, and the yoke shall be destroyed because of the anointing.

**Isaiah 10:27**

Thou lovest righteousness, and hatest wickedness: therefore God, thy God, hath anointed thee with the oil of gladness above thy fellows.

**Psalm 45:7**

Take the anointing oil and anoint the tabernacle and everything in it; consecrate it and all its furnishings, and it will be holy. Then anoint the altar of burnt offering and all its utensils; consecrate the altar, and it will be most holy. Anoint the basin and its stand and consecrate them.

**Exodus 40:9–11 NIV**

Be ye mindful always of his covenant; the word which he commanded to a thousand generations.

**1 Chronicles 16:15**

So wash and anoint yourself, then put on your clothes, and go down to the threshing floor; but stay out of the man's sight until he has finished eating and drinking.

**Ruth 3:3 AMP**

Then Samuel took the horn of oil and anointed him in the midst of his brethren: and the Spirit of the Lord came upon David from that day forward. So Samuel rose up, and went to Ramah.

**1 Samuel 16:13**

Then said he, These are the two anointed ones, that stand by the Lord of the whole earth.

**Zechariah 4:14**

Is any sick among you? let him call for the elders of the church; and let them pray over him, anointing him with oil in the name of the Lord.

**James 5:14**

The Spirit of the Lord is upon me, because he hath anointed me to preach the gospel to the poor; he hath sent me to heal the brokenhearted, to preach deliverance to the captives, and recovering of sight to the blind, to set at liberty them that are bruised.

**LUKE 4:18**

Let all that I am praise the Lord; may I never forget the good things he does for me. He forgives all my sins and heals all my diseases. He redeems me from death and crowns me with love and tender mercies.

**PSALM 103:2–4 NLT**

## *Quotes: Anointing*

The word of God is different from other words, because God's word is stuffed full of power and anointing. ~**Joyce Meyer**

Many people today are running on adrenaline and not on anointing. ~**Larry Stockstill**

The anointing of The Holy Spirit is given to illuminate His word, to open the scriptures, and to place the spiritual person in direct communication with the mind of God. ~**Charles Parham**

When the anointing of God is upon a person, it changes that individual from being a little ordinary person into a giant. ~**Sunday Adelaja**

When you come in contact with the anointing of God, it not only affects the moment, it affects all your tomorrows. ~**Creflo Dollar**

Old anointing will not suffice, to impart function to our spirit, our head must have fresh oil poured upon it from the golden horn of the sanctuary, or it will cease from its glory. ~**Charles Spurgeon**

God's anointing is not based on your performance, but if you don't open the Word, you are stupid, because that is where the words of life are. ~**Andrew Wommack**

I am not overstating this, the anointing is mandatory, if you are called to serve the Lord. Without it there will be no growth, no blessing, no victory in your ministry. ~**Benny Hinn**

True painting is only the image of the perfection of God, a shadow of the pencil with which He paints, a melody, a striving after harmony. ~**Michelangelo**

I play the notes as they are written, but it is God that makes the music. ~**Bach**

## *Scriptures: Zeal*

As many as I love, I rebuke and chasten: be zealous therefore, and repent.

**Revelation 3:19**

Not slothful in business; fervent in spirit; serving the Lord.

**Romans 12:11**

Who gave himself for us, that he might redeem us from all iniquity, and purify unto himself a peculiar people, zealous of good works.

**Titus 2:14**

The Lord will march out like a champion, like a warrior he will stir up his zeal; with a shout he will raise the battle cry and will triumph over his enemies.

**Isaiah 42:13 NIV**

For out of Jerusalem shall go forth a remnant, and they that escape out of mount Zion: the zeal of the Lord of hosts shall do this.

**2 Kings 19:31**

Look down from heaven, and behold from the habitation of thy holiness and of thy glory: where is thy zeal and thy strength, the sounding of thy bowels and of thy mercies toward me? are they restrained?

**Isaiah 63:15**

Therefore, this is what the Sovereign Lord says: "I will now restore the fortunes of Jacob and will have compassion on all the people of Israel, and I will be zealous for my holy name."

**Ezekiel 39:25 NIV**

Even so you, since you are zealous for spiritual gifts, let it be for the edification of the church that you seek to excel.

**1 Corinthians 14:12 NKJV**

And his disciples remembered that it was written, the zeal of thine house hath eaten me up.

**John 2:17**

I must work the works of him that sent me, while it is day: the night cometh, when no man can work.

**John 9:4**

My zeal hath consumed me, because mine enemies have forgotten thy words.

**Psalm 119:139**

And Caleb stilled the people before Moses, and said, Let us go up at once, and possess it; for we are well able to overcome it.

**Numbers 13:30**

## *Quotes: Zeal*

Zeal is one of the chief sources of spiritual power. In all ages, men of zeal have produced great results, this can accomplish wonders. ~**Charles Hodge**

While we are zealous for good works, let us be careful not to put them in place of Christ's righteousness. Do not advance anything which might betray others into a dreadful delusion. ~**Matthew Henry**

Zeal without knowledge is fire without light. ~**Thomas Fuller**

No one can be a good Christian, who does not with holy zeal, set out to know, delight in and live by the Word of God. ~**John R. Rice**

We can catch the spirit of Christ, zealously and enthusiastically go out each day, determined to serve God and be what we ought to be, staying on the firing line. ~**Shelton Smith**

Zeal is not static, nor does it reach what one might call its highest level and stay there. Zeal is dynamic; if it is not greater all the time, it is not zeal. ~**Mother Mary Francis**

Even if you lose your zeal, never forget the Lord has not lost his. ~**Charles Pope**

There is no greater sign of a general decay of virtue in a nation, than a want of zeal in its inhabitants, for the good of their country. ~**Joseph Addison**

Zeal is like fire, it needs both feeding and watching. ~**Unknown**

Real zeal is standing still and letting God be a bonfire in you. ~**Catherine Doherty**

Take care of giving up your first zeal; beware of becoming cool in the least degree. Be men of God who serve with diligence and zeal. ~**Charles Spurgeon**

## *Hymn: Anointing/Zeal*

**Fresh as the Dew of the Morning**
Fresh as the dew of the morning,
Bringing a sweet rest unheard.
Christ, in the gentle anointing,
Whispers his comforting word.
Stand till the trial is over,
Stand till the tempest is gone.
Stand for the glory of Jesus,
Stand till the kingdom is won.
~**William Ogden**, 1881 (public domain)

## *Personalized Prayer Weaponry*

Zeal looks with tearful eyes to the flames of hell and cannot sleep. Zeal looks with anxious gaze to the glories of heaven. Zeal devotes itself wholly to the cause of Christ.

Do not stand at the bottom of the hill when the mountain is shaking. God is moving at all times, in all places, in all who will allow. Precisely at this point is where anointing can be coupled with zeal to make a powerful impact. We can be gifted but have no anointing and our impact will be weakened. The answer is pray for your efforts to be saturated with that heavenly perfume referred to as "the anointing," rubbed in, smeared on, and poured into our earthly vessels.

Expect to be thrust upward and onward to fulfill your assignments, forever heavenward bound. We are eternal pillars in the temple of our God, prepared, polished, and placed as He sees fit. This is Christ's work done while we are earthbound. Make a difference while you're here, so you may stand before the Lord, unashamed on *that* day when we all will give an account.

# WEAPON 36

# Wisdom/Knowledge

### *Scriptures*

And the spirit of the Lord shall rest upon him, the spirit of wisdom and understanding, the spirit of counsel and might, the spirit of knowledge and of the fear of the Lord.

**ISAIAH 11:2**

Only by pride cometh contention: but with the well advised is wisdom.

**PROVERBS 13:10**

He who gets wisdom loves his own soul; He who keeps understanding will find good.

**PROVERBS 19:8 NKJV**

Who is a wise man and endued with knowledge among you? let him shew out of a good conversation his works with meekness of wisdom.

**JAMES 3:13**

Therefore, whosoever heareth these sayings of mine, and doeth them, I will liken him unto a wise man, which built his house upon a rock.

**Matthew 7:24**

This also comes from the Lord of hosts, who has made His counsel wonderful and His wisdom great.

**Isaiah 28:29 amp**

A hypocrite with his mouth destroys his neighbor: but through knowledge shall the just be delivered.

**Proverbs 11:9**

O, how I love thy law! it is my meditation all the day. Thou through thy commandments hast made me wiser than mine enemies: for they are ever with me.

**Psalm 119:97–98**

He hath made the earth by his power, he hath established the world by his wisdom, and hath stretched out the heavens by his discretion.

**Jeremiah 10:12**

For the earth shall be filled with the knowledge of the glory of the Lord, as the waters cover the sea.

**Habakkuk 2:14**

My people are destroyed from lack of knowledge. Because you have rejected knowledge, I also reject you as my priests; because you have ignored the law of your God, I also will ignore your children.

**Hosea 4:6 niv**

But you, Daniel, shut up the words, and seal the book until the time of the end; many shall run to and fro, and knowledge shall increase.

**Daniel 12:4 NKJV**

Ask me and I will tell you remarkable secrets you do not know about things to come.

**Jeremiah 33:3 NLT**

For the Lord giveth wisdom: out of his mouth cometh knowledge and understanding.

**Proverbs 2:6**

The fear of the Lord is the beginning of knowledge: but fools despise wisdom and instruction.

**Proverbs 1:7**

Gold there is, and rubies in abundance, but lips that speak knowledge are a rare jewel.

**Proverbs 20:15**

In whom are hid all the treasures of wisdom and knowledge.

**Colossians 2:3**

Happy is the man who finds wisdom, And the man who gains understanding.

**Proverbs 3:13 NKJV**

Teach us to number our days, that we may apply our hearts unto wisdom.

**Psalm 90:12**

O, the depth of the riches both of the wisdom and knowledge of God! How unsearchable are his judgments, and his ways past finding out!

**Romans 11:33**

A person's wisdom yields patience; it is to one's glory to overlook an offense.

**Proverbs 19:11 NIV**

And have no fellowship with the unfruitful works of darkness, but rather reprove them.

**Ephesians 5:11**

It is an honour for a man to cease from strife: but every fool will be meddling.

**Proverbs 20:3**

Lest Satan should get an advantage of us: for we are not ignorant of his devices.

**2 Corinthians 2:11**

For I testify unto every man that heareth the words of the prophecy of this book, If any man shall add unto these things, God shall add unto him the plagues that are written in this book: And if any man shall take away from the words of the book of this prophecy, God shall take away his part out of the book of life, and out of the Holy City, and from the things which are written in this book.

**Revelation 22:18–19**

For this cause we also, since the day we heard it, do not cease to pray for you, and to desire that ye might be filled with the knowledge of his will in all wisdom and spiritual understanding.

**COLOSSIANS 1:9**

If any of you lack wisdom, let him ask of God, that giveth to all men liberally, and upbraideth not; and it shall be given him.

**JAMES 1:5**

Therefore, if any man be in Christ, he is a new creature: old things are passed away; behold, all things are become new.

**2 CORINTHIANS 5:17**

## *Quotes: Wisdom/Knowledge*

For beautiful eyes, look for the good in others; for beautiful lips speak only words of kindness, walk with the knowledge that you are never alone. ~**Audrey Hepburn**

Honesty is the first chapter in the book of Wisdom. ~**Thomas Jefferson**

A loving heart is the truest wisdom. ~**Charles Dickens**

Start with God, the first step is learning to bow down to him. Only fools snub their noses at such wisdom and learning. ~**King Solomon**

The doors of wisdom are never shut. ~**Benjamin Franklin**

Trials teach us who we are, they dig up the soil, and let us see what we are made of. ~**Anonymous**

If you wish to enrich days, plant flowers; if you wish to enrich years, plant trees. If you wish to enrich eternity, plant ideals in the lives of others. Sometimes success is disguised as hard work. ~**Truett Cathy**

A minute of thought is greater than an hour of talk. ~**John Maxwell**

Just as radar signals the approach of a foreign missile, your anger can alert you to boundary violations in your life. ~**John Maxwell**

This is one of the marks of a truly safe person, they are confrontable. ~**Henry Cloud**

Oh, to be trapped in the beauty and freedom of youth yet recognize and obtain the wisdom of the ages. ~**Anonymous**

If you can't figure out your purpose, figure out your passion. Your passion will lead you right into your purpose. ~**T. D. Jakes**

He is no fool who gives what he cannot keep, to gain what he cannot lose. ~**Jim Elliott**

If you want children to keep their feet on the ground, put some responsibility on their shoulders. ~**Dear Abby**

Never take counsel from your fears. ~**Stonewall Jackson**

There are things I cannot force, I must adjust. There are times when the greatest change needed is a change of my own viewpoint. ~**C. M. Ward**

Never say anything about yourself that you do not want to come true. ~**Rick Godwin**

The difference between surviving, striving and thriving can be a revelation from God. ~**Mike Hayes**

Character is built by repeatedly choosing the best over the easiest. ~**Casey Treat**

Isn't it astonishing that all these secrets have been preserved for so many years so that we could discover them? ~**The Wright Brothers**

The three most important decisions you will ever make in life all start with the letter "M": **1**. Who will be your Master? **2**. Who will be your Mate? **3**. What will be your Mission? ~**Truett Cathy**

Don't be a victim of the urgent. In the long run, much of what seems so pressing now won't even matter. What you do with your children will matter forever. ~**Truett Cathy**

There are times when solitude is better than society and silence is wiser than speech. ~**Charles Spurgeon**

Never interrupt someone doing what you said could never be done. ~**Amelia Earhart**

The wisdom of God will carry you through the toughest situations of life. ~**Ravi Zacharias**

You are as weak as your secrets and as strong as your dreams. ~**Mike Hayes**

You cannot solve a spiritual problem with military or political solutions. ~**Jonathan Cahn**

Don't waste your stamina on fields that are not ripe. ~**Anonymous**

When the eagles are silent, the parrots begin to jabber. ~**Winston Churchill**

Never speak words that allow the enemy to think he is winning. ~**Jentezen Franklin**

Associate with men of good quality if you esteem your own reputation, it is better to be alone than in bad company. ~**George Washington**

If thoughts of offense are deluding your mind, know that Satan is setting a trap for you, don't take the bait. ~**Rick Renner**

Kind words are short to speak but their echo is endless. ~**John Hagee**

We need to check ourselves before we wreck ourselves. ~**Katie Souza**

The only fear a Christian should entertain is the fear of sin. All others are sent from Satan to confuse and weaken us. ~**Isabel Kuhn**

## *Hymn: Wisdom/Knowledge*

**Supreme in Wisdom as in Power**
Supreme in wisdom as in power,
The Rock of Ages stands.
Thou cannot search His mind nor trace,
The working of His hands.
~**Isaac Watts**, 1707 (public domain)

## *Personalized Prayer Weaponry*

Help us, Holy Spirit, to preserve our own souls through gaining wisdom and good sense. The fountain of godly, mature wisdom is like a bubbling spring, sparkling with fresh, pure, life-giving water. If you follow Christ, all the hounds of worldly hell will yelp at your heels. Seek His knowledge and apply His wisdom to defeat their onslaught, and your tracks will be covered. The tyrant masters will be destroyed. Step out of the mud and decay of your present circumstances. Wisdom will make you equal to each and every trial and capable of enduring any suffering with the Lord's help and power. We have infallible wisdom to direct us; therefore, help us to listen to divine counsel, receive instruction and accept correction. We are holy champions, tackling our way toward our exceeding great reward.

# Weapon 37

# Discern/Decree

### *Scriptures: Discern*

Folly is joy to him that is destitute of wisdom: but a man of understanding walketh uprightly.

**Proverbs 15:21**

And he spake unto the congregation, saying, Depart, I pray you, from the tents of these wicked men, and touch nothing of theirs, lest ye be consumed in all their sins.

**Numbers 16:26**

The Lord God is my strength, and he will make my feet like hinds' feet, and he will make me to walk upon mine high places. To the chief singer on my stringed instruments.

**Habakkuk 3:19**

And this I pray, that your love may abound yet more and more in knowledge and in all judgment; That ye may approve things that are excellent; that ye may be sincere and without offence till the day of Christ.

**Philippians 1:9–10**

And that ye may put difference between holy and unholy, and between unclean and clean.

**Leviticus 10:10**

Give therefore thy servant an understanding heart to judge thy people, that I may discern between good and bad: for who is able to judge this thy so great a people?

**1 Kings 3:9**

Whoso keeps the law is a wise son: but he that is a companion of riotous men shameth his father.

**Proverbs 28:7**

But strong meat belongs to them that are of full age, even those who by reason of use have their senses exercised to discern both good and evil.

**Hebrews 5:14**

Teach me good judgment and knowledge: for I have believed thy commandments.

**Psalm 119:66**

But the natural man receiveth not the things of the Spirit of God: for they are foolishness unto him: neither can he know them, because they are spiritually discerned.

**1 Corinthians 2:14**

He changes times and seasons; he deposes kings and raises up others. He gives wisdom to the wise and knowledge to the discerning.

**Daniel 2:21 niv**

Wisdom is the principal thing; therefore, get wisdom: and with all thy getting get understanding.

**Proverbs 4:7**

Proving what is acceptable unto the Lord.

**Ephesians 5:10**

My son let not them depart from thine eyes: keep sound wisdom and discretion: So shall they be life unto thy soul, and grace to thy neck.

**Proverbs 3:21–22**

## *Quotes: Discern*

Discernment is not knowing the difference between right and wrong. It is knowing the difference between right and almost right. ~**Charles Spurgeon**

Listen to your gut! It's where God speaks the loudest. ~**Unknown**

Life offers you a lot of invitations, be wise enough to choose which are worth attending. ~**Unknown**

God never gives us discernment in order that we may criticize, but that we may intercede. ~**Oswald Chambers**

The Holy Spirit not only helps us recognize plain truth, but also plain nonsense! ~**Anonymous**

Out of every season of life, there are some things you should take with you, and some things you should leave behind. Know the difference, discernment is the key. ~**Dale Bronner**

The rarest things in the world, next to the spirit of discernment, are diamonds and pearls. ~**Jean de la Bruyere**

God will wreck your plans when He sees your plans are about to wreck you. ~**Unknown**

We cannot afford to let down our Christian standards just to hold the interest of people who want to go to Hell and still belong to a church! ~**A. W. Tozer**

The voice of God will never contradict the word of God. ~**Unknown**

Worldly thinking will overpower spiritual discernment, if we spend two or three hours in front of the TV and only ten minutes in the Bible. ~**Charles Stanley**

God does not exist to answer our prayers, but by our prayers, we come to discern the mind of God. ~**Oswald Chambers**

Know your Holy God intimately. When you have seen His glory, His holiness, His love by drawing close to Him in prayer; then you are able to see through any counterfeits, because you know the real thing so well. ~**Andrew Strom**

A tender conscience is an inestimable blessing; that is, a conscience not only quick to discern what is evil, but instantly to shun it as the eyelid closes itself against the dust. ~**Assorted Authors**

We must learn who is gold and who is simply gold plated. ~**Unknown**

## *Scriptures: Decree*

Thou shalt also decree a thing, and it shall be established unto thee: and the light shall shine upon thy ways.

**Job 22:28**

God is not a man, that he should lie; neither the son of man, that he should repent: hath he said, and shall he not do it? or hath he spoken, and shall he not make it good?

**Numbers 23:19**

And the decree of Esther confirmed these matters of Purim; and it was written in the book.

**Esther 9:32**

When he gave to the sea his decree, that the waters should not pass his commandment: when he appointed the foundations of the earth.

**Proverbs 8:29**

I make a decree, That in every dominion of my kingdom men tremble and fear before the God of Daniel: for he is the living God, and steadfast forever, and his kingdom shall not be destroyed, and his dominion shall be even unto the end.

**Daniel 6:26**

But in the first year of Cyrus the king of Babylon the same king Cyrus made a decree to build this house of God.

**Ezra 5:13**

I will declare the decree: the Lord hath said unto me, Thou art my Son; this day have I begotten thee.

**Psalm 2:7**

And it came to pass in those days, that there went out a decree from Caesar Augustus that all the world should be taxed.

**Luke 2:1**

Surely the Lord God will do nothing, but he reveals his secret unto his servants the prophets.

**Amos 3:7**

Therefore, be ye also ready: for in such an hour as ye think not the Son of man cometh.

**Matthew 24:44**

For as the lightning cometh out of the east, and shines even unto the west; so shall also the coming of the Son of man be.

**Matthew 24:27**

Declare his glory among the heathen, his wonders among all people.

**Psalm 96:3**

And He has made my mouth like a sharp sword; in the shadow of His hand he has hidden me, and made me a polished shaft; in His quiver He has hidden me.

**Isaiah 49:2 NKJV**

Behold, I have graven thee upon the palms of my hands; thy walls are continually before me.

**Isaiah 49:16**

And I give unto them eternal life; and they shall never perish, neither shall any man pluck them out of my hand.

**John 10:28**

Thy testimonies are very sure: holiness becometh thine house, O Lord, forever.

**Psalm 93:5**

## *Quotes: Decree*

I believe that nothing happens apart from divine determination and divine decrees. ~**Charles Spurgeon**

God notices every one of us; there is not a sparrow or a worm, that continues to live apart from His decrees. ~**Charles Spurgeon**

Judicial decrees may not change the heart, but they can restrain the heartless. ~**Martin Luther King Jr.**

When angels visit early, the messengers of God's decree, they come as lightning and wind before the throne. They are living fire. ~**Emma Lazarus**

Holy scriptures could never lie or err, its decrees are of absolute and invaluable truth. ~**Galileo**

The counsels and decrees of God do not bend or bow to the frail nor the fickle will of man. ~**Matthew Henry**

You have authority in your mouth, hence do not be afraid; but rather clearly declare and decree your future, according to God's word. ~**Israelmore Ayivor**

Listen for God, listen to God and then do what He says. ~**Kenneth Copeland**

Discernment is a light of protection and direction in a world that grows increasingly dark. ~**Anonymous**

Listen to no man who has not listened to God. ~**A. W. Tozer**

The vague and continuous hope that God is too kind to punish the ungodly has become a deadly opiate for the conscience of millions. ~**A. W. Tozer**

This is a time when all God's people need to keep their eyes and their Bibles wide open, we must ask God for discernment like never before. ~**David Jeremiah**

## *Hymns: Discern/Decree*

**This Is My Father's World**
This is my Father's world,
The birds their carols raise,
The morning light, the lily white,
Declare their maker's praise.
This is my Father's world,
He shines in all that's fair,
In the rustling grass I hear Him pass,
He speaks to me everywhere.
~**Maltbie Babcock**, 1901 (public domain)

**Open My Eyes, That I May See**
Open my eyes, that I may see,
Glimpses of truth Thou hast for me.
Place in my hands the wonderful key,
That shall unclasp and set me free.
Silently, now I wait for Thee,
Ready, my God, Thy will to see.
Open my eyes, illumine me,
Spirit Divine!
~**Clara Scott**, 1895 (public domain)

## *Personalized Prayer Weaponry*

Today, I decide, declare and decree that my soul is happy in the Lord, that I will rise above the stained glass of foggy vision and soar into those unknown realms of wonder, even if only briefly. Cause my gaze to be transfixed on my Eternal Creator, who treasures, cherishes, and adores me. Let that really sink into by being. I will recognize Who is over and above me, the One who longs after me and yearns for my company. May my heart be melted beneath the sacrificial weight of Your glory. May I sit under the shadow of your wings in great delight, feeling the sacred, warming glow of Your consuming love. Anchor me to that granite Rock, while in this dry, shifting sand of a world. Let me drink from Your unending streams in every desert place in my life. I am a forever child of the forever God!

# WEAPON 38

# Giving

## *Scriptures*

Honour the Lord with thy substance, and with the firstfruits of all thine increase.

**PROVERBS 3:9**

Do not withhold good from those to whom it is due, when it is in the power of your hand to do so.

**PROVERBS 3:27 NKJV**

Delight thyself also in the Lord: and he shall give thee the desires of thine heart.

**PSALM 37:4**

All day long he craves for more, but the righteous give without sparing.

**PROVERBS 21:26 NIV**

The wicked borrow and never repay, but the godly are generous givers.

**PSALM 37:21 NLT**

Then the people rejoiced, for that they offered willingly, because with perfect heart they offered willingly to the Lord: and David the king also rejoiced with great joy.

**1 Chronicles 29:9**

And God is able to make all grace abound toward you; that ye, always having all sufficiency in all things, may abound to every good work.

**2 Corinthians 9:8**

He that giveth unto the poor shall not lack but he that hideth his eyes shall have many a curse.

**Proverbs 28:27**

I have shewed you all things, how that so labouring ye ought to support the weak, and to remember the words of the Lord Jesus, how he said, It is more blessed to give than to receive.

**Acts 20:35**

"Bring all the tithes into the storehouse, That there may be food in My house, And try Me now in this," Says the Lord of hosts, "If I will not open for you the windows of heaven And pour out for you such blessing, That there will not be room enough to receive it."

**Malachi 3:10 NKJV**

Give, and it shall be given unto you; good measure, pressed down, and shaken together, and running over, shall men give into your bosom. For with the same measure that ye mete withal it shall be measured to you again.

**Luke 6:38**

Now he that ministereth seed to the sower both minister bread for your food, and multiply your seed sown, and increase the fruits of your righteousness.

**2 Corinthians 9:10**

## *Quotes: Giving*

Tithing is God's financial plan for world evangelism and your own personal success. Tithing is what the church did before bingo. ~**John Hagee**

When we give, whether to the church or other good purposes, do so by grace. ~**Anonymous**

Giving solely because it is a rule, or done because of an expectation, will not establish a relationship with God. ~**Mike Hayes**

Christian giving is voluntary, and it is a test of sincerity and love. ~**C. I. Scofield**

No one has ever become poor by giving. ~**Anne Frank**

Learn to light a candle in the darkest moments of someone's life. Be the light that helps others see; it is this which gives life its deepest significance. ~**Roy Bennett**

We make a living by what we get, we make a life by what we give. ~**Winston Churchill**

You give but little when you give of your possessions, it is when you give of yourself that you truly give. ~**Kahlil Gibran**

You can give without loving but you cannot love without giving. ~**Amy Carmichael**

For it is in giving that we receive. ~**Francis of Assisi**

Those who are the happiest are those who do the most for others. ~**Booker T. Washington**

When you cease to make a contribution, you begin to die. ~**Eleanor Roosevelt**

Plant flowers in others' gardens and your life becomes a bouquet. ~**Unknown**

Don't tell me you are trusting God until you trust Him with your money. ~**J. Vernon McGee**

Go the extra mile, it is never crowded. ~**Unknown**

## *Hymns: Giving*

**Take My Life, and Let It Be**
Take my life and let it be,
Consecrated, Lord, to Thee.
Take my moments and my days,
Let them flow in ceaseless praise.
Take my silver and my gold,
Not a might would I withhold.
~**Frances Havergal**, 1874 (public domain)

**Give of Your Best to the Master**
Give of your best to the master,
Give him first place in your heart.
Give him first place in your service,
Consecrate every part.
Give and you will be given,
God his beloved son gave.
Gratefully seeking to serve Him,
Give Him the best that you have.
~**Howard Grose**, 1902 (public domain)

## *Personalized Weaponry*

Honestly, how could I possibly write Malachi 3:10 on the bottom of my checks as a newly divorced single mom in 1982? Granted, I had the solid biblical teaching on giving, and perhaps I thought it would inspire the people at the bank. Who knows how we often get our thinking skewed? Well, what seemed like a great witness didn't last long as *fear* set in regarding how I was going to make ends meet with three children.

I had moved us to Dallas for job opportunities, and reality clawed at our daily existence. It's incredible how many well-meaning, uninformed, and biblically illiterate Christians are roaming around. One told me, "God doesn't expect single moms to tithe." What? That's bologna, but I had to find out the hard way.

I truly hate to admit that I finally decided to tithe faithfully after years of struggling to get above the bottom of the barrel. Scrapping along, and borrowing gas money to get to work on my one-hour commute each direction in metropolitan traffic. Oh, how many times my car broke down, at home, at work, by the side of the road. It's too many to count in the blur of my memory of those days. There I was, working for the second-largest law firm in the world, yet surrounded by a type of self-imposed poverty. Never enough, forever short, laboring unnecessarily, scrapping and scratching. Even more amazingly, I was still hearing solid teaching on giving, still sighing with whispered sighs at the wondrous testimonies of faithful givers of tithes and offerings.

Yes, dull of faith in this crucial area, I finally woke up one day and announced to my daughter (who had been cabin-bound for five years with Epstein Barr virus) that I was going to tithe if we had to live on beans and rice. I would love to tell you the sky opened immediately and finances began to flow. That didn't happen, but steadily, I began to see God's hand move on our behalf as I honored Him and His word with the *first* 10 percent of my paycheck. There were a few times when I actually put the pieced-together monies in a plastic bag and proudly drop it in the offering plate.

I was able to get a slightly better car, and my daughter was shown a powerful supplement that began to renew her strength. She was able to pursue a part-time job that, a few years later, became her profession.

Just do things God's way. He doesn't need your money, but He does need your obedience. Stay with his principles and a kind of fortitude will develop and you will *not* touch what is holy unto the Lord. Your God proven faithfulness will saturate every facet of your life as you comply with His Word. Always pray fervently about where to plant your seed—in ministries that are proven. Don't just throw it around randomly.

A great man of God once said, "Got a need, plant a seed!" Supernaturally, your blessed 90 percent will stretch further than your self-gratifying 100 percent ever could.

Remember, you can't out give God, and I promise you, He will open up new vistas you never knew existed. One day, you'll realize you're actually looking for ways to give, knowing it will be multiplied back to you in money—or the things that money can't buy. All this is not to mention the sheer joy that takes root in your soul and spirit that can come from no other source but the love you show to God and to others.

May the gold of spiritual giving be your currency this day and every day!

## WEAPON 39

# Healing/Deliverance

### *Scriptures*

And said, If thou wilt diligently hearken to the voice of the Lord thy God, and wilt do that which is right in his sight, and wilt give ear to his commandments, and keep all his statutes, I will put none of these diseases upon thee, which I have brought upon the Egyptians: for I am the Lord that healeth thee.

**EXODUS 15:26**

Is any sick among you? let him call for the elders of the church; and let them pray over him, anointing him with oil in the name of the Lord.

**JAMES 5:14**

The Lord will strengthen him upon the bed of languishing: thou wilt make all his bed in his sickness.

**PSALM 41:3**

He healeth the broken in heart, and bindeth up their wounds.

**PSALM 147:3**

Yet I hold this against you: You have forsaken the love you had at first.

**Revelation 2:4 NIV**

But you belong to God, my dear children. You have already won a victory over those people, because the Spirit who lives in you is greater than the spirit who lives in the world.

**1 John 4:4 NLT**

The thief cometh not, but for to steal, and to kill, and to destroy: I am come that they might have life, and that they might have it more abundantly.

**John 10:10**

The righteous cry, and the Lord heareth, and delivereth them out of all their troubles.

**Psalm 34:17**

Confess your faults one to another, and pray one for another, that ye may be healed. The effectual fervent prayer of a righteous man availeth much.

**James 5:16**

Stand fast therefore in the liberty wherewith Christ hath made us free and be not entangled again with the yoke of bondage.

**Galatians 5:1**

Blessed are the undefiled in the way, who walk in the law of the Lord. Blessed are they that keep his testimonies, and that seek him with the whole heart. They also do no iniquity: they walk in his ways. Thou hast commanded us to keep thy precepts diligently. O that my ways were directed to keep thy statutes! Then shall I not be ashamed, when I have respect unto all thy commandments. I will praise thee with uprightness of heart, when I shall have learned thy righteous judgments.

**Psalm 119: 1–7**

My son, attend to my words; incline thine ear unto my sayings. Let them not depart from thine eyes; keep them in the midst of thine heart. For they are life unto those that find them, and health to all their flesh.

**Proverbs 4:20–22**

Ye shall not fear them: for the Lord your God he shall fight for you.

**Deuteronomy 3:22**

But he was wounded for our transgressions, he was bruised for our iniquities: the chastisement of our peace was upon him; and with his stripes we are healed.

**Isaiah 53:5**

For I will restore health to you and I will heal your wounds, says the Lord, 'Because they have called you an outcast, saying: "This is Zion; no one seeks her and no one cares for her."

**Jeremiah 30:17 amp**

But unto you that fear my name shall the Sun of righteousness arise with healing in his wings; and ye shall go forth and grow up as calves of the stall.

**Malachi 4:2**

How God anointed Jesus of Nazareth with the Holy Ghost and with power: who went about doing good and healing all that were oppressed of the devil; for God was with him.

**Acts 10:38**

Death and life are in the power of the tongue: and they that love it shall eat the fruit thereof.

**Proverbs 18:21**

His mouth is most sweet: yea, he is altogether lovely. This is my beloved, and this is my friend, O daughters of Jerusalem.

**Song of Songs 5:16**

The Lord will march forth like a mighty hero; he will come out like a warrior, full of fury. He will shout his battle cry and crush all his enemies.

**Isaiah 42:13 NLT**

A man that hath friends must shew himself friendly: and there is a friend that sticketh closer than a brother.

**Proverbs 18:24**

He sent his word, and healed them, and delivered them from their destructions.

**Psalm 107:20**

For they are life unto those that find them, and health to all their flesh.

**Proverbs 4:22**

And the prayer of faith shall save the sick, and the Lord shall raise him up; and if he has committed sins, they shall be forgiven him.

**James 5:15**

Who his own self bare our sins in his own body on the tree, that we, being dead to sins, should live unto righteousness: by whose stripes ye were healed.

**1 Peter 2:24**

Beloved, I wish above all things that thou mayest prosper and be in health, even as thy soul prospereth.

**3 John 1:2**

You must serve only the Lord your God. If you do, I will bless you with food and water, and I will protect you from illness.

**Exodus 23:25 NLT**

A merry heart doeth good like a medicine: but a broken spirit drieth the bones.

**Proverbs 17:22**

He healeth the broken in heart, and bindeth up their wounds.

**Psalm 147:3**

But I will restore you to health and heal your wounds,' declares the Lord, 'because you are called an outcast, Zion for whom no one cares.'

**Jeremiah 30:17 NIV**

## *Quotes: Healing/Deliverance*

Sorrow is God's plowshare that turns up the depths of the soul, that it may yield a richer harvest. Sorrow makes us think deeply, long and soberly. ~**Lettie Cowman**

How quickly we forget God's great deliverances in our lives. How easily we take for granted the miracles He has performed in our past. ~**Dave Wilkerson**

As long as we complain, we remain stuck in our problems, but a thankful attitude brings deliverance and makes God smile. ~**Joyce Meyer**

Deliverance can come to us only by the defeat of our old life. Safety and peace come only after we have been forced to our knees. God rescues us by breaking us, gathering our strength and wiping out our resistance. ~**A. W. Tozer**

Nobody appreciates deliverance like those who have nearly been destroyed. ~**Beth Moore**

Out of suffering have emerged the strongest souls. ~**Unknown**

God is glorified through healing and deliverance, not through sickness and suffering. ~**Kenneth Hagin**

Lord, I ask today, that you bathe those who live in pain, in the river of your healing! ~**Unknown**

When you are wounded, talk to the Man with the scars. ~**Unknown**

Difficult roads often lead to beautiful destinations. ~**Unknown**

Jesus did not heal the sick in order to coax them to be Christians. He healed them because it is His nature to heal. ~**John G. Lake**

Healing is not always obtained by saying prayers, but by obeying God. ~**John G. Lake**

These times of waiting on God, for the manifestations of the Spirit, are times when He searches the heart and tests the mind. ~**Smith Wigglesworth**

When the Holy Spirit comes into your body, soul and spirit; He comes to unveil the King, to assure you of His presence. ~**Smith Wigglesworth**

God hears and sees you, and you are not alone in your struggles. Remain firm and stable, for God has your deliverance already planned. ~**Joyce Meyer**

Healing doesn't mean the damage never existed. It means the damage no longer controls our lives. ~**Unknown**

Although the world is full of suffering, it is also full of the overcoming of it. ~**Helen Keller**

Music is a great healing balm and a great way to forget your troubles. ~**Ricky Skaggs**

The soul is healed by being with children. ~**Dostoevsky**

Broken things can become blessed things, when we let God do the mending. ~**Unknown**

I am so much better off healed than I ever was unbroken. ~**Beth Moore**

Don't hide your scars, wear them as proof that God heals. ~**Unknown**

Sometimes when you are in a dark place; you think you have been buried, but actually you have been planted. ~**Unknown**

I will not let anyone walk through my mind with dirty feet. ~**Gandhi**

You have been assigned this mountain to show others it can be moved. ~**Unknown**

His hand can cool the heat of my brow. His hand can stop the turmoil of my palpitating heart. That glorious right hand that molded the world can create my mind anew. The hand that never grows weary, the hand that bears the earth's huge pillar, can sustain my spirit. The loving hand that holds all the saints can cherish me. The mighty hand that breaks my enemies into pieces can subdue my sins! These are the reasons I need His healing hand! ~**Charles Spurgeon**

Lord God Almighty, you are Supreme, Unquestionable, Unparalleled, Limitless, Infinite, Absolute, Magnificent, Dazzling, Ingenious, Timeless, Terrible, Unsearchable, Incomprehensible, Indescribable, Unfathomable, Matchless, Unswerving, Unending, Blazing, Faultless, Awesome, Pristine and Fascinating above all. ~**Joy Dawson**

## *Hymns: Healing/Deliverance*

**There Is a Balm in Gilead**
There is a balm in Gilead,
To make the wounded whole.
There is power enough in Heaven,
To cure a sin-sick soul.
~**African American Spiritual**, 1854 (public domain)

**He Is Able to Deliver Thee**
Tis the grandest theme through the ages rung,
Tis the grandest theme for a mortal tongue.
Our God is able to deliver thee,
Our God is well able to deliver thee.
~**William Ogden**, 1887 (public domain)

## *Personalized Weaponry*

I always wanted several children, so I was thrilled when my third child, a beautiful daughter named Christie Greer, was born in 1975. There were no sonograms in those days. One would hear the cry and the announcement. She was a sweet-natured, raven-haired baby with big chocolate eyes. Oh, how I enjoyed dressing her in the frills and fancies little girls deserve! Her name means "a disciple of Christ; fully alert, watchful and vigilant."

She was a healthy child until age five, when she caught mono from a drinking fountain at school. Thus began a series of illnesses that would strip her immune system over the years. At age ten, she again contracted mono, but this time, something else came with it. The doctor had said, "Her skin feels like sandpaper, this is scarlet fever, a childhood disease that we do not see anymore." She was terribly sick, and her mouth even broke out with thrush due to all the stress of the illness. We had only been in DFW a few months when this struck, and traveling back and forth to the Carswell Air Force Base hospital was wearing on us all. My oldest son was in college at the time and with only my cousin and his family to rely on, this was a trial of suffering. If it hadn't been for my cousins, the McKinley's and their unending love and support, we would undoubtedly have not survived the big city with all its pitfalls.

Strictly through the healing power of prayer from several people and the mercy of God, Christie Greer recovered without any permanent damage, even though some ravages would reappear down the road in the form of Epstein-Barr Syndrome.

As the years marched on, after the teenage-girl phase subsided, a lovely young woman emerged who would be a pal like no other. She is now a pastor's wife, a mother of two, and quite a beauty in her own right. We await a foster adoption. She too, is a tenderhearted, unbelievably discerning woman of God and an ideal wife—supportive and loving, a wonderful mother any child would be blessed to have. This gal once replaced a dryer drum by herself and is handy with a ladder. She's also a workout queen. She's smart, tactful, hardworking, and determined, with administrative skills that are astounding.

Each child has brought me tremendous joy, stirred with seasons of pain, some intense. They're not perfect, but they're my personal treasures. They genuinely make growing older feel happier, safer, and more fulfilling.

Thank you, God, that the hand of the wicked shall not touch my righteous seed.

## Weapon 40

# Peace/Quiet/Solitude

### *Scriptures: Peace*

And the peace of God, which passeth all understanding, shall keep your hearts and minds through Christ Jesus.

**Philippians 4:7**

And let the peace of God rule in your hearts, to the which also ye are called in one body; and be ye thankful.

**Colossians 3:15**

Follow peace with all men, and holiness, without which no man shall see the Lord.

**Hebrews 12:14**

And the fruit of righteousness is sown in peace of them that make peace.

**James 3:18**

Deceit is in the heart of them that imagine evil: but to the counsellors of peace is joy.

**Proverbs 12:20**

The highway of the upright is to depart from evil; who keeps his way preserves his soul.

**Proverbs 16:17 NKJV**

The Lord will give strength unto his people; the Lord will bless his people with peace.

**Psalm 29:11**

Peace I leave with you, my peace I give unto you: not as the world giveth, give I unto you. Let not your heart be troubled, neither let it be afraid.

**John 14:27**

The glory of this latter house shall be greater than of the former, saith the Lord of hosts: and in this place will I give peace, saith the Lord of hosts.

**Haggai 2:9**

And all thy children shall be taught of the Lord; and great shall be the peace of thy children.

**Isaiah 54:13**

This is what the Sovereign Lord, the Holy One of Israel, says: "Only in returning to me and resting in me will you be saved. In quietness and confidence is your strength. But you would have none of it."

**Isaiah 30:15 NLT**

Those that be planted in the house of the Lord shall flourish in the courts of our God. They shall still bring forth fruit in old age; they shall be fat and flourishing.

**Psalm 92:13–14**

And my people shall dwell in a peaceable habitation, in sure dwellings, and in quiet resting places.

**Isaiah 32:18**

I will both lay me down in peace, and sleep: for thou, Lord, only makest me dwell in safety.

**Psalm 4:8**

## *Quotes: Peace*

Trials are conforming us to the image of Christ, if we allow a "holy alignment" to take place! We willingly release the God kind of peace into ourselves and our environment, through the help and power of the Great Sustainer. ~**Anonymous**

You cannot shake hands with a clenched fist. ~**Golda Meir**

Be real, be genuine, be human, be divine, be called as agents of God's peace. ~**Anonymous**

Fear is an inhibitor that has kept more people from fulfilling their destiny, than any other emotion. ~**Tim LaHaye**

Refuse to be average, let your heart soar as high as it will. ~**A. W. Tozer**

Faith in the heart, that is released through a peaceful mouth, can move mountains. ~**John Eckhardt**

For peace of mind, resign as the general manager of the universe. ~**Joyce Meyer**

Whatever else we say when we pray, let our restless hearts find peaceful repose in your Holy attentiveness. ~**Saint Augustine**

We were made for perfect happiness, no wonder everything short of God disappoints you. ~**Fulton Sheen**

My attitude can change my atmosphere. ~**Anonymous**

Circumstances may appear to wreck our lives and God's plans, but God is not helpless among the ruins. ~**Eric Liddell**

A born-again person ought to possess unspeakable peace in the Spirit. ~**Watchman Nee**

Envision His enveloping presence sustaining you. Stay calm and give God time to work. ~**Robert Morgan**

Let us be silent so that we may hear the whisper of God. ~**Ralph Waldo Emerson**

I am content to fill a little space if God be glorified. ~**Susannah Wesley**

Peace is not the absence of trouble, it is the ability to handle conflict, by peaceful means. ~**Ronald Reagan**

A peaceful man does more good than a learned one. ~**Pope John XXIII**

Wars are poor chisels for carving out peaceful tomorrows. ~**Martin Luther King Jr.**

We seek peace, knowing peace is the climate of freedom. ~**Dwight Eisenhower**

God cannot give us peace apart from Himself. There is no such thing. ~**C. S. Lewis**

For every minute you remain angry, you give up sixty seconds of peace of mind. ~**Ralph Waldo Emerson**

Nothing is more precious than peace, by which all war, both in heaven and earth, is brought to an end. ~**Ignatius**

May the stars carry your sadness away, may the flowers fill your heart with beauty. May hope forever wipe away your tears and may silence make you strong. ~**Chief Dan George**

## *Scriptures: Quiet*

The whole earth is at rest and is quiet: they break forth into singing.

**Isaiah 14:7**

And the work of righteousness shall be peace; and the effect of righteousness quietness and assurance forever.

**Isaiah 32:17**

Behold, a son shall be born to thee, who shall be a man of rest; and I will give him rest from all his enemies round about: for his name shall be Solomon, and I will give peace and quietness unto Israel in his days.

**1 Chronicles 22:9**

Better is a dry morsel, and quietness therewith, than a house full of sacrifices with strife.

**Proverbs 17:1**

That you also aspire to lead a quiet life, to mind your own business, and to work with your own hands, as we commanded you.

**1 Thessalonians 4:11 NKJV**

Surely, I have behaved and quieted myself, as a child that is weaned of his mother: my soul is even as a weaned child.

**Psalm 131:2**

For thus saith the Lord God, the Holy One of Israel; In returning and rest shall ye be saved; in quietness and in confidence shall be your strength: and ye would not.

**Isaiah 30:15**

But let it be the hidden man of the heart, in that which is not corruptible, even the ornament of a meek and quiet spirit, which is in the sight of God of great price.

**1 Peter 3:4**

Better is a handful with quietness, than both the hands full with travail and vexation of spirit.

**Ecclesiastes 4:6**

## *Quotes: Quiet*

Staying quiet does not mean I have nothing to say; sometimes it means you are not ready to hear my thoughts. ~**Unknown**

Sometimes the best advice you can give yourself is just be quiet and listen. ~**Unknown**

One who will not accept solitude, stillness and quiet recurring moments, is caught up in a wilderness, far removed from the original place of awareness. ~**Anonymous**

Oh, what great peace and quietness he would possess, who would cut off all vain anxiety and place all his confidence in God. ~**Thomas à Kempis**

Out of quietness with God, power is generated, that turns the spiritual machinery of the world. ~**E. Stanley Jones**

Cultivate solitude and quiet in a few sincere friends. Rather than mob merriment, noise and thousands of nodding acquaintances. ~**William Powell**

If you have not quiet in your minds, outward comfort will do no more for you, than a golden slipper on a twisted foot. ~**John Bunyan**

Many of man's miseries derive from not being able to sit in a quiet room alone. ~**Blaise Pascal**

Silence is often wiser than speech. ~**Anonymous**

## *Scriptures: Solitude*

And he withdrew himself into the wilderness and prayed.

**Luke 5:16**

Oh, that I had in the wilderness a lodging place of wayfaring men; that I might leave my people and go from them! for they be all adulterers, an assembly of treacherous men.

**Jeremiah 9:2**

And when he had sent the multitudes away, he went up into a mountain apart to pray and when the evening was come, he was there alone.

**Matthew 14:23**

But thou, when thou prayest, enter into thy closet, and when thou hast shut thy door, pray to thy Father which is in secret; and thy Father which seeth in secret shall reward thee openly.

**Matthew 6:6**

But the Lord is in his holy temple: let all the earth keep silence before him.

**Habakkuk 2:20**

Be still and know that I am God: I will be exalted among the heathen, I will be exalted in the earth.

**Psalm 46:10**

There he came to a cave and spent the night in it; and behold, the word of the Lord came to him, and He said to him, "What are you doing here, Elijah?"

**1 Kings 19:9 AMP**

It was also called Mizpah, because he said, "May the Lord keep watch between you and me when we are away from each other."

**Genesis 31:49 NIV**

## *Quotes: Solitude*

I live in that solitude that is painful in youth and delicious in the years of maturity. ~**Albert Einstein**

Be able to be alone, lose not the advantage of solitude in the society of yourself. ~**Thomas Browne**

Without great solitude, no serious work is possible. ~**Pablo Picasso**

People who cannot bear to be alone are generally the worst company. ~**Anonymous**

True silence is the rest for the mind. It is to the spirit what sleep is to the body, nourishment and refreshment. ~**William Penn**

You only grow when you are alone. ~**Paul Newman**

The more powerful and original a mind, the more it will incline toward the religion of solitude. ~**Anonymous**

## *Hymns: Peace/Quiet/Solitude*

**Wonderful Peace**
Peace! Peace! wonderful peace,
Coming down from the Father above.
Sweep over my spirit forever I pray,
In fathomless billows of love.
~**Warren Cornell**, 1889 (public domain)

**Leaning on the Everlasting Arms**
What a fellowship, what a joy divine,
Leaning on the everlasting arms.
What a blessedness, what a peace is mine,
Leaning on the everlasting arms.
Leaning, leaning, safe and secure from all alarms,
Leaning on the everlasting arms.
~**Hoffman and Showalter**, 1887 (public domain)

## *Personalized Weaponry*

Psalm 94:13 says, "That thou mayest give him rest from the days of adversity, until the pit be digged for the wicked."

Have you ever heard yourself saying, "I just need some peace and quiet"? But hardly ever do we add, "And some solitude might be nice." What exactly is solitude, anyway?

Seclusion, privacy, being alone, soul-searching, reflection. That all sounds good right about now! Can a person get too much of this? Yes, isolation is damaging in and of itself when taken to extremes. However, in this present world, with its clatter and chatter, the chaos is often deafening, and our souls crave a place of repose. A place of peacefulness is vitally necessary for our souls to function at peak levels.

Otherwise disarray and discontentment will become very loud and obtrusive.

We desperately need to be led beside still waters and to lie down in green pastures, to be restored to wholeness by truly knowing that He is our God—your God, who doesn't want you frazzled nor fragmented. Search out your quiet, peace-filled, alone place and protect it from all intruders at all times. The world can wait while you recharge, so go there before you're so harried and flustered and go often. The Lord is waiting lovingly to impart His patient parental power, to guide and direct you. He is not called the Prince of Peace for no reason. Ah, that's so much better!

## Weapon 41

# Heaven

### *Scriptures*

But as it is written, Eye hath not seen, nor ear heard, neither have entered into the heart of man, the things which God hath prepared for them that love him.

**1 Corinthians 2:9**

For the Lord God will help me; therefore, shall I not be confounded: therefore, have I set my face like a flint, and I know that I shall not be ashamed.

**Isaiah 50:7**

To an inheritance incorruptible, and undefiled, and that fadeth not away, reserved in heaven for you.

**1 Peter 1:4**

In my Father's house are many mansions: if it were not so, I would have told you. I go to prepare a place for you. And if I go and prepare a place for you, I will come again, and receive you unto myself; that where I am, there ye may be also. And whither I go ye know, and the way ye know.

**John 14:2–4**

And there shall be no more curse: but the throne of God and of the Lamb shall be in it; and his servants shall serve him.

**Revelation 22:3**

Nevertheless we, according to his promise, look for new heavens and a new earth, wherein dwelleth righteousness.

**2 Peter 3:13**

Lay not up for yourselves treasures upon earth, where moth and rust doth corrupt, and where thieves break through and steal: But lay up for yourselves treasures in heaven, where neither moth nor rust doth corrupt, and where thieves do not break through nor steal.

**Matthew 6:19–20**

But now they desire a better country, that is, an heavenly: wherefore God is not ashamed to be called their God: for he hath prepared for them a city.

**Hebrews 11:16**

And the building of the wall of it was of jasper: and the city was pure gold, like unto clear glass.

**Revelation 21:18**

Fear not, little flock; for it is your Father's good pleasure to give you the kingdom.

**Luke 12:32**

He made the earth by his power; he founded the world by his wisdom and stretched out the heavens by his understanding.

**Jeremiah 51:15 niv**

Down the middle of the great street of the city. On each side of the river stood the tree of life, bearing twelve crops of fruit, yielding its fruit every month. And the leaves of the tree are for the healing of the nations.

**REVELATION 22:2 NIV**

You alone are the Lord. You made the heavens, even the highest heavens, and all their starry host, the earth and all that is on it, the seas and all that is in them. You give life to everything, and the multitudes of heaven worship you.

**NEHEMIAH 9:6 NIV**

There is a river whose streams make glad the city of God, the holy place where the Most High dwells.

**PSALM 46:4 NIV**

Your unfailing love, O LORD, is as vast as the heavens; your faithfulness reaches beyond the clouds.

**PSALM 36:5 NLT**

The twenty-four elders fall down before him who sits on the throne and worship him who lives for ever and ever. They lay their crowns before the throne and say.

**REVELATION 4:10 NIV**

For we must all appear before the judgment seat of Christ; that everyone may receive the things done in his body, according to that he hath done, whether it be good or bad.

**2 CORINTHIANS 5:10**

Behold, I come quickly: hold that fast which thou hast, that no man take thy crown.

**REVELATION 3:11**

Blessed is the man that endureth temptation: for when he is tried, he shall receive the crown of life, which the Lord hath promised to them that love him.

**James 1:12**

He who has an ear, let him hear what the Spirit says to the churches. To him who overcomes I will give to eat from the tree of life, which is in the midst of the Paradise of God.

**Revelation 2:7 NKJV**

Him that overcometh will I make a pillar in the temple of my God, and he shall go no more out: and I will write upon him the name of my God, and the name of the city of my God, which is new Jerusalem, which cometh down out of heaven from my God: and I will write upon him my new name.

**Revelation 3:12**

And he that overcometh, and keepeth my works unto the end, to him will I give power over the nations.

**Revelation 2:26**

Even the sparrow finds a home, and the swallow builds her nest and raises her young at a place near your altar, O LORD of Heaven's Armies, my King and my God! What joy for those who can live in your house, always singing your praises.

**Psalm 84:3–4 NLT**

## Quotes: Heaven

The essence of Heaven is the vision of God and eternal increased joy in Him. Heaven is a world of love. ~**Jonathan Edwards**

At his ascension, our Lord entered Heaven, and he keeps the door open for humanity to enter. ~**Oswald Chambers**

I would rather go to Heaven alone than go to Hell in company. ~**R. A. Torrey**

The Heavenly Jerusalem, the Royal Bridal City awaits the betrothed of Christ. She is a glimmering, shimmering, gleaming gift of the Bridegroom for his beloved. ~**Anonymous**

We are traveling with our staff in hand, we are pilgrims bound for that heavenly land. ~**Fanny Crosby**

When I get to Heaven, the first face that shall ever gladden my sight, will be that of my Savior. ~**Fanny Crosby**

Heaven is an adventure that will endure forever! The enchantments of paradise shall thrill unceasingly! ~**Jerome**

The light of the city glowed with the radiance of a million stars and everything was extremely beautiful and alive with joy and happiness! Dazzling glory and bellowing light, magnificent scenes of awe-inspiring wonder, a city handcrafted for the children of God. ~**Mary Baxter**

In Heaven we shall be set free from all the ravages of sin, in a real existence enjoying real fellowship with Christ and our loved ones. It is a monumentally good place, unparalleled and unmatched in its wonder! ~**Jack Graham**

No more heartache, no more hardship, no more destruction, no more grief! Only eternal blessings under His divine rule! The dream of Heaven can be ours here and now, as we prepare for an eternal weight of glory, "beyond all comparison." ~**Jack Graham**

Victorious realities awaiting us:
**1**. We will dwell with God forever.
**2**. We will worship God.
**3**. We will work.
**4**. We will learn all about God.
**5**. We will rest.
**6**. We will eat.
**7**. We will reign with Him forever.
~**Jack Graham**

Crowns and rewards:
**1**. The Victor's Imperishable Crown (the Overcomers)
**2**. The Crown of Rejoicing (the Soul Winners)
**3**. The Crown of Righteousness (for Faithful Service)
**4**. The Crown of Glory (the Shepherds)
**5**. The Crown of Life (the Martyrs)

Aim at Heaven and you will get earth thrown in. Aim at earth and you will get neither. ~**C. S. Lewis**

Releasing the power of Heaven, laboring in the Lord, recognizing the spectacular supremacy of Christ, is our reward. ~**Anonymous**

The melodious song of the galaxies, echoes throughout the cosmic celestial refrain, "the Mighty Sovereign God reigns forever and forever." ~**Anonymous**

I want to know one thing, the way to heaven, how to land safe on that happy shore. For paradise is only the porch of heaven, it is there the spirits of just men are made perfect. ~**John Wesley**

Our heavenly bodies shall be as fire; as active and as nimble as our thoughts are. ~**John Wesley**

Heaven was man's first love; earth is only a substitute. Earth is a task garden, heaven is a playground. ~**G. K. Chesterton**

You are somewhere in your future and you look much better than you do right now. ~**Kim Clement**

You can celebrate because your name is written in heaven. ~**Rich Renner**

There are no crown bearers in heaven who were not crop bearers on earth. ~**Charles Spurgeon**

Therefore; may we be content to share in the battle, for we will soon wear a crown of rewards and wave a palm branch of praise. ~**Charles Spurgeon**

As we soak in God's presence, heaven sticks to us. ~**Dennis Walker**

God has provided heaven for our future, where eternal rewards await us. He has put eternity into our souls. ~**John Bevere**

Anticipating heaven does not eliminate pain, but it lessens it and puts it into perspective. ~**Randy Alcorn**

He who lays up treasures in heaven looks forward to eternity. ~**Randy Alcorn**

Our source of comfort isn't only that we will be with the Lord in heaven, but also, we will be with each other. ~**Randy Alcorn**

In this life we are to share Christ's cross, in the next life we will share his crown. ~**Randy Alcorn**

Heaven is the dwelling place of the One who is infinite in creativity, beauty and power. How could it be anything less than thrilling? ~**Randy Alcorn**

Nothing is more often misdiagnosed than our homesickness for heaven. What we were really made for was heaven and the person we want is Jesus. Nothing else truly satisfies us! ~**Randy Alcorn**

Where there is fulfillment, then there is beauty. When we see God as he really is, an endless reservoir of fascination, boredom is impossible. ~**Randy Alcorn**

Our minds are so much set on earth that we are unaccustomed to heavenly thinking. We have to really work at it. ~**Randy Alcorn**

Earth has an atmosphere of air. Heaven's atmosphere is glory. His presence, sometimes as dewdrops, sometimes golden drops of rain, sometimes a pillar of cloud or fire, sometimes a mist or glory dust from his garment. ~**Ruth Heflin**

Prophesy is the voice if revival, let your prophetic voice bring revival. You'll save yourself thousands of hours of vain activity. ~**Ruth Heflin**

Revival glory is standing under the cloud and ministering directly to the people. It is seeing into the eternal realm and declaring what you see, it is gathering the harvest together using only the tools of the Spirit. ~**Ruth Heflin**

Fight all forces! Oh, God, that we do not drift numb and blind and foolish into vain and empty excitements. Life is too short, too precious, too painful to waste on worldly bubbles that burst. Heaven is too great, hell too horrible, eternity too long, to putter around on the porch of eternity. ~**John Piper**

Oh, the glorious sight that met my view of that Golden City, can never be expressed by mortal tongue. ~**Maria Woodworth-Etter**

We should be looking forward to entering the spirit realm of heaven, with the same joyous anticipation as a child looks forward to Christmas. ~**Robert B. Thompson**

There are judgments to come, a beautiful, glorious heaven, a real and fiery hell. Danger awaits if we walk in disobedience before God. ~**Steve Hill**

Heaven wields above you, displaying to you her eternal glories, and still your eyes are on the ground. ~**Dante Alighier**

I don't think about retiring. I am working for the Lord Almighty, His retirement program is out of this world. ~**George Foreman**

A heavenly mind is a joyful mind. ~**Richard Baxter**

Sustain our hearts from sinking, to wait for fresh strength from heaven above. ~**Christmas Evans**

While we are here, get ready for there. ~**Anonymous**

No tempest howls along the peaceful shores of paradise. Soon we shall reach that happy shore where partings, changes and storms will be ended, and we shall see the "radiant splendor of the Exalted Lamb!" ~**Charles Spurgeon**

Heaven is a land of perfect holiness and complete security, where the wicked will not trouble us and the weary will be at rest! ~**Charles Spurgeon**

In sweet contemplation, we will drink the spiced wine of the Lord's pomegranate and taste the fruits of Paradise in that eternal world of joy! We will be privileged to go in with the divine family, to share the children's bread and to participate in all their honor and joy. We will enter the chambers of fellowship, the banquets of love, the treasures of the covenant and the storehouses of the promises and the secret of the Lord will be with us. ~**Charles Spurgeon**

## Hymns: Heaven

**In the Sweet By and By**
There's a land that is fairer than day,
And by faith we can see it afar.
For the Father waits over the way,
To prepare us a dwelling place there.
In the sweet bye and bye,
We shall meet on that beautiful shore.
In the sweet bye and bye,
We shall meet on that beautiful shore.
~**Bennett and Webster**, 1868 (public domain)

**Higher Ground**
I'm pressing on the upward way,
New heights I am gaining every day.
Still praying as I'm onward bound,
Lord, plant my feet on higher ground.
Lord, lift me up and let me stand,
By faith, on heaven's table land.
A higher plane than I have found,
Lord, plant my feet on higher ground.
~**Oatman and Gabriel**, 1898 (public domain)

**When We All Get to Heaven**
Sing the wondrous love of Jesus,
Sing His mercy and His grace.
In the mansions bright and blessed,
He'll prepare for us a place.
When we all get to heaven,
what a day of rejoicing that will be!
When we all see Jesus,
We'll sing and shout the victory!
~**Hewitt and Wilson**, 1898 (public domain)

## *Personalized Weaponry*

We, as believers in Jesus Christ, are a chosen and separated people; therefore, it stands to reason that our eternal home is exclusive, full of grandeur, and extraordinary beyond compare—a prepared place for a prepared people. It's the land of immortal joy and rejoicing. The rage and rant of tyrants will not be heard there. In it, there will be no dying, no sadness, no lonely separations, no brokenness, and no darkness of any kind. We shall be emancipated from the bondage of evil and the grip of the terrible. We will revel in the ecstasies, and our beauty will be as great as that of this place prepared for us.

What awaits the remnant, covenant family of the redeemed is, quite frankly, past our ability to express or comprehend. The wonders in store for us would take our breath away. It's a place of the original Aurora Borealis flooding the skies, the covenant rainbow above the emerald throne where Father God Jehovah sits, the sapphire sea of glass, the heavenly beings unendingly singing of the Holiness of God. There we will see the enraptured faces of saints, soaking in the resplendent light of home and the stately, venerated courtroom, the hallowed libraries where the Books of Life are kept. The consecrated, sacred temple of God, in the midst of his people will be found there.

The vast array of martyrs, the ancient prophets, the great men and women of God from every age, the faithful ones, the little children will all be joyfully reunited.

It contains the glowing city with its golden streets lined with wondrous mansions, the River of Life, the luscious trees laden with fruit for the healing of the nations.

Far greater still, our victorious Lamb upon his throne, our Kinsman Redeemer, our All in All, excitedly awaits us there. The Bema Judgment seat, where rewards and crowns are bestowed, then the Grand Finale, the Marriage Supper of the Lamb where our Heavenly Bridegroom will himself serve us!

The royal city, the New Jerusalem, the exquisite crown jewel, the metropolis of the universe, the zenith of splendor, she, the city, will be our Bridegroom's wedding gift to us.

Until that day breaks and the shadows flee, keep us in Your strong and capable hands, our Lord and Savior. Oh, long expected and awaited day begin. We long for heaven and home.

Glimpses of this colossal scene cheer our hearts and urge us on to our eternal sunrise. Press on, beloved warrior, toward your starry crown!

# WEAPON 42

# Hell

## *Scriptures*

But the fearful, and unbelieving, and the abominable, and murderers, and whoremongers, and sorcerers, and idolaters, and all liars, shall have their part in the lake which burneth with fire and brimstone: which is the second death.

**REVELATION 21:8**

The wicked shall be turned into hell, and all the nations that forget God.

**PSALM 9:17**

Who shall be punished with everlasting destruction from the presence of the Lord, and from the glory of his power.

**2 THESSALONIANS 1:9**

The way of life is above to the wise, that he may depart from hell beneath.

**PROVERBS 15:24**

And they will go away into eternal punishment, but the righteous will go into eternal life.

**Matthew 25:46 NLT**

For if God spared not the angels that sinned, but cast them down to hell, and delivered them into chains of darkness, to be reserved unto judgment.

**2 Peter 2:4**

The Lord preserveth all them that love him: but all the wicked will he destroy.

**Psalm 145:20**

And whosoever was not found written in the book of life was cast into the lake of fire.

**Revelation 20:15**

Therefore, Death expands its jaws, opening wide its mouth; into it will descend their nobles and masses with all their brawlers and revelers.

**Isaiah 5:14 NIV**

Enter by the narrow gate; for wide is the gate and broad is the way that leads to destruction, and there are many who go in by it.

**Matthew 7:13 NKJV**

And fear not them which kill the body but are not able to kill the soul: but rather fear him which is able to destroy both soul and body in hell.

**Matthew 10:28**

And the smoke of their torment ascendeth up for ever and ever: and they have no rest day nor night, who worship the beast and his image, and whosoever receiveth the mark of his name.

**Revelation 14:11**

But Abraham said, 'Son, remember that in your lifetime you received your good things, and likewise Lazarus evil things; but now he is comforted and you are tormented.

**Luke 16:25 NKJV**

Hell and destruction are before the Lord: how much more then the hearts of the children of men?

**Proverbs 15:11**

## *Quotes: Hell*

The searing flames, the total isolation, the rotting stench, the deafening screams of agony, the terrorizing demons, avoid this place at all cost; it is for real!!! ~**Bill Wiese**

Nobody will go to hell for rejecting a Gospel they have never heard. ~**Robert Jeffress**

We need to fully understand what we are fighting for and what we are fighting against. There is a Heaven to gain and a Hell to shun. Both are literal and eternal. ~**Anonymous**

Not believing in Hell doesn't lower the temperature down there one degree. ~**Neil Anderson**

How well I have learned there is no fence to sit on between Heaven and Hell. There is a deep wide chasm and men should not choose the pit. ~**Johnny Cash**

Hell, a land where repentance is impossible and useless, even if it were possible. ~**Charles Spurgeon**

If there are a million roads into Hell, there is not one leading out. ~**Leonard Ravenhill**

The most fervent prayer meetings are coming from Hell. ~**Leonard Ravenhill**

Almost saved is altogether lost. There are many in Hell who were almost saved. It is being in the kingdom that saves the soul, not being near to it. ~**Charles Spurgeon**

Hell is a place void of all good, because all good comes from God. ~**Bill Wiese**

Satan's chief tactic is deception and he does it by telling people lies about God. ~**Peter Wagner**

Christ took our hell so that we might take His Heaven. ~**Donald Barnhouse**

Satan's greatest success is in making people think they have plenty of time before they die to consider their eternal welfare. ~**John Owen**

The proof of how real Jesus knew Hell to be, is that He came to earth to save us from it. ~**Peter Marshall**

The safest road to Hell is the gradual one, the gentle slope, soft underfoot, without sudden turnings, without milestones, without signposts! ~**C. S. Lewis**

After the present age is ended, God will judge His worshippers, for a reward of eternal life. The godless, for a fire equally perpetual and unending. ~**Tertullian**

God save us from living in comfort while sinners are sinking in Hell. ~**Charles Spurgeon**

The preaching of Christ is the whip that flogs the devil. The preaching of Christ is the thunderbolt, the sound of which makes all Hell shake. ~**Charles Spurgeon**

The lost enjoy forever the horrible freedom they have demanded. ~**C. S. Lewis**

Hell is the highest reward that the devil can offer you, for being a servant of his. ~**Billy Sunday**

I would rather go into the kingdom of Heaven through the poorhouse than down to Hell in a golden chariot. ~**Dwight L. Moody**

The road to Hell is paved with good intentions. ~**Martin Luther**

The national anthem of Hell is, "I did it my way!" ~**Unknown**

The saddest road to Hell, is the one that runs under the pulpit, past the Bible and through the middle of warnings and invitations. ~**J. C. Ryle**

We face "utter barrenness outside of Christ." ~**Unknown**

If we had more hell preached from the pulpit, we would have less hell in the pew. ~**Billy Graham**

Our Blessed Substitute has broken the arrows of hell. The Mighty Breaker destroys every indictment and accusation of the redeemed. ~**Unknown**

Hell is absolute hatred because heaven is absolute love. **Unknown**

Christ, who came meek and mild, to save us from pain and suffering, was the one who talked more about hell than any other person in scripture. ~**D. James Kennedy**

## *Personalized Weaponry*

Consolidated evil fuels Satan's government. The corridors of hell reek with evil that is active, organized, never resting, and always anxious and seeking to destroy.

Hell is a dreadful place where there is not a glimmer of light or hope. No one can die or be annihilated to escape. The body and soul, with its senses and awareness, will remain intact to be tortured, yet not consumed, by fire. This is not fiction, my friend, but as God lives, it is solid, stern truth.

The chains rattle forever; the flames eerily spell out forever. There is weeping and gnashing of teeth because of great pain and agony, due to cursing of God. Souls there are ruined, lost, and forever separated from all that is good, bright, and happy. They are damned for rejecting the very One who came to save them from this horror, Jesus Christ!

Hell enlarges itself rapidly with yawning jaws, never satisfied but always hungry for more souls to be eternally destroyed. Do not dance on the brink of hell, like a spider on a single thread, thinking your unrepentant sins are nothing. Do not be lulled into a fool's paradise with soft slumbers and smooth excuses this side of death's door. Do not be fascinated and bewitched by sin; it will surely and gladly validate your ticket to the dark abyss. Your damnation is your own choice, not God's. He has provided a way of escape through Jesus Christ. Will you receive him?

## *Hymns: Hell*

**Blest Be the Lamb**
The Lamb that freed my captive soul,
From Satan's heavy chains.
And sent the Lion down to howl,
Where Hell and horror reign.
~**Isaac Watts**, 1712 (public domain)

**Terrible Thought! Shall I Alone**
Shall I, amidst a ghastly band,
Dragged to the judgment seat,
Far on the left with horror stand,
My fearful doom to meet?
~**Charles Wesley**, *Hymns for Children*, 1763
(public domain)

## Weapon 43

# Witness/Testimony/ Evangelism

### *Scriptures*

But when the Comforter is come, whom I will send unto you from the Father, even the Spirit of truth, which proceedeth from the Father, he shall testify of me: And ye also shall bear witness, because ye have been with me from the beginning.

**John 15:26–27**

And for me, that utterance may be given unto me, that I may open my mouth boldly, to make known the mystery of the gospel, for which I am an ambassador in bonds: that therein I may speak boldly, as I ought to speak.

**Ephesians 6:19–20**

Be not thou therefore ashamed of the testimony of our Lord, nor of me his prisoner: but be thou partaker of the afflictions of the gospel according to the power of God.

**2 Timothy 1:8**

They arrested the apostles and put them in the public jail. But during the night an angel of the Lord opened the doors of the jail and brought them out.

**Acts 5:18–19 niv**

And this is the record, that God hath given to us eternal life, and this life is in his Son.

**1 John 5:11**

I will declare thy name unto my brethren: in the midst of the congregation will I praise thee.

**Psalm 22:22**

And my tongue shall speak of thy righteousness and of thy praise all the day long.

**Psalm 35:28**

But God forbid that I should glory, save in the cross of our Lord Jesus Christ, by whom the world is crucified unto me, and I unto the world.

**Galatians 6:14**

The fruit of the righteous is a tree of life; and he that winneth souls is wise.

**Proverbs 11:30**

Thus will I magnify myself and sanctify myself; and I will be known in the eyes of many nations, and they shall know that I am the Lord.

**Ezekiel 38:23**

And the lord said unto the servant, Go out into the highways and hedges, and compel them to come in, that my house may be filled.

**Luke 14:23**

And they overcame him by the blood of the Lamb, and by the word of their testimony; and they loved not their lives unto the death.

**Revelation 12:11**

Now then, we are ambassadors for Christ, as though God were pleading through us: we implore you on Christ's behalf, be reconciled to God.

**2 Corinthians 5:20 NKJV**

Knowing therefore the terror of the Lord, we persuade men; but we are made manifest unto God; and I trust also are made manifest in your consciences.

**2 Corinthians 5:11**

The law of truth was in his mouth, and iniquity was not found in his lips: he walked with me in peace and equity and did turn many away from iniquity.

**Malachi 2:6**

But sanctify the Lord God in your hearts: and be ready always to give an answer to every man that asketh you a reason of the hope that is in you with meekness and fear.

**1 Peter 3:15**

But you will receive power when the Holy Spirit comes on you; and you will be my witnesses in Jerusalem, and in all Judea and Samaria, and to the ends of the earth.

**Acts 1:8 NIV**

Go ye therefore, and teach all nations, baptizing them in the name of the Father, and of the Son, and of the Holy Ghost: Teaching them to observe all things whatsoever I have commanded you: and, lo, I am with you always, even unto the end of the world. Amen.

**Matthew 28:19–20**

He that believeth and is baptized shall be saved; but he that believeth not shall be damned.

**Mark 16:16**

And I, if I be lifted up from the earth, will draw all men unto me.

**John 12:32**

So shall my word be that goeth forth out of my mouth: it shall not return unto me void, but it shall accomplish that which I please, and it shall prosper in the thing whereto I sent it.

**Isaiah 55:11**

I will make thy name to be remembered in all generations: therefore, shall the people praise thee for ever and ever.

**Psalm 45:17**

## *Quotes: Witness/Testimony/Evangelism*

Every Christian is either a missionary or an imposter. **~Charles Spurgeon**

To belong to Jesus is to embrace the nations with Him. ~**William Cary**

The best remedy for a sick church is to put it on a missionary's diet. ~**David Livingston**

God forbid that I should travel with anybody a quarter of an hour without speaking of Christ to them. ~**George Whitefield**

His voice leads us not into timid discipleship but into bold witness. ~**Charles Stanley**

Let us arise and march to the place of duty and there declare what great things God has shown us. ~**Alistair Begg**

Every day you are a witness, the total package of your actions, attitudes and character do not lie. ~**Winkie Pratney**

Be ready to share your story when God gives you the opportunity. One faithful witness is worth a thousand mute professors of religion. The Spirit goes ahead of us when we witness, granting us words and courage. ~**Billy Graham**

The work of the church is not survival, she exists to fulfill the Great Commission. ~**Brother Andrew**

What an incredible witness it is to a lost and fearful society; when a Christian acts like a child of God, living under the loving sovereignty of the Heavenly Father. ~**Henry Blackaby**

At times our own light goes dim and is rekindled by a spark from another person. Each of us has cause to think, with deep gratitude, of those who have stoked the flame within us. ~**Phillips Brooks**

God wants us to set up memorials in our hearts, testifying to the provisions He has given us. ~**Michael Youssef**

Come out of your holy huddle, to engage an unbelieving world. ~**Anonymous**

Go straight for souls and go for the worst. ~**William Booth**

Surely there is no greater joy than that of saving souls. ~**Lottie Moon**

I have a firm conviction; I am immortal until my work is done. ~**Lottie Moon**

I wish I had a thousand lives that I might give them all to Christ. ~**Lottie Moon**

May God give you a fresh apostolic anointing and renewal. May you be abundantly fruitful in building His kingdom and in reaping the end-time harvest. ~**T. L. Lowery**

Your story is the key that can unlock someone else's prison. ~**Unknown**

Do you realize, that God expects you to consider the fact, that you are working for Christ on your job? ~**Bill Gothard**

Talk about your blessings more than you talk about your burdens. ~**Tim Tebow**

Talent is God given. Be humble. Fame is man given. Be careful. Conceit is self-given. Be more careful. ~**John Wooden**

Golf is just an avenue for Jesus to use me, to reach as many people as I can. ~**Bubba Watson**

The spirit of Christ is the spirit of missions. The nearer we get to Him, the more intensely missionary we become. ~**Henry Martin**

My heart is to help people, but sometimes I wear myself out, by not asking You first. Help me, Lord, so I don't burn out and end up resenting the people I want to help. Teach me to say "no" graciously. ~**Jennifer LeClaire**

Missionary work should never be an afterthought of the church, because it is Christ's first thought. ~**Henry van Dyke**

## *Hymns: Witness/Testimony/Evangelism*

**Before the Throne of God Above**
Before the throne of God above,
I have a strong, a perfect plea.
A great High Priest whose name is Love,
Whoever lives and pleads for me.
My name is graven on his hands,
My name is written on his heart.
I know that while in heaven he stands,
No tongue can bid me thence depart.
~**Bancroft and Bradbury**, 1867 (public domain)

**I Love to Tell the Story**
I love to tell the story,
Of unseen things above,
Of Jesus and his glory,
Of Jesus and his love.
I love to tell the story,
Because I know 'tis true,
It satisfies my longings,
As nothing else can do.
~**Hankey and Fischer**, 1866 (public domain)

**O for a Thousand Tongues to Sing**
O for a thousand tongues to sing,
My Great Redeemer's praise.
The glories of my God and King,
The triumphs of his grace!
~**Wesley and Glaser**, 1739 (public domain)

## *Personalized Weaponry*

For the last few years before my retirement, I was working in a hospital. The Lord had always made sure I was placed where I could come into contact with the right people. Those who were at least ready for planting the seeds of salvation, or watering and tending or harvesting.

Normally I was out in the public eye, but this season I was in a small, secluded, secured area with up to four women at a time. I was working a late evening shift, ending at 11:00 p.m., which meant the last several hours, as things quieted down, were ideal for some degree of visiting.

We had recently acquired a new employee, a young Hispanic woman named Carrie. She and I just seemed to gel, and a friendship developed, which provided me the great opportunity to share the Gospel with her. Coming from a strong Catholic background, she was hungry for many conversations. As God would have it, none of the other staff members were working with me except Carrie. It was a perfect time and place to talk, with only the two of us and no rushing involved. The circumstances were ideal. There was no one around to interrupt us, and we could still do our work. I had times in the past when I could witness to a person, but it might be brief, and sometimes I couldn't really follow through. But this was one of those golden opportunities, a divine appointment, a holy setup where everything came together beautifully in an ordered space of time.

The Lord enabled me to take my time and answer all her questions, and I joyfully report to you Carrie wholeheartedly received the Lord. Soon afterward, she moved with her family out of state, but on numerous occasions she had told me, "The change in me was permanent and lasting, I thank God he sent me an angel like you to bring me the Good News of his Word. I will forever love you and remember what you taught me." What a joy to share with others the Good News of Yeshua Messiah!

God has specifically ordained us to be alive, programmed it into our DNA, to be here in this hour as witnesses to our generation. The wheels of evangelism, testimonies, and witnessing never stop turning. He never leaves Himself without a witness on the earth.

Come and join us, you workers in His vineyard, intercessors, harvesters, revivalists, sowers, reapers, and gatherers of the sheaves of humanity. Come, you appointed ones, come tread the emblazoned trail of evangelism. Lead the charge. Be radical for God. Be a righteous renegade. Secure the victory!

# Weapon 44

# Laughter

### *Scriptures*

Even in laughter the heart is sorrowful; and the end of that mirth is heaviness.

**Proverbs 14:13**

He who sits in the heavens shall laugh; The Lord shall hold them in derision.

**Psalm 2:4 NKJV**

Rejoice with them that do rejoice, and weep with them that weep.

**Romans 12:15**

A feast is made for laughter, and wine maketh merry: but money answereth all things.

**Ecclesiastes 10:19**

All the days of the afflicted are evil: but he that is of a merry heart hath a continual feast.

**Proverbs 15:15**

This is the day which the Lord hath made; we will rejoice and be glad in it.

**Psalm 118:24**

Then he said unto them, Go your way, eat the fat, and drink the sweet, and send portions unto them for whom nothing is prepared: for this day is holy unto our Lord: neither be ye sorry; for the joy of the Lord is your strength.

**Nehemiah 8:10**

The light of the eyes rejoiceth the heart: and a good report maketh the bones fat.

**Proverbs 15:30**

My brethren count it all joy when ye fall into diverse temptations.

**James 1:2**

Make thy face to shine upon thy servant: save me for thy mercies' sake.

**Psalm 31:16**

If I say, I will forget my complaint, I will leave off my heaviness, and comfort myself.

**Job 9:27**

Finally, brethren, whatsoever things are true, whatsoever things are honest, whatsoever things are just, whatsoever things are pure, whatsoever things are lovely, whatsoever things are of good report; if there be any virtue, and if there be any praise, think on these things.

**Philippians 4:8**

With good will doing service, as to the Lord, and not to men.

**Ephesians 6:7**

Till he fill thy mouth with laughing, and thy lips with rejoicing.

**Job 8:21**

The Lord shall laugh at him: for He seeth that his day is coming.

**Psalm 37:13**

A time to weep, and a time to laugh; a time to mourn, and a time to dance.

**Ecclesiastes 3:4**

Then was our mouth filled with laughter, and our tongue with singing. Then said they among the heathen, The Lord hath done great things for them.

**Psalm 126:2**

And Sarah said, God hath made me to laugh, so that all that hear will laugh with me.

**Genesis 21:6**

A merry heart does good, like medicine, but a broken spirit dries the bones.

**Proverbs 17:22 NKJV**

Strength and honour are her clothing; and she shall rejoice in time to come.

**Proverbs 31:25**

Blessed are ye that hunger now: for ye shall be filled. Blessed are ye that weep now: for ye shall laugh.

**Luke 6:21**

## *Quotes: Laughter*

The Lord loves us and fills us with joy and laughter when we are connected to Him. Laughing is an amazing gift from God. It helps us cope with sadness and everyday life. Laughter releases stress, improves your mood, boosts immunity and can even relieve pain. ~**Unknown**

Even if you are on the right track, you will get run over, if you just sit there. ~**Will Rogers**

Some people seem to go through life standing at the complaint counter. ~**Unknown**

Today, they are making movies that I wouldn't want Trigger to see! ~**Roy Rogers**

God is never late, but He has missed several golden opportunities, to be early. ~**E. V. Hill**

God made women to be outdoors too! They do not know what they are missing, staying cooped up in the house. ~**Annie Oakley**

The reason women don't play football is because eleven of them would not want to be wearing the same outfit in public. ~**Phyllis Diller**

I had way too many kids, my playpen looked like a bus stop for midgets. ~**Phyllis Diller**

I don't have false teeth, do you think I would pay good money for teeth that look like this? ~**Carol Burnett**

Having a baby is like taking your lower lip and pulling it over your head. ~**Carol Burnett**

Doing housework won't kill you, but why take the chance? ~**Phyllis Diller**

The best way to get rid of kitchen odors, just be sure to eat out always. ~**Phyllis Diller**

I couldn't keep up with my laundry, so I buried it in the backyard. ~**Phyllis Diller**

Always laugh when you can; it is cheap medicine. ~**Lord Byron**

As soup is to the body, so laughter is to the soul. ~**Jewish Proverb**

Laughter is an instant vacation. ~**Milton Berle**

Life is much better when you are laughing. ~**Unknown**

There is nothing in the world so irresistibly contagious, as laughter and good humor. ~**Charles Dickens**

Laughter sparkles like a splash of water in sunlight. ~**Unknown**

Hearty laughter is a good way to jog internally without having to go outdoors. ~**Norman Cousins**

Laughter is the most beautiful and beneficial therapy God has ever granted humanity. ~**Chuck Swindoll**

Never go to a doctor whose office plants have died. ~**Erma Bombeck**

My second favorite household chore is ironing. My first is being hit in the head on the top bunk until I faint. ~**Erma Bombeck**

No one ever dies from sleeping in an unmade bed. I have known mothers who make their children's bed after they leave, this is sick. ~**Erma Bombeck**

I picked out the nicest, sturdiest playpen, brought it home, and after the kids had fun playing, I climbed out. ~**Erma Bombeck**

A woman who likes stomping around in the country on a clear frosty morning, with a good gun and a pair of good dogs, knows how to enjoy life. ~**Annie Oakley**

Confidence is going after Moby Dick in a rowboat and taking the tartar sauce with you. ~**Zig Ziglar**

Laughter is America's most important export! ~**Walt Disney**

## *Hymns: Laughter*

**Let a Smile Be Your Umbrella**
Whenever skies are gray,
Don't you worry or fret.
A smile will bring the sunshine,
And you never will get wet.
So let a smile be your umbrella,
On a rainy, rainy day
~**Sammy Fain**, 1927 (public domain)

**Mirth**
With white and crimson laughs the sky,
With birds the hedgerows ring,
To give the praise to God most High
And all the sulky fiends defy,
Is a most joyful laughing thing.
~**Christopher Smart,** 1791 (public domain)

## *Personalized Prayer Weaponry*

We pray for laughter to be as much a part of our daily routine as eating and drinking. It has to become embedded in our very being by practice and choice. To be lighthearted is an acquired gift that will grow musty if not used regularly and with intention. We understand it's contagious. Who hasn't heard a hearty belly laugh coming from someone and become involved in laughing too, over who knows what?

But we say, "I don't have anything to laugh about. My life is one sad heap of heartache and trouble." Maybe this is fact for the moment, but the truth overrides the facts. We can find some small, even insignificant thing to smile about. Laughter can be switched on like a warm and welcoming light in a dark room. Charge the atmosphere of your life with excitement and expectancy, and you can ignite that fuse with laughter. Don't allow anyone to dull your sparkle, sprinkled with resounding laughter. The Lord God Himself invented laughter and bestows it on his creation to ease life's burdens. Make it easier on yourself and others – *or* make it harder.

## WEAPON 45

# Blessing/Favor

### *Scriptures: Blessing*

Every good gift and every perfect gift is from above, and cometh down from the Father of lights, with whom is no variableness, neither shadow of turning.

**JAMES 1:17**

But my God shall supply all your need according to his riches in glory by Christ Jesus.

**PHILIPPIANS 4:19**

Blessed is the man that walketh not in the counsel of the ungodly, nor standeth in the way of sinners, nor sitteth in the seat of the scornful. But his delight is in the law of the Lord; and in his law doth he meditate day and night.

**PSALM 1:1–2**

My God, my rock; in him will I trust. He is my shield, and the horn of my salvation, my high tower, and my refuge, my Saviour; thou savest me from violence.

**2 SAMUEL 22:3**

And God is able to make all grace abound toward you; that ye, always having all sufficiency in all things, may abound to every good work.

**2 CORINTHIANS 9:8**

And God is able to make all grace abound toward you; that ye, always having all sufficiency in all things, may abound to every good work.

**EXODUS 23:25**

The Lord is my shepherd; I shall not want. He maketh me to lie down in green pastures: he leadeth me beside the still waters.

**PSALM 23:1–2**

Blessed are the peacemakers: for they shall be called the children of God.

**MATTHEW 5:9**

Beloved, I wish above all things that thou mayest prosper and be in health, even as thy soul prospereth.

**3 JOHN 1:2**

How joyful is the man whose quiver is full of children! He will not be put to shame when he confronts his accusers at the city gates.

**PSALM 127:5 NLT**

Teach me thy way, O Lord; I will walk in thy truth: unite my heart to fear thy name.

**PSALM 86:11**

But as for you, ye thought evil against me; but God meant it unto good, to bring to pass, as it is this day, to save much people alive.

**Genesis 50:20**

Yea, and if I be offered upon the sacrifice and service of your faith, I joy, and rejoice with you all.

**Philippians 2:17**

A merry heart maketh a cheerful countenance: but by sorrow of the heart the spirit is broken.

**Proverbs 15:13**

## *Quotes: Blessing*

Don't think of things you didn't get after praying, think of the countless blessings God gave you, when you didn't even ask. ~**Unknown**

What seems to us as bitter trials are often blessings in disguise. ~**Oscar Wilde**

Give thanks for the unknown blessings that are already on the way. ~**Native American Proverb**

Don't just count your blessings, be the blessing other people count on. ~**Unknown**

Those blessings are the sweetest that are won in prayer and worn with thanksgiving. ~**Thomas Goodwin**

May we be strengthened with the understanding, that being blessed, does not mean we shall always be spared the difficulties and the disappointments of life. ~**Anonymous**

The reason so many people miss out on their blessings is because they decide to settle for a meager dinner, instead of waiting on the feast God has for them. ~**Tiffany Langford**

Kind words are such a blessing to the needful, if one but knew the pleasures that they bring. ~**Anonymous**

With so much uncertainty in the world, aren't we blessed to have the perfect word of God in our hands, to treasure every day of our lives? ~**Anonymous**

As the chosen favorites of heaven are much forgiven, much delivered, much instructed, much enriched, and much blessed; therefore, as uniquely favored, let us take seriously the slightest sin against our Lord and Master. ~**Charles Spurgeon**

## *Scriptures: Favor*

For his anger lasts only a moment, but his favor lasts a lifetime! Weeping may last through the night, but joy comes with the morning.

**Psalm 30:5 NLT**

May the favor of the Lord our God rest on us; establish the work of our hands for us—yes, establish the work of our hands.

**Psalm 90:17 NIV**

For the Lord God is a sun and shield; the Lord bestows favor and honor; no good thing does he withhold from those whose walk is blameless.

**Psalm 84:11 NIV**

Will the Lord wait, that he may be gracious unto you, and therefore will he be exalted, that he may have mercy upon you: for the Lord is a God of judgment: blessed are all they that wait for him.

**Isaiah 30:18**

Thou hast granted me life and favour, and thy visitation hath preserved my spirit.

**Job 10:12**

Let us therefore come boldly unto the throne of grace, that we may obtain mercy, and find grace to help in time of need.

**Hebrews 4:16**

And Jesus increased in wisdom and stature, and in favour with God and man.

**Luke 2:52**

Good understanding giveth favour: but the way of transgressors is hard.

**Proverbs 13:15**

Who hath saved us, and called us with an holy calling, not according to our works, but according to his own purpose and grace, which was given us in Christ Jesus before the world began.

**2 Timothy 1:9**

So shalt thou find favour and good understanding in the sight of God and man.

**Proverbs 3:4**

Who found favour before God, and desired to find a tabernacle for the God of Jacob.

**Acts 7:46**

The Lord make his face shine upon thee and be gracious unto thee.

**Numbers 6:25**

For thou art the glory of their strength: and in thy favour our horn shall be exalted.

**Psalm 89:17**

Blessed be the God and Father of our Lord Jesus Christ, who hath blessed us with all spiritual blessings in heavenly places in Christ.

**Ephesians 1:3**

And Mizpah; for he said, The Lord watch between me and thee, when we are absent one from another.

**Genesis 31:49**

## *Quotes: Favor*

The favor of God has nothing to do with luck or chance, it is the well thought-out plans of our Loving Benefactor. ~**Anonymous**

I have the supernatural favor of God working in my life; it is incomprehensible, just waiting to be revealed and unveiled. ~**Anonymous**

God is working behind the scenes, arranging and rearranging things in your favor. He is making a way where there seemed to be no way! ~**Unknown**

What a great favor God does to those He places in the company of good people. ~**Saint Theresa**

May your future be saturated with God's favor, as you give up those things that are holding you back and rise to the destiny that He has for you. ~**John Hagee**

Just one touch of God's favor can put you twenty miles down the road. ~**Joel Osteen**

No hater can stop God's favor, God will give them VIP seats to watch, as He enlarges your territory. ~**Unknown**

There is absolutely nothing you can do to save yourself or to earn God's favor. ~**Francis Chan**

Memories of our lives, of our works and our deeds, will continue on in others. ~**Rosa Parks**

We are the most blessed generation to ever live on this planet. God has poured out on us more revelation than any other before us. ~**Charles Capps**

## *Hymns: Blessing/Favor*

**There Shall Be Showers of Blessings**
There shall be showers of blessing,
This is the promise of life.
There shall be seasons refreshing,
Sent from the Savior above.
Showers of blessings we need,
Mercy drops around us are falling,
But for the showers we plead.
~**Daniel Whittle**, 1883 (public domain)

**He Hideth My Soul**
He hides our soul in the cleft of the rock
That shadows a dry, thirsty land
He hides our life in the depths of his love,
And covers us there with his hand
and covers us there with his hand.
~**Fanny Crosby**, 1890 (public domain)

## *Personalized Weaponry*

John Brandon, my firstborn son, was expected to make his arrival in September 1965 but came two days earlier. I was a young mom of twenty, with no experience at all, and I had no help or motherly advice. When my water broke several days before my due date, I immediately went to the hospital and was told, "Not yet, go home." This was *bad* advice!

Three days later, labor started, and I endured hours of what I would later be told was a dry birth, which can be extremely dangerous. None of the pain meds were working successfully, so thankfully, after nine hours, I delivered my healthy, beautiful son.

Less than four months later, before he was able to receive the appropriate vaccination, he came down with a bad case of the measles. His temp was soaring, and he was covered with a raging rash and showing signs of dehydration and lethargy as we rushed him to the ER. The protection of the Lord spared my son! The blessing of his life has been enormous: he taught me about motherhood as we grew up together, and he was the first little person to call me by that treasured name—Mother.

His agreeable and pliable disposition would follow him into adulthood. I was always amazed by how he never touched an open candy dish and how he thrilled his grandpa by quoting the "Pledge of Allegiance" at two. Little man, mature beyond his years. He was my good-natured little sidekick through all the endless short tours when his dad was gone, and to this day, he's a stable, solid man of God, full of love and loyalty. Over the years, he's been a pillar of strength, plowing through times of adversity like a champ. Yet a genuine tenderheartedness would shine through the lionhearted persona. Children surely are a blessing from the Lord and a mighty inheritance. "My righteous seed shall inherit the earth and shall possess the gates of the enemy."

Brandon's name means "a beacon of light, sent by God," and he has always been an unfaltering example of solid character to his siblings, who are eight and ten years younger. He is laden with a quiet, gentle strength that assisted him in a determined way to work his way through college. He willingly supported us during those lean years, proving what we were all made of. Even as a youngster, his neatness was surprising, and his well-mannered and teachable spirit was evident, not to mention his love of the outdoors and athletics. Both my sons are avid fisherman and love a good cookout. All my children are business savvy, adventurous, and willing to help others, not to mention polite, respectful, and friendly. I am thoroughly proud of each individual one and the express blessing and contribution they are to my life and to each other's.

My children seem to share some of the same gifts and callings, yet each is distinctly imprinted with undeniable and irreplaceable characteristics that have brought enrichment and abundant love to our family unit.

## WEAPON 46

# Honor/Respect

### *Scriptures*

And every creature which is in heaven, and on the earth, and under the earth, and such as are in the sea, and all that are in them, heard I saying, Blessing, and honour, and glory, and power, be unto him that sitteth upon the throne, and unto the Lamb for ever and ever.

**REVELATION 5:13**

Whoever offers praise glorifies Me; And to him who orders his conduct aright I will show the salvation of God.

**PSALM 50:23 NKJV**

Honour the Lord with thy substance, and with the firstfruits of all thine increase.

**PROVERBS 3:9**

Whoever oppresses the poor shows contempt for their Maker, but whoever is kind to the needy honors God.

**PROVERBS 14:31 NIV**

So that all will give honor to the Son just as they give honor to the Father. The one who does not honor the Son does not honor the Father who has sent Him.

**John 5:23 AMP**

Honour thy father and thy mother: that thy days may be long upon the land which the Lord thy God giveth thee.

**Exodus 20:12**

Be kindly affectioned one to another with brotherly love; in honour preferring one another.

**Romans 12:10**

Let the elders that rule well be counted worthy of double honour, especially they who labour in the word and doctrine.

**1 Timothy 5:17**

Let nothing be done through strife or vainglory; but in lowliness of mind let each esteem other better than themselves.

**Philippians 2:3**

What? Know ye not that your body is the temple of the Holy Ghost which is in you, which ye have of God, and ye are not your own? For ye are bought with a price; therefore, glorify God in your body, and in your spirit, which are God's.

**1 Corinthians 6:19–20**

And you shall proclaim on the same day that it is a holy convocation to you. You shall do no customary work on it. It shall be a statute forever in all your dwellings throughout your generations. When you reap the harvest of your land, you shall not wholly reap the corners of your field when you reap, nor shall you gather any gleaning from your harvest.

You shall leave them for the poor and for the stranger: I am the Lord your God.

**Leviticus 23:21–22 NKJV**

Honour all men. Love the brotherhood. Fear God. Honour the king.

**1 Peter 2:17**

Nevertheless, let every one of you in particular so love his wife even as himself; and the wife see that she reverence her husband.

**Ephesians 5:33**

Children obey your parents in all things: for this is well pleasing unto the Lord.

**Colossians 3:20**

And, ye fathers, provoke not your children to wrath: but bring them up in the nurture and admonition of the Lord.

**Ephesians 6:4**

## *Quotes: Honor/Respect*

You will never do anything in this world without courage, it is the greatest quality of the mind, next to honor. ~**Aristotle**

Every good citizen makes his country's honor his own and cherishes it not as precious but as sacred. ~**Andrew Jackson**

We treat our people like royalty, if you honor and serve those who work for you, they will honor and serve you. ~**Mary Kay Ash**

America's honor is at stake, go out and preserve the greatest country in the history of the world. ~**Rick Santorum**

No person was ever honored for what he received, honor has been the reward for what he gave. ~**Calvin Coolidge**

Man's greatest honor and privilege is to do the will of God. ~**Unknown**

Listen to your elders' advice, not because they are always right, but because they have more experience at being wrong. ~**Unknown**

Never throw mud. You may miss the mark and you'll have really dirty hands. ~**Joseph Parker**

Everyone should be respected as an individual, but no one idolized. ~**Albert Einstein**

There is always the danger of doing the work for work's sake. This is where respect, love and devotion come in, we work as to the Lord; therefore, as beautifully as we can! ~**Mother Teresa**

One of the most sincere forms of respect is actually listening to what other people have to say. ~**Bryant McGill**

Respect is a wealth you can lavishly spend on others. ~**Bryant McGill**

I always prefer to believe and expect the best of everybody, it saves me so much time and trouble. ~**Rudyard Kipling**

Treat other people exactly as you want to be treated by them. ~**The Golden Rule**

Respect for ourselves guides our morals; respect for others, guides our manners. ~**Laurence Sterne**

## *Hymns: Honor/Respect*

**Come In, Thou Blessed, Honored Lord**
Come in, Thou blessed, honored Lord!
By earth, by Heaven, by all, adored!
We hail Thee welcome!
Take Thy throne and
in Thy Zion reign alone.
~**Joseph Proud**, 1690 (public domain)

**Immortal, Invisible, God Only Wise**
Immortal, invisible, God only wise,
In light inaccessible hid from our eyes.
Most blessed, most glorious,
the Ancient of Days
Almighty, victorious,
Thy great name we praise!
~**Walter Smith**, 1876 (public domain)

## *Personalized Prayer Weaponry*

Today, Lord, we seek to, first and foremost, honor and respect Your Holy Name, Your Holy Word, and Your Holy Blood. This constitutes the whole of Your being. You are truly the apex of all reality, and we earnestly desire that reality above all else.

Remind us often that You are the forever and always Promise Keeper, and we need not wonder exactly what promises You have made. We simply scour and devour Your Word, for there, the promises are available for us at any moment of the day or night.

As we honor and respect You, our lives will reflect that same momentum toward others, and especially those of the household of faith. Cause us to rejoice in the truth that You are energizing us and creating not only the power but the desire to bring You delight. May the cloud by day and the pillar of fire by night eternally settle over us.

Like that eternal flame, may our love, honor, and respect grow to heights never before experienced as we serve You and others. Let our honor know no bounds nor boundaries but be thrust ever upward to the very gates of glory.

# Weapon 47

# Israel

## *Scriptures*

Pray for the peace of Jerusalem: they shall prosper that love thee.

**Psalm 122:6**

And give him no rest, till he establish, and till he make Jerusalem a praise in the earth.

**Isaiah 62:7**

Thou shalt arise and have mercy upon Zion: for the time to favour her, yea, the set time, is come.

**Psalm 102:13**

For Zion's sake will I not hold my peace, and for Jerusalem's sake I will not rest, until the righteousness thereof go forth as brightness, and the salvation thereof as a lamp that burneth.

**Isaiah 62:1**

As the mountains are round about Jerusalem, so the Lord is round about his people from henceforth even forever.

**Psalm 125:2**

I will bless those who bless you, and whoever curses you I will curse; and all peoples on earth will be blessed through you.

**Genesis 12:3 NIV**

I have set watchmen upon thy walls, O Jerusalem, which shall never hold their peace day nor night: ye that make mention of the Lord, keep not silence.

**Isaiah 62:6**

And I John saw the holy city, new Jerusalem, coming down from God out of heaven, prepared as a bride adorned for her husband.

**Revelation 21:2**

God himself is in Jerusalem's towers, revealing himself as its defender.

**Psalm 48:3 NLT**

Nor by the earth; for it is his footstool: neither by Jerusalem; for it is the city of the great King.

**Matthew 5:35**

## *Quotes: Israel*

God's divine presence dwells where Christ was crucified and resurrected. Where the Gospel spread to the whole world and where his blessed feet will touch the Mount of Olives when He returns again. ~**Day Star**

Israel was not created in order to disappear. Israel will endure and flourish, a child of hope and a home of great people, not to be broken by adversity or demoralized by success. ~**John F. Kennedy**

The most formidable and remarkable race, which has ever appeared on the earth, are the Jews. ~**Winston Churchill**

I will insist that the Hebrews have contributed more to civilized man than any other nation. ~**John Adams**

I had faith in Israel before it was established. I have it now. I believe it has a glorious future before it, not just another sovereign nation, but as an embodiment of great ideals of our civilization. ~**Harry Truman**

Jerusalem is a port city on the shores of eternity.
~**Yehuda Amichai**

Israel is the gateway to marked blessings, embedded in the fabric of God. ~**Anonymous**

Israel is a land of stability and democracy, in a region of tyranny and unrest. ~**Ronald Reagan**

Jerusalem, eternal Holy City of The Great King, postured as a diamond on the velvet couch of earth, the forever lasting nation, nurtured by the Strength of Israel. ~**Anonymous**

The stones of Jerusalem are saturated with holiness, with the blood of Jesus, with the tears of those who pray for the salvation of Israel. The link to Jerusalem is a spiritual connection that cannot be created anywhere else in the world. The Holy City, where the first temple stood, where Christ himself shall return, one glorious day. ~**Anonymous**

History has shown us time and again that what is right is not what is popular. ~**Benjamin Netanyahu**

Peace is purchased from strength. It is not purchased from weakness or unilateral retreat. ~**Benjamin Netanyahu**

The Jews take precedence among the races and are the first to be waited on at the God feast. ~ **Charles Spurgeon**

Jesus would have us entertain a deep regard for that nation, that God chose of old and out of which Christ came. He puts those first who knew Him first. ~**Charles Spurgeon**

May it be pleasing in your eyes, to bless your people Israel, at every season, every hour with your peace. ~**Shalom Rab** (traditional prayer)

## *Hymns: Israel*

**The Holy City**
Last night I lay asleeping,
there came a dream so fair,
I stood at old Jerusalem,
beside the temple there.
I heard the children singing
and ever as they sang,
I thought the voice of angels
from heaven in answer rang.
Jerusalem! Jerusalem,
lift up your gates and sing,
Hosanna in the highest,
Hosanna to the King!
~**Weatherly and Maybrick**, 1892 (public domain)

**Israel, Israel, God is Calling**
Israel, Israel, God is calling,
Calling thee from lands of woe,
Babylon the great is falling;
God shall all her towers overthrow,
Come to Zion, come to Zion,
And within her walls rejoice.
~**Richard Smyth**, 1914 (public domain)

## *Personalized Weaponry*

Just the other day, I was trying to remember when Father God Jehovah grafted Israel into my heart. In my younger years, I was taught nothing about Jerusalem—or Israel, for that matter. Gradually, line upon line, precept upon precept, I began hearing and absorbing solid, scriptural teaching on the Jewish people and the "Glorious Land."

It had never dawned on me back then that all the disciples except Luke were Jewish. Joseph, Mary, and Christ Himself were 100 percent Jewish. How did this tiny country no bigger than the state of New Jersey and her original, covenant, and ancient people affect me in the here and now? They had great impact on me, whether I realized it or not.

Jehovah himself called Israel his Son and placed His name on Jerusalem as the Holy, Eternal City. From satellite imagery, the mountains surrounding the city, reveal God has engraved His name, "YHVH," in 3D on the hills. It's carved out by the valleys north of the city and in two places, Shiloh and Jerusalem. On top of Mount Moriah, He has etched the first letter of his sacred name, "YOD." His love for this small piece of real estate is formidable, and scholars have often referred to Jerusalem as the navel of the earth.

**Warning:** I should interject that if you are anti-Semitic or a hater of the Jews, you are on thin ice with Yahweh, and do not call yourself a Christian. God's Word has much to say about the subject, and the bottom line is: blessing or cursing. Consider what the Lord said to Abraham, the Jewish patriarch, in Genesis 12:2–3 NIV: "I will make you into a great nation, and I will bless you; I will make your name great, and you will be a blessing. I will bless those who bless you, and whoever curses you I will curse; and all peoples on earth will be blessed through you."

If you desire to see your life expand exponentially, both spiritually and naturally, begin to actively look for ways to bless Israel and her people. Search for groups or ministries who help in tangible ways to bring relief and happiness to her residents. Pray for the peace of Jerusalem daily, and unprecedented blessing and favor will flow your direction. The smiles of heaven will search you out and chase you down!

"I have installed my king on Zion, my holy mountain" (Psalm 2:6 NIV).

"The singers as well as the players of flutes will say, 'All my springs and sources of joy are in you [Jerusalem, City of God]'" (Psalm 87:7 AMP).

"Glorious things are said of you, City of God" (Psalm 87:3 NIV).

It is time for the restoration of all things!

**Warning:** The church has *not* replaced the nation of Israel. Replacement Theology is not endorsed by the Lord; in fact, quite the contrary, it is a heretical teaching that has infiltrated the modern-day church. It will bring repercussions, both on a people, a nation, individuals, or a practicing church body.

## Weapon 48

# America/Patriotism

### *Scriptures*

But ye are a chosen generation, a royal priesthood, a holy nation, a peculiar people; that ye should shew forth the praises of him who hath called you out of darkness into his marvelous light.

**1 Peter 2:9**

Now the Lord is that Spirit: and where the Spirit of the Lord is, there is liberty.

**2 Corinthians 3:17**

I will run the way of thy commandments, when thou shalt enlarge my heart.

**Psalm 119:32**

In my distress I prayed to the LORD, and the LORD answered me and set me free.

**Psalm 118:5 NLT**

Stand fast therefore in the liberty wherewith Christ hath made us free, and be not entangled again with the yoke of bondage.

**GALATIANS 5:1**

And I will walk at liberty: for I seek thy precepts.

**PSALM 119:45**

In whom we have boldness and access with confidence by the faith of him.

**EPHESIANS 3:12**

If my people, which are called by my name, shall humble themselves, and pray, and seek my face, and turn from their wicked ways; then will I hear from heaven, and will forgive their sin, and will heal their land.

**2 CHRONICLES 7:14**

Blessed is the nation whose God is the Lord; and the people whom he hath chosen for his own inheritance.

**PSALM 33:12**

The king's heart is in the hand of the Lord, as the rivers of water: he turneth it whithersoever he will.

**PROVERBS 21:1**

I exhort therefore, that first of all, supplications, prayers, intercessions, and giving of thanks, be made for all men; For kings, and for all that are in authority; that we may lead a quiet and peaceable life in all godliness and honesty.

**1 TIMOTHY 2:1–2**

By the blessing of the upright the city is exalted: but it is overthrown by the mouth of the wicked.

**Proverbs 11:11**

For promotion cometh neither from the east, nor from the west, nor from the south.

**Psalm 75:6**

When the Son of man shall come in his glory, and all the holy angels with him, then shall he sit upon the throne of his glory.

**Matthew 25:31**

Woe unto them that call evil good, and good evil; that put darkness for light, and light for darkness; that put bitter for sweet, and sweet for bitter.

**Isaiah 5:20**

And because iniquity shall abound, the love of many shall wax cold.

**Matthew 24:12**

There is a generation that are pure in their own eyes, and yet is not washed from their filthiness.

**Proverbs 30:12**

## *Quotes: America/Patriotism*

My dream is of a place and a time, when America will once again be seen as, the last best hope on the earth. ~**Abraham Lincoln**

If we ever forget that we are One Nation Under God, then we will be a nation gone under. ~**Ronald Reagan**

There is a famine in America. Not a famine of food but of love, truth and the word of God. ~**Mother Teresa**

One flag, one land, one heart, one hand, one nation evermore. ~**Oliver Wendell Holmes, Sr.**

America is the greatest forge for good in the history of the world. ~**John McCain**

The great tragedy in America, is not the destruction of our national resources, but the failure to utilize our Human Resources. Most men and women go to their graves with their music still in them. ~**Oliver Wendell Holmes, Sr.**

My countrymen, we hold a rich deposit in trust for ourselves and for all mankind. It is the fire of liberty. If it becomes extinguished, our darkened land will cast a mournful shadow over the nations. If it lives, its blaze will enlighten and gladden the whole earth. ~**Francis Scott Key**

Patriotism is supporting your country at all times and your government when it deserves it. ~**Mark Twain**

No president or politician can fix America. The only way the USA can be fixed is, if the American people fix themselves spiritually. Repent, turn, trust and obey God, not man! ~**Unknown**

I do not believe there is a problem in this country or the world today, which could not be settled, if approached through the teaching of the sermon on the Mount. ~**Harry S. Truman**

Intelligence, patriotism, Christianity and a firm reliance on Him who has never yet forsaken this favored land, are still competent to adjust in the best way, all our present difficulties. ~**Abraham Lincoln**

America is the first culture in jeopardy of amusing itself to death. ~**John Piper**

A nation that turns away from prayer, will ultimately find itself, in desperate need of it. ~**Jonathan Cahn**

America will never be destroyed from outside, if we falter and lose our freedom, it will be because we destroyed ourselves. ~**Abraham Lincoln**

The reason America is a special nation is because it was founded by people, who were first on their knees, before they were on their feet. We are a nation rooted in faith. ~**Mike Huckabee**

I always carry a small American flag with me when I travel out of the country so people will know I am from America. ~**George Foreman**

This is our land, our heritage and with God's help, we shall reclaim this nation for Christ. No power on earth can stop us. ~**D. James Kennedy**

Pray for inspiration, repentance, revival and restoration for America. May the quickenings, the outpourings, the stirrings, the awakenings of yesteryear find a mighty culmination of eruption in the Holy Spirit's fire. May they sweep multitudes into the kingdom of God. The clarion call goes out, awake, oh, sleeper the harvest is ripe. May the church be a healing force to change our nation. ~**Anonymous**

Once we roared like lions for liberty. Now we bleat like sheep for security. The solution for America is not government but men whom God controls. ~**Norman Vincent Peale**

America is too young to die, she needs to fulfill her God-given ordained assignment. ~**Lance Wallnau**

God has reset the clock for the church to take back territory. ~**Lance Wallnau**

Do not let us squander our Christian heritage. ~**Lance Wallnau**

Then, in that hour of deliverance, my heart spoke, does not such a country as America, and such defenders of this country, deserve a wondrous song? ~**Francis Scott Key**

I tremble for my country, when I reflect that God is just, that his justice cannot sleep forever. ~**Thomas Jefferson**

## *Hymns: America/Patriotism*

**My Country, 'Tis of Thee**
Our Father's God, to Thee,
Author of liberty,
To Thee we sing.
Long may our land be bright,
With freedom's holy light.
Protect us by Thy might,
Great God, our King!
~**Samuel F. Smith**, 1832 (public domain)

**Battle Hymn of the Republic**
Mine eyes have seen the glory
of the coming of the Lord.
He is trampling out the vintage
where the grapes of wrath are stored.
He has loosed the fateful lightning
of His terrible swift sword.
His truth is marching on.
~**Julia Ward Howe**, 1862 (public domain)

**Great God of Nations**
Great God of nations, now to Thee,
Our hymn of gratitude we raise;
With humble hearts and bending knee,
We offer Thee our song of praise.
Thy name we bless, Almighty God,
For all the kindness Thou hast shown.
To this fair land the Pilgrims trod,
This land we fondly call our own.
~**Woodhull and Greatorex**, 1829 (public domain)

## *Personalized Weaponry*

A few years ago, I came across a definition of the name "America" that made me stop and think. "Lovable," endearing, deserving of love. Wow, with all the current rivers of crime, hatred, dishonor, murder, corruption, vileness, and the fast unraveling of our homeland, I wanted to further investigate this and other meanings.

Research revealed a plethora of information and descriptions. "The land beyond the sunset, rich in gold, the land of strong wind, the fountainhead of life and movement, place of master workmen, the kingdom of heaven on earth."

The early Puritans and Pilgrims believed that the New World was formed by the Hand of God. They considered it a perfectly selected land where religious freedom could be found and propagated. We have been a country full of a giving nature when disaster strikes. Eighty percent of all missionary outreach comes from America. Israel and America are the only two landmasses destined purposefully to fulfill God's covenant plans. Yet America has become sick and putrid to the core and has experienced a great fall.

As a native-born daughter of the republic, I love my country, even though she is swimming in sin and beset by enemies from within and without. My duty is to pray for God's intervention to stop her hemorrhaging and collapsing, to continue the brief reprieve that God's mercy is extending. I pray for the summoning of the true remnant Christians to stand strong, not stand down. Our heritage is replete with unspeakable bravery, staggering fortitude, and undeniable resolve. Take hold of the victory torch and *run*!

Sovereign God, grant us a continued window of opportunity, even for a short time, to become appreciative of Your great love and longsuffering. Cleanse our land and bring in a mighty harvest of souls, as a reward for Your suffering.

## WEAPON 49

# Rest/Meditation

### *Scripture*

Be still and know that I am God: I will be exalted among the heathen, I will be exalted in the earth.

**PSALM 46:10**

He that dwelleth in the secret place of the Most High shall abide under the shadow of the Almighty.

**PSALM 91:1**

Return unto thy rest, O my soul; for the Lord hath dealt bountifully with thee.

**PSALM 116:7**

Thus saith the Lord, Stand ye in the ways, and see, and ask for the old paths, where is the good way, and walk therein, and ye shall find rest for your souls. But they said, We will not walk therein.

**JEREMIAH 6:16**

Thou wilt keep him in perfect peace, whose mind is stayed on thee: because he trusteth in thee.

**Isaiah 26:3**

When thou liest down, thou shalt not be afraid: yea, thou shalt lie down, and thy sleep shall be sweet.

**Proverbs 3:24**

But now the Lord my God hath given me rest on every side, so that there is neither adversary nor evil occurrent.

**1 Kings 5:4**

And God blessed the seventh day and sanctified it: because that in it he had rested from all his work.

**Genesis 2:3**

Remember the sabbath day, to keep it holy. which God created and made.

**Exodus 20:8**

Come unto me, all ye that labour and are heavy laden, and I will give you rest.

**Matthew 11:28**

And I said, Oh, that I had wings like a dove! for then would I fly away and be at rest.

**Psalm 55:6**

I will both lay me down in peace, and sleep: for thou, Lord, only makest me dwell in safety.

**Psalm 4:8**

There remains, then, a Sabbath-rest for the people of God; for anyone who enters God's rest also rests from their works, just as God did from his. Let us, therefore, make every effort to enter that rest, so that no one will perish by following their example of disobedience.

**Hebrews 4:9–11 NIV**

Truly my soul waiteth upon God: from him cometh my salvation. He only is my rock and my salvation; he is my defense; I shall not be greatly moved.

**Psalm 62:1–2**

Let the words of my mouth, and the meditation of my heart, be acceptable in thy sight, O Lord, my strength, and my redeemer.

**Psalm 19:14**

Blessed is the man that walketh not in the counsel of the ungodly, nor standeth in the way of sinners, nor sitteth in the seat of the scornful. But his delight is in the law of the Lord; and in his law doth he meditate day and night.
And he shall be like a tree planted by the rivers of water, that bringeth forth his fruit in his season; his leaf also shall not wither; and whatsoever he doeth shall prosper.

**Psalm 1:1–3**

My meditation of him shall be sweet: I will be glad in the Lord.

**Psalm 104:34**

I have set the Lord always before me: because he is at my right hand, I shall not be moved.

**Psalm 16:8**

When I remember thee upon my bed and meditate on thee in the night watches.

**Psalm 63:6**

I will speak of the glorious honour of thy majesty, and of thy wondrous works.

**Psalm 145:5**

Thy word have I hid in mine heart, that I might not sin against thee.

**Psalm 119:11**

And Isaac went out to meditate in the field at the eventide: and he lifted up his eyes, and saw, and, behold, the camels were coming.

**Genesis 24:63**

This book of the law shall not depart out of thy mouth; but thou shalt meditate therein day and night, that thou mayest observe to do according to all that is written therein: for then thou shalt make thy way prosperous, and then thou shalt have good success.

**Joshua 1:8**

You will keep him in perfect peace, whose mind is stayed on You, because he trusts in You.

**Isaiah 26:3 NKJV**

Meditate upon these things; give thyself wholly to them; that thy profiting may appear to all.

**1 Timothy 4:15**

I call to remembrance my song in the night: I commune with mine own heart: and my spirit made diligent search.

**Psalm 77:6**

In addition to the Scriptures above, I will speak Psalm 91 over myself and my loved ones. I will read and meditate this wonderful scripture of covenant protection daily.

## *Quotes: Rest/Meditation*

Rest and be thankful. ~**William Wadsworth**

Take rest; a field that has rested gives a bountiful crop. ~**Anonymous**

You have permission to rest. You are not responsible for fixing everything that is broken. You do not have to try to make everyone happy. For now, take time for you, it's time to replenish. ~**Anonymous**

Rest time is not waste time, it is economy to get a fresh strength, it is wisdom to take an occasional furlough. In the long run, we shall do more by doing less. ~**Charles Spurgeon**

The bosom of God's love is even a sweeter resting place, than even the rock of His promises. ~**Hannah Whitall Smith**

You have made us for yourself, oh Lord, and our heart is restless until it rests in You. ~**Saint Augustine**

Let us start by taking a smallish nap or two. ~**Winnie the Pooh**

Rest is a weapon given to us by God, the enemy hates it because he wants you stressed and occupied. ~**Unknown**

If you have no time to rest, it's exactly the right time. ~**Mark Twain**

In these times, God's people must trust Him for rest of body and soul. ~**Dave Wilkerson**

How sweet is rest after fatigue! How sweet Heaven will be when our journeys have all ended. ~**George Whitefield**

Water rests only when it gets to the lowest place, and so do men hence, be lowly. ~**Henry Drummond**

Were our spirits hearty, we would be able to meet the most disturbing situation with peace and rest. ~**Watchman Nee**

In His time, God gives us rest from every test. ~**Woodrow Kroll**

The reason we come away so cold from reading the Word is; because we do not warm ourselves at the fire of meditation. ~**Thomas Watson**

When we find a man meditating on the words of God, my friends, that man is full of boldness and success. ~**Dwight L. Moody**

Meditation is rehearsing God's words over and over in our minds, searching for their hidden treasures to feed our souls. ~**Unknown**

In the inner stillness, where meditation leads, the Spirit securely anoints the soul and heals our deepest wounds. ~**Saint John**

Biblical meditation is the powerful practice of pondering, personalizing and practicing scripture. ~**Robert J. Morgan**

The sweet spices of divine works must be beaten into powder by meditation and laid up in the cabinets of our memories. ~**Abraham Wright**

Meditation is a lost art today and Christians suffer grievously from the ignorance of this practice. It is an activity of holy thought, consciously performed in the presence of God, under the eye of God, by the help of God, as a means of communing with God. ~**J. I. Packer**

By nature, our brains choose to scroll worthless graffiti, but meditation colors and fills our minds with masterpieces. ~**Robert J. Morgan**

Biblical meditation has a way of turning our attention from our problems that we are facing, to the face of God we serve. ~**Robert J. Morgan**

The more you read the Bible and the more you meditate on it, the more you will be astonished by it. ~**Charles Spurgeon**

The Hebrew word for meditate means to be intense in the mind. Meditation without reading is wrong and bound to err, reading without meditation is barren and fruitless. ~**Thomas Watson**

We live in a world starved for solitude, silence and privacy; and, therefore, starved for meditation and true friendship. ~**C. S. Lewis**

## *Hymns: Rest/Meditation*

**Near to the Heart of God**
There is a place of quiet rest,
Near to the heart of God.
A place where sin cannot molest,
Near to the heart of God.
Oh Jesus, blest Redeemer,
Sent from the heart of God,
Hold us who wait before Thee,
Near to the heart of God.
~**Cleland McAfee**, 1903 (public domain)

**How Sweet Is My Rest**
How sweet is the comfort and rest of my soul,
Where peace doth so tranquilly flow.
Though storm-cloud and tempest and dark billows roll,
All my heart with his sunlight doth glow.
How sweet is my rest, how richly I'm blessed!
Oh, how sweet is the rest of my soul!
~**Barney Warren**, 1893 (public domain)

**Alone with Jesus**
Alone with Jesus, oh, how sweet,
The seasons spent low at his feet.
In humble, fervent, secret prayer,
My soul will ever be feasting there.
There, I drink with my Savior
Of the joy that never ends.
~**Charles Naylor**, 1900 (public domain)

## *Personalized Prayer Weaponry*

Rest in the assurance that God's everlasting strength will be your support and sustenance. When you feel zapped and drained, your triune being is telling you to pull away and rest. The blessedness of listening to the voice of wisdom when your world is swirling is incalculable. Coming back from the front lines is not only necessary but demanded for further development of excellence. There will be time for turbo-power, violent prayer and possessing the gates of the enemy, but for now, it's time to dream the dreams of God. Let the Scripture glow with the splendor of revelation, as the Holy Spirit calls you away for deeper, more intimate communion with Him. Help us, Lord, to choose the better thing that will never be taken from us. Let us meditate on the five great mysteries: Father, Son, Holy Spirit, Creation, and Redemption!

## Weapon 50

# Signs/Wonders/Miracles

### *Scriptures*

God also bearing them witness, both with signs and wonders, and with diverse miracles, and gifts of the Holy Ghost, according to his own will?

**Hebrews 2:4**

Remember his marvelous works that he hath done, his wonders, and the judgments of his mouth.

**1 Chronicles 16:12**

Which doeth great things and unsearchable; marvelous things without number.

**Job 5:9**

Thou art the God that doest wonders: thou hast declared thy strength among the people.

**Psalm 77:14**

How great are his signs! and how mighty are his wonders! his kingdom is an everlasting kingdom, and his dominion is from generation to generation.

**Daniel 4:3**

By stretching forth thine hand to heal; and that signs and wonders may be done by the name of thy holy child Jesus.

**Acts 4:30**

Call unto me, and I will answer thee, and show thee great and mighty things, which thou knowest not.

**Jeremiah 33:3**

This beginning of miracles did Jesus in Cana of Galilee and manifested forth his glory; and his disciples believed on him.

**John 2:11**

Truly the signs of an apostle were wrought among you in all patience, in signs, and wonders, and mighty deeds.

**2 Corinthians 12:12**

Beloved, believe not every spirit, but try the spirits whether they are of God: because many false prophets are gone out into the world.

**1 John 4:1**

Behold, I and the children whom the Lord hath given me are for signs and for wonders in Israel from the Lord of hosts, which dwelleth in mount Zion.

**Isaiah 8:18**

And the spirit of the Lord shall rest upon him, the spirit of wisdom and understanding, the spirit of counsel and might, the spirit of knowledge and of the fear of the Lord.

**Isaiah 11:2**

## *Quotes: Signs/Wonders/Miracles*

God has written you into the storyline of faith heroes and it is of epic and triumphant proportions, filled with miracles, battles, signs and wonders. ~**Lisa Bevere**

If you don't believe in miracles, perhaps you have forgotten you are one! ~**Unknown**

Is not the Gospel its own sign and wonder? Is it not the miracle of miracles, that God gave his only begotten son, that whosoever believes in Him shall not perish? ~**Charles Spurgeon**

Life is full of wonders, but you can't have rainbows without rain, lightning and thunder. ~**Anonymous**

Let anyone laugh and taunt if he so wishes, I am not keeping silent nor am I hiding the signs and the wonders that were shown to me by my Lord. ~**Saint Patrick**

How quickly we forget God's great deliverances in our life, how easily we take for granted the miracles He has performed in our past. ~**Dave Wilkerson**

We live on the blue planet that circles around a ball of fire next to a moon that moves the sea and you don't believe in miracles? ~**Unknown**

You haven't fully preached the Gospel of Christ if you haven't done it with signs, wonders and miracles like Paul and Jesus. ~**Todd Bentley**

God moves in mysterious ways, His wonders to perform. He plants his footsteps in the sea and rides upon the storm! ~**William Cowper**

God has always worked wonders through His prophets, to increase the faith of his chosen people, or to correct their disobedience. ~**Mother Angelica**

Miracles come in moments, be ready and willing. ~**Wayne Dyer**

A grateful heart is a magnet for miracles. ~**William Hazlitt**

## *Hymn: Signs/Wonders/Miracles*

**O Render Thanks and Bless the Lord**
O render thanks and bless the Lord,
Invoke his sacred name.
Acquaint the nations with his deeds,
His great and matchless deeds proclaim;
His wondrous works in hymns rehearse,
Make them the subject of your verse.
~**Tate and Brady**, 1754 (public domain)

## *Personalized Weaponry*

It was a spring day, a Sunday to be precise, almost seventeen years ago. I know because my oldest granddaughter was due in May. My family as well as the congregation, gathered in a junior high auditorium, as our church, at the time, was looking for a larger, more permanent facility.

With a normal service proceeding, and with no warning, I was thrust into an "open vision," which means with my eyes wide open I was immediately in another dimension. All senses were active but focused on what was before me and not on the service around me.

The atmosphere was dry, a desert place to be sure, with a gentle breeze cooling the arid land. I was distinctly aware; all my senses were more active and enhanced than normal. Looking around, I recognized the Tabernacle in the Wilderness, with white pieces of cloth gently moving back and forth as if dancing to an unheard, melodious song.

My feet were strangely warmed by the sand between my toes, and there was a hushed silence. There was definitely a large crowd standing quietly outside the tent of meeting, waiting for what, I did not know.

Without conversation or direction, certain people began walking toward the opening, and I was among the throng. I proceeded past the various outer court pieces toward curtains that opened to reveal the Holy Place. At that point, never stopping to relish the beauty of that divine place, I proceeded to boldly walk into the Holy of Holies, where the Ark of the Covenant slowly opened up from the center outward like a jewelry box, and stairs radiating with Shekinah glory beckoned me to climb them. Then, instantly, it was all gone. I had seen a glimpse of the Glory, and what a wonder it was! What were all the implications? I still don't know but portions have been revealed from time to time along the journey.

## WEAPON 51

# Rapture/Second Coming

### *Scriptures*

And if I go and prepare a place for you, I will come again, and receive you unto myself; that where I am, there ye may be also.

**JOHN 14:3**

But of that day and that hour knoweth no man, no, not the angels which are in heaven, neither the Son, but the Father.

**MARK 13:32**

Because thou hast kept the word of my patience, I also will keep thee from the hour of temptation, which shall come upon all the world, to try them that dwell upon the earth.

**REVELATION 3:10**

Behold, I shew you a mystery; We shall not all sleep, but we shall all be changed, In a moment, in the twinkling of an eye, at the last trump: for the trumpet shall sound, and the dead shall be raised incorruptible, and we shall be changed.

**1 CORINTHIANS 15:51–52**

For God hath not appointed us to wrath, but to obtain salvation by our Lord Jesus Christ.

**1 Thessalonians 5:9**

Which also said, Ye men of Galilee, why stand ye gazing up into heaven? this same Jesus, which is taken up from you into heaven, shall so come in like manner as ye have seen him go into heaven.

**Acts 1:11**

Being confident of this very thing, that he which hath begun a good work in you will perform it until the day of Jesus Christ.

**Philippians 1:6**

Marvel not at this: for the hour is coming, in the which all that are in the graves shall hear his voice.

**John 5:28**

Watch ye therefore, and pray always, that ye may be accounted worthy to escape all these things that shall come to pass, and to stand before the Son of man.

**Luke 21:36**

Looking for that blessed hope, and the glorious appearing of the great God and our Saviour Jesus Christ.

**Titus 2:13**

For God hath not called us unto uncleanness, but unto holiness.

**1 Thessalonians 4:7**

So that ye come behind in no gift; waiting for the coming of our Lord Jesus Christ.

**1 Corinthians 1:7**

When Christ, who is our life, shall appear, then shall ye also appear with him in glory.

**Colossians 3:4**

To the end he may stablish your hearts unblameable in holiness before God, even our Father, at the coming of our Lord Jesus Christ with all his saints.

**1 Thessalonians 3:13**

So, Christ was once offered to bear the sins of many; and unto them that look for him shall he appear the second time without sin unto salvation.

**Hebrews 9:28**

And when the Chief Shepherd shall appear, ye shall receive a crown of glory that fadeth not away.

**1 Peter 5:4**

And Enoch also, the seventh from Adam, prophesied of these, saying, Behold, the Lord cometh with ten thousands of his saints.

**Jude 1:14**

And, behold, I come quickly; and my reward is with me, to give every man according as his work shall be. I am Alpha and Omega, the beginning and the end, the first and the last.

**Revelation 22:12–13**

Behold, he cometh with clouds; and every eye shall see him, and they also which pierced him: and all kindreds of the earth shall wail because of him. Even so, Amen.

**Revelation 1:7**

And his feet shall stand in that day upon the mount of Olives, which is before Jerusalem on the east, and the mount of Olives shall cleave in the midst thereof toward the east and toward the west, and there shall be a very great valley; and half of the mountain shall remove toward the north, and half of it toward the south.

**Zechariah 14:4**

Then shall the King say unto them on his right hand, Come, ye blessed of my Father, inherit the kingdom prepared for you from the foundation of the world.

**Matthew 25:34**

And out of his mouth goeth a sharp sword, that with it he should smite the nations: and he shall rule them with a rod of iron: and he treadeth the winepress of the fierceness and wrath of Almighty God.

**Revelation 19:15**

Watch therefore: for ye know not what hour your Lord doth come.

**Matthew 24:42**

For as the lightning comes from the east and is visible even in the west, so shall the coming of the Son of Man be.

**Matthew 24:27**

## *Quotes: Rapture/Second Coming*

If you don't like or believe the word rapture, call it the Great Catching away or the Great Assembly or the Great

Ingathering. The rapture is not a blessing for salvation; it is a reward for faithfulness. ~**Perry Stone**

Throughout scripture, there is a principle of the righteous escaping danger, judgment and wrath. ~**Perry Stone**

*Rapturo* is Greek for snatching away. This is the literal, visible and bodily return of Christ. It will be the greatest escape in the history of the world. ~**Jack Van Impe**

The rapture is not Christ's appearance on the earth but a meeting in the heavens, an intermediary evacuation of believers from earth before the storm. Seven years later Christ again comes to earth, touching down on the Mount of Olives with His Saints. ~**Jack Van Impe**

I believe the rapture is the next great event on the prophetic calendar and could happen at any moment, it is an eminent time of blessing, comfort and consolation. ~**Mark Hitchcock**

Our divine appointment is to be caught up to be with Christ; the appointment for the world is the day of the world, the day of wrath. One cannot keep both appointments. ~**John Walvoord**

Indicators of the approaching rapture are great deception, dispute among nations, great devastation, great lawlessness, a great turning from God and His ways, great despair and great distraction. ~**Anonymous**

Why would Christ leave his bride on earth to endure his wrath? One is forced to ask how the Lamb of God died and rose again to save the church from wrath and then make her pass through the wrath reserved for His enemies. Such inconsistency is possible in the minds of men but not in the acts of the Son of God. ~**J. F. Strombeck**

The rapture, a selective event for believers only.
The rapture is a spectacular event.
The rapture is a sequential event.
The rapture is a strengthening event.
The rapture is a signless event.
The rapture is a surprise event.
The rapture is a sudden event.
~**David Jeremiah**

The harvest is ready and the Lord will come back to reap a bountiful mature body of believers. ~**Aimee Semple McPherson**

The early Christians were looking, not for a cleft in the ground called a grave, but for a cleavage in the sky called glory! ~**Alexander MacLaren**

Nothing is more prominently brought forward in The New Testament than the second coming of Christ. ~**John Nelson Darby**

One of your most important responsibilities is to help prepare the world for the second coming of the Savior. ~**Unknown**

God is doing great things in the last days. We are living in very solemn times and God is doing a strange work of judgment. Jesus is coming soon and we will need to trust God to hide us away from the coming storm. ~**Maria Woodworth Etter**

There is a wasting of power, a failure to grasp the end time. The church and most pastors are not really concerned about the people and the nations. There needs to be preaching of "fire in the belly" to wake up the body of Christ and the lost sinners. ~**Oral Roberts**

The Rapture is going to burst like a thunderclap upon an unsuspecting world, huge numbers of people who know not because they chose not to know! The climax of the saved souls' righteousness being filled, will bring Christ our Savior, vaulting over the gates of Heaven with a mighty shout to gather us home. ~**Oral Roberts**

Blessed day! When will you dawn? Rise, unsetting sun! ~**Charles Spurgeon**

We are very near the final climactic events that will end with the second coming of Christ. ~**Hal Lindsey**

What are the practical duties of true believers in the prospect of the second coming of Christ? Our Lord mentions three things: Watch, pray, work. ~**J. C. Ryle**

For the first time ever, everything is in place for the battle of Armageddon and the second coming of Christ. ~**Ronald Reagan**

Even though it has been nearly two thousand plus years since Christ's first coming, the second coming is certain as well. ~**David Jeremiah**

Bible teaching about the second coming of Christ was once thought of as doomsday preaching, but not anymore. It is the only ray of hope that shines as an ever-brightening beam in a darkening world. ~**Billy Graham**

The Bible indicates as the time for Christ's return approaches, evil and chaos will intensify, evil men and imposters will go from bad to worse, deceiving and being deceived. ~**Billy Graham**

Oh, that our Lord would come today! He is coming, He is on the road and traveling quickly. The sound of His approach should be music to our hearts, ring out, you bells of hope. We sigh for the return of your sweet smile. ~**Charles Spurgeon**

Christ is coming again, He has not deserted us, our leader is merely on another part of the battlefield, but He will return! There remains a great unity between Christ, the King, and the lowest soldier on the field. He cares for us, His heart is with us and He is praying for us. ~**R. L. Hymers Jr.**

## *Hymns: Rapture/Second Coming*

**Blessed Assurance**
Perfect submission, perfect delight,
Visions of rapture burst on my sight.
Angels descending bring from above,
Echoes of mercy, whispers of love.
~**Fanny Crosby**, 1873 (public domain)

**Lo, He Comes with Clouds Descending**
Lo, he comes with clouds descending,
Once for our salvation slain.
Thousands, thousands, saints attending,

Swell the triumph of His train.
Hallelujah! Hallelujah! Hallelujah!
Christ the Lord returns to reign.
~**Charles Wesley**, 1758 (public domain)

**O the Bliss, the Holy Rapture!**
O the bliss, the holy rapture!
When from earth we glide away,
To the realms of endless splendor,
To the soul's eternal day.
To the golden fields of Eden,
With the pure and blessed above.
Where the saints of all the ages,
Sing of His redeeming love.
~**Fanny Crosby**, 1920 (public domain)

## *Personalized Weaponry*

The Great God of magnanimous creativity has fashioned you with a void that only He can fill. This is where true fulfillment and contentment rest. Nothing else fits precisely inside that God-shaped vacuum. He is our exceeding great reward, and we are wired for love by his uniqueness. The King of all Glory resides in each and every believer, by means of the Holy Spirit, and the gracious acts of the Trinity. Overwhelming victory is available as we stand still and see the salvation of the Lord. His wonderful dealings with us bring cohesiveness and consistency found nowhere else. The convergence of our prayers forbids our faith to droop. We go from a barren branch to an exhilarated enforcer by His power and might, vibrating and pulsating for His pleasure and delight. Hide yourselves in Christ's wounds and allow Him to pour fresh oil from the golden horn of the sanctuary upon you.

This is *your* watch, so go forth with militant action, your training manual in hand, and present yourselves to your Commander-in-Chief, energized and determined to obey His every word.

Even though this manual has been written primarily for mature believers, or at least those desiring to become so, if you have found your interest piqued, or perhaps a strange stirring in your heart to be a part of the *ranks of the righteous,* and the *brotherhood of blood,* please feel free to pray the sinner's prayer below.

## *Prayer of Salvation*

Lord Jesus, thank You for loving me and dying for me on the cross. Your precious, redeeming blood washes me clean of every sin. I want You to be my Lord and my Savior now and forever. I believe You rose from the dead and that You are very much alive today. Because of Your finished work, I am now a beloved child of God, and heaven is my home. Thank you for giving me eternal life and filling my heart with Your peace and joy. Amen.

# *Maranatha!*

## *Our Lord comes quickly,*

## *Prepare to meet your God*

## *"Fight on, dear warrior, fight on!!"*

# The Heavenly Commander's Conclusion

Who doesn't love a sweet, tender love story? Most especially one that's replete with God's fingerprints marking every moment—an exhilarating, enchanting retelling of a peculiarly supernatural encounter. He was a shy, scholarly classmate of Comanche/ Apache heritage, she was a lively yet studious girl of Irish/French bloodline. During those early years, they never dated, didn't run with the same crowds, never met at school functions, never communicated. They were on parallel paths, never intersecting.

Enter, the determined will of the Lord, the ultimately precise hand of the Matchmaker, most excellent. I've discovered that when it's your time, beautiful surprises lie in wait. When you relinquish control, abandoning the vague ideas that you know what's best, then and only then can the Personal Trainer of time take over. When the time is right, God will reveal his purposes, and promises will be fulfilled accurately and precisely.

At those moments, all the second hand, sloppy substitutes, the make-dos, the caving-in compromises will evaporate, and God's best number one choice will be manifested. You will discover, to your delight, sparkles of golden light sprinkled on your path to light your way. No, you will not miss it. There will be no more disappointments or sad endings. Relational let-downs will be a thing of the past.

Because the Lord is not bound by the dimension of time,

what is sixty years of waiting to Him? To us, it's grueling and often dreary, and we fill our days with dreams of a true love. The uniqueness of this new relationship springs from a mystical connection that only the Holy Spirit could have crafted for us. We stepped out of a longed-for dream into a heavenly reality of an ordained love, one that was customized, personalized, and hand-picked.

As you read this astonishing account, allow the Lord to pour a fresh surge of faith and trust into your prayers for a mate. Our love story was not going to go untold or unwritten but will be used to strengthen those believing for that special someone.

There will be seasons of battles, great and small, attempting to demolish your desires or even whisper doubts that your dreams are dust. Evict those dream-stealers and vision-killers. Allow and welcome the Great Vinekeeper to gloriously interrupt your life and bring forth the plantings ripened by the sun of His Divine Love.

Susan and Ed Chappabitty reside in the Lawton-Fort Sill, Oklahoma, area and are celebrating their first year of marriage at age seventy-four! Both grew up within blocks of each other but never dated, even though both attended the same schools from seventh grade to their sophomore year at Cameron College. Both were previously married yet remained single for thirty-five years and living in different states. By a divine intervention, dreams, and direct confirmation, they connected in 2018 and were married in Rockwall, Texas, in 2018. Ed is a Vietnam veteran and a decorated war hero. He was a family practice, M.D. at the Lawton Indian Hospital for twenty-five years. Susan worked for thirty years in corporate reception/communication systems in Dallas, Texas. They are blessed with four children and six grandchildren.

CPSIA information can be obtained
at www.ICGtesting.com
Printed in the USA
FSHW021344090420
69008FS